MY LIFE OF LANGUAGE

MY LIFE OF LANGUAGE

A MEMOIR

Paul W. Ogden

Gallaudet University Press
Washington, DC

Gallaudet University Press
Washington, DC 20002
http://gupress.gallaudet.edu

Cover photo courtesy of Stefani Santos.

Library of Congress Cataloging-in-Publication Data

Names: Ogden, Paul W., author.
Title: My life of language : a memoir / Paul W. Ogden.
Description: Washington, DC : Gallaudet University Press, [2017] |
    Includes bibliographical references.
Identifiers: LCCN 2017039434 | ISBN 9781944838140 (pbk. : alk. paper) |
    ISBN 9781944838157 (ebook)
Subjects: LCSH: Ogden, Paul W. | Deaf--United States--Biography. |
    Teachers of the deaf--United States--Biography. | Deaf--Education--
    United States.
Classification: LCC HV2534.O43 A3 2017 | DDC 371.91/2092 [B] --dc23
LC record available at https://lccn.loc.gov/2017039434

∞ This paper meets the requirements of ANSI/NISO Z39.48-1992
(Permanence of Paper).

To the Reverend Dunbar H. Ogden, Jr. He often found it challenging to communicate verbally with us, his deaf sons. Yet he taught us to be comfortable with everyone and compassionate toward everyone, regardless of race, education, disability, and religion.

CONTENTS

PREFACE

I HAVE BEEN profoundly deaf from birth. For nearly that long, it seems, I have also been a professional educator of deaf students. Nothing gives me the same sense of satisfaction as guiding, teaching, and advising young deaf people who are finding their way in the world—unless it is helping those who care about, work with, and are invested in the lives of these same young people.

My own journey as a young deaf person led me to this passion. The trials and triumphs of my early years, at a time when society often looked on deaf people in ignorance or with shame, fueled a desire within me to try to make the path a little smoother for future generations. Now I am ready to share with you the story of those years and the lessons I acquired along the way.

The experience of being deaf is profound, one that cannot be described in a single word or phrase. Rather, it is a range, a spectrum of conditions. The term "deaf" is applied to people who are profoundly deaf, with little or no hearing, to people who are only slightly hard of hearing, and to everyone in between. There is a similar range of approaches to educating and communicating with deaf people. This book is not just for those with a specific level of deafness or about promoting one of those education methods over another. It is for anyone with a connection to deaf or hard of hearing children and anyone with an interest in what it means to grow up deaf in a hearing world.

Successful communication takes many forms. We may bond with others through our ears, our eyes, physical touch, and more. Often our experience, our attitude, and even the environment make all the difference. A mealtime, for example, is a golden opportunity to make and maintain friendships. There is something in the shared experience of replenishing ourselves with a sandwich, a salad, a bowl of soup, or even a cup of coffee that breaks down barriers and encourages relaxed and heartfelt communication. I realized this when I was a young adult, a few years after my niece Stephanie and nephew

Christopher were born. As they grew older, I noticed how difficult it was for me to connect with them when others were around. I decided I would take one or the other out to lunch or dinner during my visits, just the two of us. At these meals, we talked for hours about people and events in their lives, a practice they both appreciated and that we continue to this day. We had found a path to high-quality communication.

I was in graduate school when I spied a poster on the wall of a faculty member's office. It depicted a painting by Monet, *The Artist's Garden at Vétheuil.* Immediately, I fell in love with the pastoral scene. I delighted in the sensation of being in the garden, of feeling embraced and supported. It reminded me of the Garden of Eden, a place where life begins, a place where people live in harmony and peace. It also brought back memories of my family—my mother, father, and brothers, who lovingly gave me my first lessons in communication. As I grew up, I sensed that all of us seek such a garden, a place where we can understand and be understood, a perfect world for living and loving. For me, it depicts a world of perfect communicating.

All of us are still on the path toward understanding and perfect communication. Perhaps this book can be another stepping-stone for you, whether you are hearing or deaf. I hope the following pages give you joy, laughter, hope, guidance, sensitivity, encouragement, and inspiration.

ACKNOWLEDGMENTS

MANY PEOPLE along the way have coaxed and urged me to finish this work. They have been extraordinary coaches who love words. There are more people to thank than can be recognized here. Among them: Brian Riley, Jim Lund, Kathy Yoshida Doerksen, Pamela McCallon Warkentin, and my students, staff, and faculty colleagues at California State University in Fresno. They listened patiently to my life stories and responded from the heart.

Special appreciation goes to my brother Dunbar and his wife, Annegret, for their enthusiasm and moral support for not only this book but all my book projects. Behind the work, and within it, lives the inspiration and the memory of my parents, Dunbar and Dorothy Ogden, and my brothers David and Jonathan. The person who has been my true foundation is my wife, Anne Keenan Ogden. Her love and patience have sustained me through the writing process and cheered me up through all the months and years. The best deal we have for our passions during very hectic times is that she quilts and travels while I teach and write books.

My deep appreciation goes to Ivey Pittle Wallace at Gallaudet University Press. With her rigorous crafting and shaping as an editor, I have gained confidence in the words on the page. Very special thanks go to these people for their sharp proofing skills: Kim Holly, Ellen Morse, and Marilyn Weinhouse, whose insightful comments also added clarity to the manuscript. With her art photography on the cover, Stefani Santos invites the reader to open the book and read on.

INTRODUCTION FOR PARENTS

IMAGINE YOU ARE standing behind an airport window, watching passengers deplane. Suddenly you see a young, wide-eyed stranger stepping uncertainly down the portable stairway, wrapping her jacket tightly around herself. This is the person you've been waiting for. She is a foreign exchange student on her first visit to America and you are her host.

When this new arrival reaches the airport, she glances around, taking it all in. You sense that she is nervous. You know she doesn't speak English, so you step forward to greet her with a smile and a welcoming hug. As you do, you feel the weight of your responsibility. It's up to you to introduce this young woman to her new world.

This is only a made-up story, of course. But for parents, teachers, and other family, friends, and professionals who are charged with raising and teaching deaf children, it is an apt illustration of what both sides will face. A young deaf boy or girl may often feel like a stranger in a foreign land, unable to grasp common language practices and pick up the simple but vital bits of information that allow us to easily connect and communicate. A parent or teacher, meanwhile, is this child's guide. If we are that parent or teacher, our task is to support, to encourage, and to teach—to be a good "host."

Many years ago, my parents faced this unexpected challenge. On the day I was born, my mother held me in her arms for the first time, gazed into my eyes, and confronted a sudden, shocking realization: that her newborn son might be deaf. The clue was the loose way I held my head, an indication I had no sense of balance. It is a common characteristic of babies with hearing loss, a sign my mother already knew well because my older brother Jonathan also is deaf.

I wonder about the questions that must have run through my mother's mind at that moment. *What will this mean for him and our family? Will he be able to carry on a conversation with other children and make friends? Where will we send him to school? Will he find*

The author and his parents.

success in a career, marry, and raise a family? Is my baby ready for the challenges ahead?

These are many of the same questions that mothers and fathers ask today when they discover that one of their children is deaf. Perhaps you are one of these parents. That moment of realization is life changing. Undoubtedly, deafness was not part of your plan. Yet all parents must eventually accept their children for who they are, including their unique traits, gifts, and passions, and let go of some of their own parental expectations. Deafness may be an unexpected challenge, but it need not be a tragedy. I encourage you to not dwell on this "setback" and the lost future you'd imagined and instead to embrace your child and see his or her potential. Follow your instincts and don't worry too much about making mistakes. Trial and error are part of the process. You may face tough choices in deciding what is best for your child, but I encourage you to keep the long view in mind, even if it is upsetting in the short term. The priority is to commit yourself to opening the world to your child.

The world has come a long way since my birth in 1949, though those of us without hearing still face many impediments to communicating in our modern world. Back then, email, texting, and even teletypewriters hadn't been invented yet. More troubling was society's attitude toward anyone who was different. Deaf people were often shunned or kept out of sight. Many parents even felt ashamed that they had produced a deaf child. Few people went out of their way to accommodate the needs of a nonhearing person. I faced some of these obstacles when I entered the world—but I also possessed several advantages, chief among them the wisdom and experience of my family. They were indeed good hosts.

I was fortunate because my parents already knew about the importance of nonverbal communication. Many parents with deaf children remain totally unaware of their children's nonverbal communication skills and their potential effectiveness. Sometimes this ignorance is a manifestation of the parents' intense wish that their child be "normal." These parents are expressing a common self-deception. Desperately hoping that the child will seem like other kids, they focus on teaching one mode of expression and exclude everything else. Often, what they are really saying to their child, perhaps subconsciously, is "Forget about other ways of communicating. Just communicate the way we do."

Some parents and instructors committed to oralism—the method of communicating and teaching deaf children through lipreading, speech, and mimicking the mouth shapes and breathing patterns of speech—even put a condition on their communication with deaf children. They respond only if these children express their messages in a clear, spoken way, with words everyone can understand. How discouraging! Consider how you would react if someone you felt close to—a relative, say, from another country—suddenly burst out in fury, "Don't talk to me in English, ever! Learn to speak my language or don't speak to me again!"

This type of misunderstanding or impatience on the part of parents and teachers can shatter a deaf child's feelings of security. To grow strong and independent, children need to feel totally accepted, and they need to be encouraged to express themselves, even if this sometimes leads to conflict. Many parents of deaf children unknowingly threaten that sense of security by making their love and acceptance conditional on the child's learning to communicate only through speech and lipreading. Children whose efforts at nonverbal communication or sign language are devalued and discouraged may come to feel that only when they learn the art of spoken communication will their parents truly love and accept them fully.

Ultimately, all communication is a kind of guessing game between people. Recognize it as such and play it with your deaf child. Play your hunches with each other. That's what we all do, all the time, when we talk with each other. Deaf children can acquire language and the cognitive tools related to it beginning even in infancy. The secret is to immerse them in language, whether it is spoken, gestural, or sign language and to show them—by whatever means necessary—how communication works. From the day of birth, "talk" to him or her with your voice, mouth, eyes, face, hands, and touch. Add an element of humor and fun to your instruction, and above all, pay close attention!

I want to pass on my parents' wisdom and experience to you. This book is my story. It relates both triumph and family tragedy, moments of shocking ignorance and cruelty and incidents of heartwarming compassion. But it is more than just the details of my journey. It also contains the knowledge and insights I gained while growing up in a family with both deaf and hearing children and while serving as a professor of deaf education for more than thirty-five years. Whether you are a parent, teacher, interpreter, or friend of a deaf person—or are simply interested in learning more about the deaf community and one member's rites of passage—this book is for you.

I have spent a lifetime studying the art of communication. What I have learned is that whether deaf or hearing, we all struggle to understand and have a desperate need to be understood. My hope is that the following chapters will ease your efforts to communicate successfully with those you work with, live with, and love. In telling my story, I have changed some names and identifying details to protect the privacy of individuals. I have written events as I remember them, but others may remember them differently.

PART ONE

MAKING SENSE OF A SILENT WORLD

I

A NEW PLAN

Children shouldn't have to sacrifice so that you can have the life you want. You make sacrifices so your children can have the life that they deserve.

Ritu Ghatourey

MY STORY begins eleven years before I entered the world. My brother Jonathan Herr Ogden was born into a loving family on February 8, 1938. Our father, Dunbar Ogden, Jr., was the minister of a Presbyterian church in Portsmouth, Ohio. Our mother, Dorothy Coblentz Ogden, stayed at home to raise our two older brothers, Dunbar (born 1935) and David (born 1936).

My mother was musically inclined. She graduated from the Conservatory School of Music, affiliated with the University of Cincinnati. She earned a bachelor of arts degree in music, with high honors, even though it was quite unusual for a woman to attend and graduate from college in the early 1930s. After college and before marrying my father, she taught high school music. In our family's early years, when Dunbar and David took music lessons, my mother entertained the idea of raising a family orchestra. While Jonathan was on the way, she dreamed about playing the piano while each of her three children played other musical instruments along with her.

When Jonathan was born, however, he didn't seem very strong. He didn't sit up when he should have been able to. My parents attributed this weakness to the fact that he arrived so soon after his brothers. But as time went on, they noticed he was not picking up sounds as he should. One day my mother observed that whenever Jonathan saw her he threw his arms up, indicating he wanted to be picked up. But when his face was turned away, he didn't respond to her even when she called him. She was a few feet behind him and called and called. There was

1

no reaction. But when she came within his line of vision, he dropped everything and extended his arms toward her.

In the late 1930s, there was almost no accurate information on deafness or any special public services for parents of deaf children. The fact that Jonathan was deaf eluded my parents until he was about three. During the long, emotional process of determining why Jonathan seemed to have hearing and learning difficulties, one doctor declared that Jonathan was mentally retarded. It was a difficult diagnosis for my parents to shake off, but finally another doctor ruled it out.

My father's younger brother, Fred, lived in Boston and was interning to become an ear, nose, and throat doctor. He was able to get the family in touch with one of the leading specialists in the United States. There in Boston, after many tests, the doctor told my parents with finality that Jonathan was profoundly deaf. He said that it was nerve deafness for which there was no cure and that they should not waste their time searching for one. The doctor then told them something that would positively influence, for life, their treatment of Jonathan and me. He said that the best thing they could do for Jonathan was to give him the finest education possible, to prepare him to live a self-sufficient and independent life.

The truth sank slowly into my parents' minds. It took them a long while to get over the shocks they had experienced in their journey from doctor to doctor. It was especially tough for my father, a church pastor. He was a conceptualizer, the kind of person who organized things. He constructed frameworks within which things were to be done. It was his attempt to make everything in life logical. He had little tolerance for surprises. At first, my father couldn't cope with the idea that deafness fit somewhere into his family's life and into life in general.

The adjustment was a little easier for my mother. She was a balanced, even-tempered, pragmatic person who was rarely flustered or upset. She was also selfless and kind, able to fit into nearly any situation. Rather than be nervous about new experiences, my mother was at peace. A large family of males felt natural to her, since she'd grown up with an older brother and played a major part in bringing up her two younger brothers. She knew, however, that raising a deaf child meant adapting to significant changes.

During Jonathan's early years, my parents talked to several doctors about our family history. Since there was no serious childhood illness that would have affected Jonathan's hearing, his deafness was considered a fluke. The only explanation the doctors could give my parents was that it was a "freak of nature." The example they used was that when ten acorns were planted, nine might grow into perfect oak trees while one developed poorly.

The final diagnosis from the Boston ear specialist came as a terrible blow to my parents. Yet they finally accepted his diagnosis *and* his advice. Soon they began the slow collection of information and skills they would need to raise and educate a profoundly deaf child.

Jonathan was born without a sense of balance, just as I would be eleven years later. The nerves having to do with hearing are also connected to those having to do with one's equilibrium. It took both of us a long time to master the skill of walking unaided and confidently. After Jonathan fell and cut himself several times when learning to walk, my parents got a harness for him. The harness was equipped with a long cord. Every time Jonathan stumbled, they pulled up on the cord to keep him from falling flat on his face. My parents' experiences with Jonathan and the harness saved me from falls when I began learning to walk. In many ways, I was spared scars that Jonathan had to suffer.

With Jonathan and then again with me, my parents learned how important it was to take us out on walks. These frequent exercises gave us an increasing mastery over our imbalance. We learned to walk by eye adjustment—that is, by looking at the horizon and adjusting accordingly. If I were put in a completely dark room, I would not know which way was up and which way was down. My eyes would be unable to find the horizon on which I rely for balance.

Almost from the beginning of Jonathan's life, Mother began to devote many hours each day to teaching him to lipread. She had very little professional knowledge of what she was doing and was not always sure he understood what she said, but she kept trying. At the time, the prevailing wisdom was that the best way for deaf children to communicate was through speech and lipreading. Sign language had yet to earn its place among educators as a respected and viable alternative.

One day Jonathan sat on the floor in the bedroom. My mother knew he loved to take a bath and play in the tub filled with little toys. She turned to him, caught his eye, and asked, "Jonathan, do you want to take a bath?"

Jonathan jumped up, ran to the bathroom, turned on the faucets, and started to undress. A huge smile lit my mother's face. It was her first communication breakthrough with Jonathan. She now had the wonderful satisfaction of knowing that he had lipread and understood her. That small moment of victory made everything she had done up to that point worthwhile. It encouraged her to keep going.

My mother had many techniques for teaching language to Jonathan. For instance, she cut out pictures, pasted them on cardboard, and wrote the names of the objects on the bottom. She taped labels to pieces of furniture and other practical objects—all with the idea of stimulating language and communication in Jonathan. She practiced with him by asking him to bring things to her so that he had to lipread her and know what she said. She worked on numbers and was always printing something for him on cards she made from the cardboard inside dress shirts that came from the dry cleaners.

Years later, when I was about a year old, a family friend mentioned correspondence courses for parents on teaching and raising deaf children, available through the John Tracy Clinic in Los Angeles. John Tracy was the deaf son of Spencer Tracy, the actor, and his wife, Louise. My mother soon started the courses and received weekly letters, but by then there was little she hadn't already learned. The correspondence did, however, show my mother that all the things she had been doing for Jonathan were indeed recommended, and this gave her much-needed confidence.

My mother had no firsthand help of any kind in teaching Jonathan. She learned from different professionals, teachers, and friends but mostly by trial and error. Since there were no educational materials to help her with Jonathan, she created them herself. She felt that teaching him to lipread was the most important thing she could do for him. She had to give him language and a means to communicate.

2

THE LANGUAGE OF LIFE

The limits of my language mean the limits of my world.

Ludwig Wittgenstein

During Jonathan's early years, my mother realized that she faced a continuous teaching job. She couldn't ignore the responsibility; she and my father both felt it was important to prepare Jonathan for the adjustment into hearing society. Remembering the Boston specialist's advice and recognizing their own strong commitment to education, they began to visit schools around the country for people who are deaf.

They were not impressed with the quality of teachers and education in most of the schools they visited. They saw that teachers often lacked the specialized skills needed to work with children who are deaf. They also noticed that some of the teachers seemed to have no respect for their pupils. Once, for example, my mother visited a class in which a seven-year-old girl asked her how old she was. The teacher immediately slapped the girl's face and told her not to ask adults about their age. The poor little girl didn't understand the teacher. My mother was shocked by the harshness of the punishment.

At another school, my parents didn't like the superintendent's attitude toward his pupils. He treated many of the children as if they were mentally retarded. In one class, the teacher wanted a little girl to demonstrate something in front of other children. My parents noticed that the little girl flinched as if she thought the teacher was going to hit her. They knew that it was not good for the children to be afraid of their teacher. To them, it was obvious that confidence was one of the most important qualities a deaf child needed to survive and learn.

But perhaps my parents' most consistent reaction during their visits to many schools for the deaf was dismay, at how little language the children seemed to have and at how poor their reading was. Both my parents came from families where everyone loved to read. They wanted Jonathan to love reading as much they, Dunbar, and David did. My mother had always enjoyed reading to the boys at bedtime. My father even read to them at breakfast. My parents wondered how the deaf children they saw would acquire the incentive to read if they were not learning any vocabulary in the classroom.

In 1940, when Jonathan was two years old, my father accepted a new pastorate and the Ogden family moved to Staunton, Virginia. Although there was a school for the deaf in Staunton, my parents' research, combined with the advice of friends and other knowledge-able people, led them to decide that the best school for Jonathan was Central Institute for the Deaf (CID) in St. Louis, Missouri. So, in 1943, when Jonathan was five years old, he began attending CID, a thousand miles away.

Every time Jonathan left for St. Louis, it was emotional and heart-breaking for the whole family. Jonathan came home only for Christmas and the summer, since, by train, the trip was too long for short vacation holidays such as Thanksgiving and Easter.

When he was a little older, Jonathan made the eighteen-hour train ride by himself. But when he first started at CID, my father went with him. It was an awful experience for them both. Jonathan became physically sick. When he tried to tell me about it, the memory was so distressing that he couldn't express himself. Meanwhile, when my father took Jonathan to CID, he found it difficult to leave. When my father finally had to say goodbye, he was overcome with emotion at the thought of leaving his small son all alone. Once outside, he hung around the school, looking through the dining room windows to catch a glimpse of Jonathan in his chair at the table. My father cried whenever he told this story, saying how small and helpless Jonathan looked sitting there. It really broke my father up to leave him.

Although my mother rarely cried in public, she always wept when seeing Jonathan off at the railway station. When the train started to pull away, the boys ran beside it as fast as they could, trying to keep up. When it finally outdistanced them, they returned to our parents and the family began the drive home, all except for little Jonathan.

Despite the trauma of these separations, my parents stuck to their decision rather than choose the easier path of keeping Jonathan close to home. They were determined to give him the language skills and education they felt he needed to succeed in life.

During Jonathan's first year away at school, my mother visited several times to learn for herself how to work with him. She wanted him to continue to learn at home and not lose ground during vacation periods. At CID, my mother saw that the children used language and read much more than at any other school. The teachers seemed to know how to correct their language errors and how to guide them in their reading. In their own thoughts about how to educate Jonathan, my parents had already concluded that reading and vocabulary were even more important than speech itself. My mother was also soon to learn firsthand how difficult it was to teach speech to someone who couldn't hear himself speak.

Back home in Staunton, my mother asked the superintendent of the Virginia School for the Deaf and the Blind if she could sit in on a speech class for the teachers at the school, taught by an instructor from Canada. At the end of the semester the superintendent asked my mother to be the speech teacher to five children who had just started at the school. She was surprised and flattered and agreed to teach basic speech for a semester—one hour every day for a few months. It was not a gratifying experience, however, for the longer she taught the more incompetent she felt. There was so much about teaching speech to deaf children that she didn't know.

School officials asked my mother to stay on and become a speech teacher. She declined. She felt bad that the school viewed her as a potential teacher even though she was so poorly qualified. It only drew attention to how poorly qualified most teachers of deaf children really were. In the 1940s, many people teaching deaf children had no training of any kind in areas of deafness. Often, they'd had little or no teaching experience in hearing schools either. During her visits and work at the school, my mother noticed that these "teachers," who knew nothing about deafness, did not relate well to deaf children and contributed almost nothing to the students' education. They seemed to be hired only to babysit and discipline the children.

On the other hand, my mother respected the teachers at CID very much. As time went on, she grew hesitant about interfering with what Jonathan was learning in speech, even though she now knew a lot about speech therapy from her work at the Virginia School for the Deaf and her visits to CID. But the more she learned, the more strongly she felt that one had to have specialized training and to be certified before teaching deaf children. With Jonathan she did some teaching, but once he started school, she made sure she didn't do anything but reinforce what he had learned at CID. Everything she learned and did for him, she was also learning and doing—unknowingly—for me.

3

DOING WHAT WORKS

If you tell people where to go, but not how to get there, you'll be amazed at the results.

George S. Patton

In 1948, ten years after Jonathan's arrival, my parents began talking about having another child. They both loved children and thought it would be nice for Jonathan to have a younger brother or sister who could support him after his two older brothers left home, or after they themselves were gone. If they had another baby, there would always be someone to look after Jonathan. They felt no fear, only anticipation, at the prospect of another child. A doctor said there was virtually no chance that they would have another deaf baby. My parents were convinced that the next child would be hearing and healthy.

My father wanted a girl this time. He would name the baby Dorothy Louise after my mother. She, however, wanted another boy, since she was more confident about raising boys.

I arrived at King's Daughters Hospital on February 15, 1949, very much a male—and also, as my mother suspected immediately, with no more ability to hear than Jonathan. Either the hair cells of the cochlea in my inner ears or the auditory nerve that transmits signals from my inner ears to the auditory cortex of my brain were damaged (I've never learned which). I was born profoundly deaf.

My mother waited six weeks to tell my father. He was again beset by a reality he wasn't prepared for. He tried to fit this new family "tragedy" into some logical place in his world. But it wasn't easy for him, the great believer in order and harmony. It wasn't easy at all.

For one thing, there was no such thing as genetic counseling in those days. My father mused and worried about how strange it was for our family to have two deaf children. There was no one he could

9

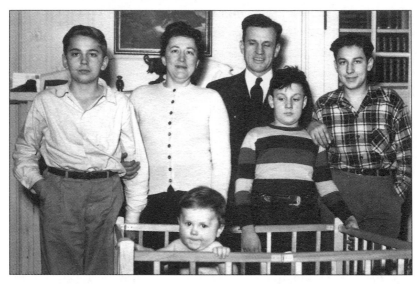

First family photo. Ten-month-old Paul with his family (L to R: thirteen-year-old David, Mother, Father, eleven-year-old Jonathan, fourteen-year-old Dunbar).

turn to for a logical explanation. He knew there was no deafness in his family or my mother's. Uncles on both sides of the family were genealogy experts and they could find no record of deafness going back three hundred years.

Satisfied that there was no evidence of inherited deafness, my father decided that Jonathan and I were products of our mother's thyroid condition. She had suffered from an overactive thyroid while pregnant with Jonathan and had almost miscarried him. Several years after he was born, she had an operation to remove part of the gland to eliminate an overactive rate of metabolism.

My mother started my education right away. With Jonathan, my parents had to gather and sift through all the information they could find about deafness before they could proceed with home instruction. With me, all they had to do was bring down from the attic the boxes of instructional materials they'd collected for my brother. Their experience with Jonathan saved me years of frustrating interaction with my family and professionals.

From Jonathan, my family learned that deafness affects hearing and speech but *not* the impulse to communicate. They knew that I also would have a great desire and need to communicate with others. After all, as humans, our satisfaction and success in life has everything to do with our ability to send and receive messages and interact with others. We all long to be understood—by our friends, our bosses, our parents, our children, and most certainly by our boyfriend, girlfriend, husband, or wife. Nothing is more frustrating than trying to express a vital message or our innermost thoughts and realizing that our coworker, teenager, or lover isn't getting it—or worse, that he or she isn't even trying to understand!

When communication succeeds between us and another person, however, it unlocks the potential of the relationship. We discover points of common delight. Ideas pour out and build on each other. A bond forms. Even when we disagree, communication creates a connection that often leads to mutual trust and respect. An effective exchange allows us to see circumstances from another's perspective. And when communication flows at an intimate level, it can open the door to love.

Jonathan introduced my family to the idea that communication can take place without hearing and speech. My parents and brothers had learned that hands and arms, faces, postures, gestures, and expressions are as important to communication as lips, tongues, and vocal cords. We have our eyes, which read those gestures and postures, the thousand avenues of facial and body expression. And we have our lips to form unspoken words.

However highly my family valued words, they knew that some people overvalued speech as a means of transmitting information. My family didn't think of speech as the only means of communication. Their experience and intuition taught them that a large percentage of social conversation among hearing people is nonverbal in nature and that only a small portion of the total energy used in communicating is expended in the utterance of words. They also learned that everyone transmits and reads body language, for the most part unconsciously. Jonathan's deafness made my family aware of their bodies as well as their speech. They learned to sharpen their perceptions about gestures, postures, and facial expressions and to loosen up and use these elements when communicating with Jonathan. By the time I came along, my family, especially my mother and brothers, were experts at nonverbal communication.

In my early years, as with any young child, much of what I needed to get across to my family and others involved primarily my feelings.

These messages came through in body language, and my family responded to me immediately. All families respond to their babies' expressive motions, but they usually treat such movements as basically informative only. The baby smiles: it is content. The baby cries: it is wet or hungry. Their babies' expressions and gestures give them pleasure, but it is not until the children learn to talk that many parents think of them as communicating beings.

My family had a special reason to concentrate on my vocabulary of body movements, gestures, and sounds. By learning to read my body language and noises, they came a step closer to participating in an ongoing conversation with me that was as valid and informative as any spoken exchange. Eventually, we developed a system of signs and signals that seemed to be born out of our subconscious.

My family wanted me to learn to speak, but they intuitively supported *all* my communication efforts. Their positive attitude about nonverbal methods enhanced our overall communication. With my family's support, not pressure, I picked up words and started communicating very quickly.

It helped that my family was naturally physical. My mother held and hugged me often. My brothers and father wrestled with each other and me because my father was strong and had been a wrestler in college. From the very beginning, my brothers added me to their horseplay. We played physical games and boxed each other around—activities that sometimes led to fights among the older boys, though they were surprisingly careful with me.

It was a graphic way to communicate. It showed me how much they loved me and that they treasured me as part of the family. I remember especially my father playing "airplane." He lay on his back on the floor with his feet straight up in the air, and one of us—the "airplane"—balanced on our stomach on the soles of his feet. I also remember him flipping us. As he lay on his back supporting me by the shoulders with his hands, my hands would be on his knees while he kept my body straight up in the air. Then he would flip me over so that I would land back on my feet. We did many other daring acrobatics, and my mother would watch with fear and trepidation.

My father played these physical games with me until I was about twelve. It seemed to make up for all the time he didn't spend communicating with me. My father was out of the house most of the time, and because of his impatient nature he had more difficulty than the rest of the family in understanding my sounds, gestures, and beginning words. The older I got, however, the easier it was for him to understand me.

My mother worked with me on jigsaw puzzles. She started with simple ones and went on to larger and more complicated puzzles. This was an important mental exercise in spatial relations. During our time with these puzzles I imitated and lipread my mother, and as I did so I learned to use my voice. I formed many words on my lips and eventually burst out with my own voice. To begin with, my father and brothers often had trouble understanding my speech. But as time passed they could usually decipher the words by watching my face. Therefore, while I was learning to lipread them, my family was learning to lipread me as well.

It was a matter of trial and error. In a way, it was like all the other games we played. We boys touched and pummeled each other and made up physical tricks almost constantly. It was contact, it was recognition, it was love—and it was a form of communication.

Verbal language is also physical. My family learned to listen to me by watching me and figuring out what I was saying. This meant a lot of lipreading and it became very accurate. Since I imitated what I saw on the lips of others but not the inner mechanics of sounds when I spoke, it took more work on the listener's part. I used an exaggerated way of saying things with the lips, tongue, and teeth. But an average listener couldn't understand my words since I was imitating visual cues, not sounds. In fact, no one outside my family could understand me, so my family interpreted for me. It was amazing how my family lived with so many of my mispronunciations. But they were unconcerned at the time with fine-tuning my speech. My parents' major objective had been achieved—to get me to use my voice to communicate. It was a goal they had set with certainty, based on their early years with Jonathan, eleven years before.

Almost anyone, even the uninitiated, can understand the mouthing of words and the sounds I make now. The crucial point is whether they're interested in hearing me or not. Some people are embarrassed by the process. Others, it seems, don't want to be bothered. This is a pity, because just as they might learn something about the rest of the world by speaking with a foreigner, they would also learn from "talking" with a deaf person.

When Jonathan was very young, as with me later, my parents explained to Dunbar and David that excessive use of sign language would cut Jonathan off from most hearing people. They told the boys that when they felt like using a homemade sign for a word Jonathan already knew, such as "snipping" two fingers together to indicate scissors, they should put their hands behind their back. That was the rule while talking to Jonathan: if he had already learned to lipread a word, then they would not substitute a sign if he failed to lipread it. Instead, they should repeat the word. If that failed, they should stop and work on it with him again, or find another word (though they often used the gesture eventually).

This process required looking Jonathan squarely in the face and enunciating clearly and slowly, "Do you want a bath?" rather than just pointing to him and then pointing to the bathtub. It caused the whole family to slow down and think about how they communicated. In some ways, I believe they profited from it as much as Jonathan and I did.

My older brothers communicated with us in other ways, which often included a barrage of visual pranks and body language. They used pantomime to act out stories, events, and jokes. One favorite game began with Dunbar or David pointing excitedly off to the side. Jonathan or I would look, and then one of the brothers would bop us on the right shoulder. Or, while we were turning around, one of the two would make our piece of cake disappear, then start looking under the table for the cake! We received more than our share of this kind of teasing, but I at least usually liked the attention.

It would have been much easier, of course, for Jonathan and me had the rest of the family signed for words like "scissors." But my parents and brothers encouraged us to practice lipreading so that we would become better at it. My family certainly never resorted to punishing Jonathan or me for using *some* signs, as some families did. Instead, they always tried positive encouragement as a way of getting us to talk and lipread more.

My parents' decision to discourage sign language within our household reflects one side of the philosophical coin in deaf education. Many educators favor teaching sign language to deaf children. Others prefer oralism, while still others teach and practice both methods. The foundation of my parents' approach was a fierce commitment to communication and family unity. They did not know that a vibrant deaf community used sign language, and they continued to trust the prevailing view of professionals regarding signing. Even so, they could not bring themselves to discourage my brothers from using the gestures and facial expressions that helped Jonathan and me stay within the web of communication that bound our family together.

In doing so, my parents unknowingly expressed a belief that I have grown to feel strongly about—parents and teachers should use whatever works, be it physical contact, speech, lipreading, signing, or a combination of each. Deaf people need to communicate, no matter the means.

4

BAND OF BROTHERS

Your chances of success in any undertaking can always be measured by your belief in yourself.

Robert Collier

My family noticed right away a big difference between Jonathan and me in our psychological makeup. From early on, Jonathan was quiet. Whenever he came home from CID, he was subdued and had almost a hurt look on his face. He endured many things in silence. I, on the other hand, was always laughing or talking, eager to do things with everyone. I was out of bed early each morning and ready for adventure. I was "the Teddy Bear," crying and yelling boldly from an early age.

While Jonathan was mostly docile and a good little boy, I was more rebellious and expressed my opinions. To my family, it was obvious that I was full of mischief. I was restless and wanted to move all the time. Like many deaf children, I was thought to be hyper-active. In reality, I was frustrated. Since I wasn't able to participate in meaningful, give-and-take conversations in the same way as the hearing members of my family, I wanted some kind of return in terms of physical interaction with other people. I was always longing for something but didn't know exactly what it was.

As surprising as it may seem, I didn't understand that I was different from my parents and older brothers—that they were hearing and Jonathan and I were deaf. The concept was beyond my comprehension. I believe that before I connected the dots, I was affirming that I was alive, acting out the knowledge that I did exist and that I was part of everything I saw. I reached out to anything I saw and wanted to touch, feel, smell, and explore. Because of this restlessness, my family felt freer in their efforts to communicate with me, feeling that they could more easily risk the trial and error approach.

My brothers gave me an active social life. Thanks to them, I never felt like an outsider in my own family, as many deaf children do. I had a different relationship with each of my brothers. When all of us were together, the energy could be overwhelming—sometimes too much for my parents!

One of my earliest memories—I was probably two—is of wanting to get on top of the garage at the back of our home. The garage was uphill and about thirty feet from the house. I remember pointing to the top of the garage. I wanted to get up there. My parents, of course, didn't think it was a good idea. Finally, however, Dunbar responded to my pleas and told me I could do it with his help.

The fact that I had no sense of balance certainly must have entered his mind, but it didn't stop him. Perhaps it even convinced him to take me up. He encouraged me to climb up the ladder, so I went up with him climbing behind. He formed a sort of cage against the ladder, surrounding me with his arms so I wouldn't fall. When we got to the top, I crawled along the ridge. Dunbar still surrounded me on all fours, crawling along above me as I crawled. We kept going like this to the peak of the roof, where we finally sat down. As I looked around at the yard below, I must have been very proud of myself, thinking, *Wow, I am high up here, aren't I?*

Dunbar was at home for the first two and a half years after I was born, before he graduated from high school in June 1951. He used to pick me up and carry me under his arm like a package. He hauled me from place to place when my parents were busy. Since he was the oldest child, my parents depended on him for help.

Before he left home, Dunbar began teaching me to swim at Lake Shenandoah near Staunton. He wanted me to be able to do anything he did, since I always wanted to be with him. He was never ashamed of his baby brother, as many teenagers might have been. I suspect he gained a bit of notoriety with me as his sidekick.

In the middle of Lake Shenandoah was a diving tower with what we would today call a zip line. A cable ran from the top of the tower down to the edge of the lake. Along the cable was a wheel, and from the wheel a handle dangled. The more adventurous swimmers would climb the three-story tower, stand on tiptoe to grab the handle, and ride the cable down into the water. You could either let go of the handle partway down and fall into the water from above or continue the long incline until your ride ended in a dramatic splash.

Dunbar and I would swim out to the tower, Dunbar with his hand under my stomach so I wouldn't sink. At the tower, we climbed the ladder three stories to the top. Dunbar used the same technique as when we climbed the roof of our family garage, enclosing me in his human cage. At the top of the tower, I got on Dunbar's back. He put a leather belt from his pants around me, tying me to him. I wrapped my arms around his neck and legs around his waist. He then reached up and grabbed the pulley handle, and we sailed off through the air and down the thrilling ride. As soon as we hit the water, Dunbar quickly unfastened the belt and shoved me above the surface. I always laughed so hard I had to gasp for air.

The other high school kids at the lake said they would never jump off in tandem as we did, but Dunbar took pleasure in showing off his brave kid brother. We'd climb out of the water, laugh, and repeat the stunt. I suspect my folks never knew about our little game, but I loved the excitement of "Doing Daring Deeds with Dunbar." Those wild jumps gave me a physical confidence that someone who lacked balance might otherwise not have. After climbing on the roof and jumping off the tower, staying on my feet was getting to be no problem at all.

My interactions with David and Jonathan were those of siblings, physical and sometimes quite rough. Despite our fourteen-year age difference, however, my relationship with Dunbar grew to be more like one of equals and friends. He attended Davidson College in North Carolina, but when he returned home, he tended to spend more time interacting with me, taking me places and showing me things.

David was my wild brother. He indulged in mischievous and dangerous antics, especially when his favorite audience, Jonathan and me, was around. He had a preoccupation with guns and sometimes used them recklessly. There was the time he fired a .22 caliber bullet into a phone book in his bedroom and made bets with us on how deep the bullet would go. There was also the episode at the zoo at Hot Springs, Arkansas, when he snuck over a barrier, grabbed a crocodile by the tail, swung it over his head, and tossed it into the pond.

One night when I was about eight, my parents told me to answer the doorbell. On our porch stood a tall, ugly man whose face was badly disfigured. He gestured for me to come with him. I refused but froze in panic. I couldn't move and couldn't take my eyes off him. Just as I was working up the courage to bolt, I realized it was David standing there in shabby clothing with a stocking over his face.

If David was wild and nutty, he was also a strong and manly big brother that I looked up to. I remember vividly the time he gave a verbal thrashing to several teenage boys who had threatened me. David wasn't all mischief. He had high spirits and a lively imagination. He was a fantastic storyteller. I loved to sit in front of him, reading his lips, facial expressions, and gestures, savoring every detail. He told thrilling tales of monsters and horrors. I was petrified by his realism. I think he mostly made them up, sometimes inspired by his favorite horror movies. Often, the storytelling took place at night, and David turned down the lights to make the room spooky. From time to time, he acted out how a character in the story walked, ate, and behaved. Although I was scared, I loved every minute of it.

Jonathan, meanwhile, was more serious. We communicated primarily by lipreading, with exaggerated speech, facial expressions, and gestures. It was comfortable and easy. Jonathan loved talking about what he'd learned from his high school classes and friends. One day he explained the power of persuasion to me. He could serve someone a glass filled with 7 Up, he said, yet tell them it was filled with alcohol.

David, holding George, the rat, by the tail, Dunbar clutching Paul's arms, and Jonathan.

Soon that person would act as if he were intoxicated, even though he hadn't downed any alcohol at all. It was a fascinating concept for me.

Jonathan had a passion for gadgets, movie and still cameras, and cars. Once, an acquaintance from church took us out in his sports car. I noticed the speedometer showed that the maximum speed was two hundred miles per hour. Jonathan later explained how that speed wasn't possible for this model.

Although Jonathan was close to David (he was almost his sidekick as I was to Dunbar), he often shared his insights about people with me. He would relay conversations, not necessarily the actual words but his interpretation of what was said.

All my brothers treated me as an important member of the family. Although I didn't understand it at the time, this was a tremendous boost for my self-esteem and confidence. For anyone with a disadvantage—physical, social, or economic—confidence is a huge factor that can allow us to overcome it.

The disability that is most difficult to overcome, however, one that plagued my family, is the psychological sort.

5

KEEPING THE FAITH

From their experience came pain; and from their pain came
purpose; and from their purpose came beauty.

J. Arcangel

In 1952, when I was three years old, my father sank into a deep depression. Perhaps he was overwhelmed by what he felt were the injustices of having two deaf children. Or perhaps it was the pressures at his church in Staunton. The church was certainly not paying him enough salary, $4,500, to make him feel at ease about his family expenses, especially since $1,000 of it went to Jonathan's schooling at CID each year. With Dunbar at Davidson, David about to begin studies at Hampden-Sydney College in Virginia, and me slated to attend CID in a couple of years, finances must have weighed heavily on our father.

Father's depression was further precipitated, however, by a chemical imbalance, though we wouldn't know this until twenty-five years later. At that time doctors didn't even understand there was such a thing as a chemical imbalance in the nervous system. Father's depressions had occurred before, when he was in college. It would happen to him again in later life, a periodic psychological plague that had a physical cause.

On the advice of doctors in our community, Father was placed in Johns Hopkins Hospital, a major center for the treatment of depression. After a few months, my mother took him from the hospital to stay for six weeks in the home of friends in Pennsylvania to give her time to decide what to do next. My father's brother Fred, now a medical doctor, then encouraged my father to stay with him and his family in Fayetteville, Arkansas, while he recovered.

During all of this, the people at my father's church grew impatient and decided to get another minister. My mother, therefore, had to move out of the church manse in Staunton. It was a time of great upheaval for us and a time when we relied on my mother's strength to hold the family together. Mother hired a moving van and moved us into her mother's home in Springfield, Ohio. Along with all the other things on her mind, my mother kept herself busy by continuing to teach me.

The period after my father's hospitalization was one of Mother's hardest times. She simply had no idea what would become of us, but her Christian faith and her family's love sustained her. During this time, she wrote a poem that reflected her mood. It read:

> Where there is Faith.
>   There is Love.
>   Where there is Love.
>   There is Peace.
>   Where there is Peace.
>   There is God.
>   Where there is God.
>   There is no Need.
>   D.C.O. 1953

Small children are susceptible to tensions and upheavals in the family, and I was no exception. I was three when my mother and I moved into her mother's house in Springfield. My Grandmother Cobolentz, who had been a widow for eight years, lived in a large house that my grandfather built in 1912. It was a duplex. Each side had two stories plus a full basement and attic. All the rooms were huge with high ceilings. I was frightened in the large house at night, and since the halls were lengthy and full of boxes of our things from Staunton, going from room to room meant a long, scary walk in the dark.

One evening my mother and I were in the bathroom, where I brushed my teeth and got ready for bed. I started alone for the bedroom. On the way in the darkness, I tripped and fell. Hearing me fall, my mother came running. Not knowing where I was, she fell on top of me, fracturing my leg.

Parents are always shocked and dismayed when their child decides to have a major trauma exactly when everything else is crashing down around their ears. I think it's natural that little ones, feeling the tension around them, would decide to join in the action and add their little bit to the disaster. For the next six weeks in Springfield, my poor mother had to carry me and my heavy cast around. It must have made me twice as heavy as before.

My mother sometimes wrapped me up, put me in a baby carriage, and took me on long walks. I loved the railway station and watching the trains pull into town and out again. Once as we watched a switch engine, the engineer motioned for us to get on. These walks were filled with little adventures.

At the end of the six weeks, I went back to the hospital for my run-in with the diabolic doctor and his power saw. I didn't believe my mother's explanation that it was for removing the cast. I was convinced it was to remove my leg. I screamed and fought, my eyes closed. Without sound or sight, I felt the vibrations of the power saw buzzing up and down my leg. I was sure the doctor was working hard to cut my leg off. I was much relieved when the ordeal was over and a bit surprised that my limbs remained intact.

While my father was in Arkansas, living with his brother and fighting to recover from his depression, our life in Springfield was complicated. Through it all, I never questioned my father's absence. Our family's future looked bleak, but my mother continued to pray for her husband's recovery and for blessings on her four sons. Mother kept up constant correspondence with my brothers and kept the family together as best she could. She knew that my father was a comparatively young man. In her heart, she felt God had important work for him to do.

She also wondered why she and my father had been given two sons who were then regarded as handicapped. The thought always came that perhaps God had chosen them as our parents because he knew they would respond to our needs with faith, love, and concern. She felt inadequate to deal with this situation on her own, but with God's guidance and inspiration she was able to create the materials necessary to teach us. She learned that continuously asking "why" was unproductive, while asking "how" produced results. My mother had the combination of personality and potential to move on with what she saw as the business of her life.

My Uncle Fred, whose support and love were unwavering during my family's difficult years, began encouraging my father to preach as a guest where needed in various rural churches. Mount Vernon

Presbyterian Church, near Fayetteville, was one of these. The congregation was looking for a new pastor, and eventually they hired my father on a full-time basis. Gradually, he resumed his role as a pastor, and in 1953 we all moved to Pea Ridge, Arkansas, at the edge of the Ozarks. I was four years old.

Two years later, in the summer of 1955, my father's depression fully lifted at last. I often wonder whether my father's situation would have been eased by the treatments, medications, and therapies available today. But we had a treatment even more effective than these—the strength and faith of my mother. From this I learned that one needs to persevere in the face of problems. By having faith and relying on friends and family for support, we can overcome challenges that, at first, seem daunting.

6

PRACTICAL MATTERS

He is wise who can instruct us and assist us in the business of daily virtuous living.

Thomas Carlyle

Throughout the family turmoil during my early years, my mother continued working with me, teaching me all she believed I needed to know. By age four I was a facile lipreader and my vocabulary was expanding rapidly. I rarely had the "Help me find that thing" episodes I'd had when I was a little younger. I now had many words to express myself with, and I made use of them all. This was unusual for someone so young and profoundly deaf, but it was due to my family's conscientious effort to help me become an independent person.

Many have said that when dealing with people with disabilities, the worst thing you can do for them is to overprotect. With children, especially those who are disadvantaged, challenging them will make them stronger. But challenging doesn't mean leaving them to fend for themselves. It requires continual awareness and effort to give them the skills and direction they need to succeed.

When we stayed with her, Grandmother Coblentz was critical of the way my mother treated me. "You're giving him too much attention," she said. "He always wants your time. He knows all the ways of getting your attention. You're spoiling him rotten."

My mother knew Grandmother was right—I did know all the tricks—but she refused to change her ways. She understood that when Dunbar or David came home from school, she could ask "How was school?" as a greeting and keep ironing. But when Jonathan or I arrived, she put down her iron and greeted us face to face, sometimes from her knees at eye level. It was a way to acknowledge us rather than leave us feeling ignored.

It was in Pea Ridge that I started learning about the world outside my family in a real way—what many deaf children learn at a much later age. Too many families overlook the practical aspects of their deaf children's education, even when they are careful to see that their academic life is in order. Perhaps subconsciously they believe their children will be dependent on others all their lives. But children who learn to conduct the daily transactions of life—cashing checks, making purchases, paying visits—are training for independence. My family understood this basic fact well.

The people in rural Pea Ridge were warm and friendly to me. The town was so small that it had only a few stores, a post office, a bank, and a gas station, all of which were surrounded by farmlands.

When I was four, I went to the local bank with my father. I saw him write a check and turn it in to a teller, who in turn gave him some money. The next time I was at the bank I found a little piece of paper and scribbled on it. Then I handed it to a lady at the teller's window. She gave me a nickel. I was thrilled with the nickel and showed it to everyone. My parents didn't want the tellers to get into the habit of passing out money every time I scribbled something, so they persuaded the bank people to stop. In a way, they had to guide my educators as well as my education.

Every time I walked by the local barbershop, I ran inside, knowing that the barber, a friend of my father's, would give me a stick of gum. I looked forward to shaking hands with him before he gave me the gum. He recognized me as an individual. As a little deaf boy, I suppose I was somewhat of an oddity, maybe like a mascot to some people. This had its disadvantages as well as advantages, but mostly it worked in my favor, since people often paid attention to me when they may not have otherwise. This did not always please my parents, since they felt that if I were to make it on my own someday, favoritism now might slow me down.

A few times I insisted that my mother let me go by myself to the dime store to buy something. She wanted me to learn to be independent but was concerned about my crossing the street. From time to time she let me go. She would give me a dime and pretend to be busy with something. I would walk across the street, not knowing that my mother was watching me furtively and anxiously from the living room window. She was very conscious of allowing me this slightly dangerous but necessary exercise in independent living.

It was my father who impressed on me the importance of being careful while crossing a street. I was a little terrified when he explained how a car could swoop down and run me over. I looked many times in both directions before crossing the street. It's hard to explain the disadvantage not hearing can create for such simple, everyday activities.

Despite my parents' efforts, some of the adults in Pea Ridge favored me over the other children in town. Many children were invited to participate in the annual Easter egg hunt. We raced against each other to find as many eggs as possible in an open field. But the adults stationed in different places secretly tipped me off about where the eggs were hidden, so I found many of them quite easily. In the end, I won first prize.

Looking back, I'm grateful that I didn't live in Pea Ridge all my life. If I had, I might have turned into a spoiled adult who puts no effort into cultivating friends and developing a vocation but rather expects the world to come to his or her doorstep as it had in childhood. I surely would have missed out on many challenges. As with a hearing child, though perhaps in a more exaggerated way, successfully training a deaf child to become an independent adult involves striking the perfect (and maybe impossible) balance between encouragement and indulgence.

For my fourth birthday, my mother decided to host a big party for me. She invited children from the neighborhood to our house. Many were also about four, though some were a little older. My mother wanted me to get to know the kids and hoped they would become my friends. While we played games, however, many of the kids disappeared. I couldn't find them. Where were they? Why did they run off? I felt frustrated because they ran away from me. I didn't understand *why* they were teasing me. But my mother knew. She was so upset that she decided never to invite those children again.

The favoritism I experienced from adults was not always shared by children, who often misunderstood my deafness to mean that I was strange. I realize now that many of those kids had heard from their parents that I was deaf and that I was "handicapped." These parents failed to educate them, so I became an oddity to be shunned. There was one girl, however, one or two years older than I was, who came to our house many times. She was nice to me and we played together often. I give a lot of credit to her parents for teaching her to regard me as a human being, not as a freak. Her parents invited my family to their farm to ride horses, so I have many fine memories of that girl and those times. Almost out of instinct, some people seem to relate easily to a deaf person, or to anyone different, while others for unknown reasons simply cannot. One lesson of that birthday party was that my deafness was a fact of my life despite the free-flowing communication that characterized our family life.

My lack of hearing sometimes had strange and startling consequences. One such consequence could easily have become a tragedy. Our house in Pea Ridge was in the country next to my father's church. One day, again when I was four, my father asked if I wanted to go with him to a neighbor's house to get some fresh eggs. I agreed to go but had to wait for him to get ready. I sat down to wait for my father on the rear bumper of our family car, my legs dangling in the air, and quickly became engrossed in watching other children playing in the street.

All of a sudden, I felt the car vibrate. It started backing up and I, still seated there, held onto the bumper tightly with both hands. My father was backing the car into the street before taking off for the dirt road that led to the neighbor's chicken farm. A hearing child would almost certainly have picked up auditory clues to my father's departure—the slamming of the house door, exchanged goodbyes, even his footsteps. In this case, my full attention was on the other children.

Here my parents had overlooked a cardinal rule for communicating with people who are deaf: never assume that information has been conveyed "somehow." Deaf people—and especially deaf children— need to pick up information directly, not incidentally from the environment. I was trying with all my might to hold on to the bumper, praying I wouldn't fall off. It seemed as though we traveled a long way before the car finally stopped. The vibrating ended. I jumped off the bumper and ran up to my father, who was startled to see me.

I tried to express my anger to him in simple words and gestures, many of which included pointing at the rear bumper. My father was speechless for a few seconds before he rushed up and hugged me. He thought I had changed my mind and decided not to go with him after all. Later, with the excitement of gathering eggs, I forgot all about the scare I had experienced. My father, of course, did not.

Another day, my mother and I walked from our little house to a neighboring church where my father was asked to conduct a funeral. I understood that we were going to a service for someone who had died. On the way I asked my mother, "Why the man die?"

My mother explained that the man was so old that he just died. I was not satisfied with this explanation at all, so I asked her again. When she gave me the same answer, I got impatient and asked again. "How the man die? Sick, car hit, gun, knife, fire?"

"No," she said, "he didn't die like that. He was very old. He was eighty-seven years old."

"How he die? He hurt and die?" I persisted.

"No, nothing happened. He died in his sleep because he was so old."

"Someone kill him in bed?"

"Paul, nothing happened to him," my mother said. "He lived many, many years and he became very old. His body was worn out and fell apart. He just went to sleep and died because he was very old."

I stopped pestering my mother for an explanation, but I was a little stunned to know that people did die in their sleep and that they dropped dead for no reason other than being old. It was an abstract concept I had trouble digesting. This new discovery was a little scary.

I was discovering much more about the world around me. Because my mother played many cognitive, linguistic, and thought-provoking games with me, I developed cognitive structures and processes at an early age. The more I learned, the more active and restless I was in response to life in general. I learned to see relationships in the environment clearly and to have them confirmed through communication with my family. Through travels and activities my family conducted outside of the home, I acquired many concepts of time and place—ideas that are too often poorly conveyed to deaf children.

Even though my family had only a modest standard of living, we managed to take memorable trips and vacations. It was part of an upbringing intentionally designed to widen vistas for all four boys, both hearing and deaf. Wherever possible, my family thought of ways to get ideas, concepts, and things through to me. Some of these techniques took imagination. To refer to days in the future, for instance, my mother used the term "sleeps"—two days from now would be two sleeps from now. She knew that the idea would have to be linked to something familiar to me in my soundless world. With a deaf child, you have to work hard to find concrete examples of abstractions, such as time or a distant place. It's easy to gloss over something by using a few words to describe it, but my family learned to communicate in unique and memorable ways.

When we talked about a place that was far from home, my brothers acted out driving a long way and for many days. Thanks to their gestures, I understood at an early age whether a place was far or close, and so gained a more accurate view of the world. A bit of pantomime helped facilitate learning many concepts. How, for example, do you get across the notion of "happy" to a deaf child? You act out experiences—a birthday party, a surprise gift, eating ice cream. Whenever you see a situation where he or she smiles, you use the word. That is much more detailed and effective than just saying, "To be happy is like feeling good."

With a deaf child, the spoken word and concept grow together eventually, but it takes time. A hearing child has another way of reaching the same definition. He or she simply parrots a word overheard from adults and throws it out there, using it out loud to test it in a multitude of situations until the word and its subtle shades of meaning and association are fully understood.

I am especially indebted to my family for the infinite number of word games they played with me as a natural part of daily life. At an early age, I was able to understand abstract basic relationships apart from the physical environment and to gain information simply because they talked and pantomimed to me. They knew how to use my language. If one word didn't work, they'd try another. Then they'd slip in a new one. By the time I was five, I had developed many strategies for understanding and had progressed in my general cognitive development. Although I didn't have perfect speech, I was able to communicate almost anything I wanted to.

My early language evolved from a well-integrated, nonverbal communication system at home. My brothers always made conversations interesting. They were never shy about going to any lengths to help me understand. If we went to the zoo and saw an elephant, for example, they'd tell me all about elephants. Then, to spice things up, David would say that some could flap their ears and fly, and Dunbar would add that many are pink, and then they'd pick me up and make me "fly." Jonathan, meanwhile, would tell me the elephant was so strong that he could knock down everything around him. He would imitate the elephant's walk and swing his "trunk."

My parents and brothers were responsive to my existence and needs in everyday life. They talked with me, acted upon their talk, and expected feedback from me. They responded to me as a partner in meaningful social communication. They used eye contact to reinforce our communication. They didn't talk to me only about what they wanted me to know. They also responded to what I had to say. Through communication, I became socialized—a part of the social order—and learned that I could affect my environment through communication.

PART TWO

SCHOOL DAYS IN ST. LOUIS

❙

LEAVING HOME

Love knows not distance; it hath no continent; its eyes are for the stars.

Gilbert Parker

In 1954, as I neared the age of five, Jonathan approached sixteen, the age limit for the Central Institute for the Deaf. The CID faculty felt that because he was not an excellent lipreader, he would suffer educationally and socially by going to a regular hearing school. For his part, Jonathan was fed up with the oral instruction at CID. He had become frustrated with the speech drills and lipreading lessons and felt strongly that he was not learning anything of value.

While my parents corresponded with the people at CID about Jonathan's future, Jonathan insisted that the place for him was the Arkansas School for the Deaf in Little Rock. The school was a long distance from Pea Ridge, but Jonathan's eagerness to go there helped ease my parents' conscience about sending him so far away from home again.

At this same time, it was agreed that I would benefit from attending CID. The people at CID were so impressed with my progress in home instruction that they offered a scholarship to offset part of the tuition, as they had for Jonathan. My education would emphasize speech, lipreading, and auditory training for my first four years and then expand in subsequent years to include traditional academic study. My parents thought it would be wonderful if both Jonathan and I were at CID at the same time, for him to help me adjust to school life, but it wasn't to be. I started at CID in September 1954, just a few months after Jonathan ended his eleven years of study there.

My parents drove me from Arkansas. I vividly remember sitting in the backseat of the Chevrolet after we reached St. Louis, looking for my black cowboy boots with red spots on them.

35

"Where my boots?" I asked my mother. This was an important day and I had to look my best. I was proud of those boots. I sensed tension and apprehension in the car, more between my parents than with me. This trip felt different than all the others we'd made in my short life. We looked the city over from the Chevrolet as we drove down Kingshighway Boulevard.

Suddenly, in front of us was the school, a huge, four-story brick building taking up nearly a whole block. It took my mother and father two or three trips to unload and carry my suitcases and footlocker up to the second floor of the school. I looked around, not knowing exactly what to expect. I did know I was going to school there, but I didn't understand that I was going to be *left* there, alone. I was so excited about this new adventure that I just assumed my family would be staying too. We walked up the stairway to the spacious room that was to be my dormitory. There were ten beds in the room, five on one side and five on the other. At the foot of each bed was a metal locker, two feet by two feet by three feet. The third side of the room was lined with ten wardrobe closets.

I looked up and saw a small, round lady. I was introduced to Mrs. Morton. "Paul," she said, "welcome," and she hugged me. I could lipread her easily. She was to be the housemother for the ten boys in my room, ages three through six. I remember the smell of Mrs. Morton, a distinctive combination of body odor and cigarettes. She wore dark, round glasses. She acted as if she had known me for a long time, probably because she had known Jonathan. As Mrs. Morton showed us around the room, the other nine boys followed and watched with curiosity. I was shown my bed, my metal locker, and my wall closet. My mother put some things in the locker and hung clothes in the wall closet. I was beginning to get the idea. The housemother showed us to the large, boys' bathroom, where nine towels hung on hooks. Someone had written a boy's name above each hook.

After we moved my things in, my parents and I went out for supper. At the restaurant, my parents explained that they would see me at Christmas. "Time will go fast," my mother said. "Many sleeps will go fast. We will all be together again at Christmas. In December you will come home!"

I was not really paying attention to the conversation, nor had I fully absorbed the reality of separation from my family. I was excited by the dormitory and what seemed like a new adventure. The gravity of the situation would visit me later. That evening my parents and I went back to the dorm room again. They hugged me. "Goodbye! Goodbye!" they said. I remember how tense they seemed. I know now they were holding back their tears. "Goodbye!" I said, waving with excitement. They were gone.

The other boys in the dormitory were curious about me. We got acquainted. To the hearing, the communication of that group of deaf children must have been a comic opera indeed. We all began gesturing and moving our lips in exaggerated emphasis of the words, pointing to our lips and pantomiming everything we said. It struck me at that time that the way these boys talked was different from the way my family moved their lips. My family's speech was smoother and more natural.

Soon, it was time to prepare for bed. The boys knew what they were supposed to do and I fell in line, following them to the bathroom where we cleaned up and brushed our teeth. We then went to bed. I wasn't homesick or even upset that my parents had left me. Everything was new and different from what I normally experienced, and I was thoroughly infected with the spirit of adventure.

The next morning I sensed a lot of excitement. We washed up, put on our school clothes, formed a straight line, and followed Mrs. Morton down the stairway to breakfast. To my amazement, there were a hundred people in the dining room—boys, girls, adults, and black women serving meals (the term "African American" was still many years away). I learned later there were five levels of students at the school, ranging from age five to age sixteen. Altogether, eighty pupils lived in the dormitories. Another eighty to ninety children lived at home and attended CID during the day. During my years at CID the population was roughly 160 to 170 pupils at any given time.

In the large dining room at that first breakfast, I followed Mrs. Morton with the other boys from my dormitory to the first table at the end of the long row. The tables were set according to dormitory levels. I was fascinated with the mystery of being in a new atmosphere. I could see right away that it was special to be seated at the last table at the other side of the dining room. Once you arrived there, you were the oldest and most mature. The instant I saw those teenage children, I looked up to them.

After the newness wore off, though, the first few weeks in that dining room were an awful experience for me. No longer was I the focus of attention. I had entered my first dictatorship. I was about to experience the world as it really was.

From time to time we had hot oatmeal and Mrs. Morton expected all her boys to like their oatmeal the same way. That included lots of white sugar. I had never put sugar on cereal before and hated it from the first. At home, we had always had butter and milk on our cereal. I refused the sugar: "No, no, no sugar." My frustration grew as I realized that Mrs. Morton was not listening to my protests.

"Paul, eat your cereal," Mrs. Morton said. I had to eat my cereal or whatever we had for breakfast and do whatever she bid. I tried to verbalize my family's home customs, but I felt a wall go up between us. I was used to being in a household where communication was total, but here at the table I was faced with a person who, after working for years with deaf children, no longer made any attempt to understand preferences.

After breakfast on that first day we lined up to walk back to our dormitory and to the bathroom to brush our teeth. At eight o'clock, Mrs. Morton led each of us to our different classrooms. Mine was only a few yards from the dormitory. It was the first one in the hall and was for first- and second-year students. Mrs. Morton led me by the hand to my new teacher, Mrs. Olmstead, who gave me a warm smile and big hug. My brother had been in Mrs. Olmstead's class eleven years earlier, though I didn't learn this until a few years later. I sensed right away that she was wonderful—warm, patient, loving, and kind.

There were four other kids in the classroom. Two, Rusty Hooten and Rochelle Berlin, remained with me throughout my years at CID. I have no recollection of the other two, for they dropped out of school within a few years. We sat in our little chairs in what seemed to me to be a huge room. When I returned to visit the same classroom fifteen years later, I was shocked, of course, to see how small it really was. But on that first day I was small too.

So my classroom education began. On our first day and for many days to come we formed a semicircle and faced the teacher, who sat with a large blackboard behind her. Mrs. Olmstead was generous with hugs and affection, and I always felt positive feelings toward her. She was also easy to lipread and enunciated slowly so that the words formed on her lips were clear to me.

The basic philosophy was that only oral communication took place in the classroom. For emphasis, Mrs. Olmstead pointed to her chin with her index finger to remind us to keep our attention on her lips. The gesture meant "Listen to this. You must hear this."

Mrs. Olmstead carried a long stick, which she used to tap our laps to get our attention. When we looked up, she'd say, "Would you say or do...?" and then give us a specific command. These simple commands enabled us to flex our energetic muscles while also exercising our lip-reading skills and pouring new words into our vocabulary. They might go on for a few minutes: "Turn around. Catch the ball. Throw the ball. Give me the blue car. Jump up and down. Say 'mumumumum.' Say 'la la la la.' Clap your hands."

Since oral education was the school's philosophy, we had speech and lipreading lessons every day. To me, these "games" were great fun, for I was already a good lipreader and I could follow everything Mrs. Olmstead said. There was a great deal of interaction between teacher and students. Mrs. Olmstead always gave the impression that she could be reached easily, unlike Mrs. Morton, who seemed not to care to communicate with us.

Mrs. Olmstead was a scientific educator. She knew how to get and keep our attention. How? She bribed us. On her desk was a fishbowl full of M&Ms. If we did our speech lesson particularly well, Mrs. Olmstead gave us one of those bright little candies. I remember vividly that bowl of M&Ms, as well as my fantasy of running up and grabbing a handful of the sweet treats. Usually, we earned only one M&M at a time and could go up before the class and pick the color of our choice. With the rest of the class watching with envy, we'd pop it in our mouths and savor it, trying to make that moment and the M&M last as long as possible. It was a rare achievement to get more than five in a day.

We remained with the same teacher all day long in the same classroom for a year. We focused on the basic communication skills of speech, lipreading, and listening. The longer we worked with Mrs. Olmstead, the better we understood her and the more naturally she spoke to us, which meant less enunciation and more speed. At first, we did all exercises orally, but later in the year Mrs. Olmstead showed us large cards on which were printed the word and sentence commands. We repeated the words after her and followed the commands if she asked us to do so.

My interaction with other deaf children was also a big part of my new life. Some of those I met at CID that first year became lifelong friends. One was Rusty. We communicated orally—that is, we lipread and talked, which is what CID and our prior training at home encouraged us to do. We also gestured along with our speech, but hard as it is for some to believe, we did not use sign language at all. Hearing people with no exposure to deaf speech would probably not have understood much of what we said. Our speech was not perfect. However, we were more conscious than hearing children of the way we made ourselves understood by enunciation and lip movement.

When it came to hearing people, we talked a bit differently, focusing on making our speech as intelligible as possible. Therefore, we learned two distinct ways of talking, and the distinction is with me to this day. When I am with deaf people, I don't try as hard to make myself easy to lipread and nor do I speak as clearly. When I am with hearing people, my shift is in speech quality. For this reason, I usually find it difficult to talk to hearing and deaf people at the same time.

Although CID discouraged sign language, we used gestures often. I remember several gestures well. If we didn't like someone, for instance, we flicked the middle finger off our thumb outward toward the disliked person (that may sound familiar to people who sign). If we liked someone, we made a petting motion up and down with a flat palm. If we were playing in a group and someone displeased us, we'd look at that person and flick out our fingers at him. The other kids, if they agreed, would start flicking too. On other days, we'd like that person again and would use the petting motion to show approval. I've thought of that gesture as like smoking a peace pipe, whereas the negative gesture sometimes got us into arguments or fights.

The younger kids were, of course, the least verbal. They frequently resorted to pushing and shoving each other in frustration. We became less physical and more verbal in our conflicts as we got older. Hearing children are much the same, but children who are deaf are often slower to learn proper, diplomatic ways to vent anger through verbal expression if they did not pick up good communication skills at home at an early age. Research shows that even babies can sign, some as early as six months old.

One of my strongest impressions of my first year at CID, besides the M&Ms, was of a magnificent calendar on the classroom wall. At the beginning of each day, we stood in a semicircle in front of the calendar. It featured colorful stickers on different days of the month, such as holidays or special days for us to remember. Standing there at the calendar, we recited such things as: "Today is Monday. Tomorrow will be Tuesday. Yesterday was Sunday. In one week, we will go to the movies. Yesterday, Rusty and I had some ice cream." These exercises were designed to help us with time concepts as well as proper grammar.

The most important part of the calendar work was figuring out how much longer it would be before we would see our families again. Instead of "days" we used the same term my mother used, "sleeps," to measure how often we'd have to sleep through the night before a given day would arrive. While pointing with our index fingers to the calendar days, we'd say, "Sleep, sleep, sleep," eagerly counting down the time before we would be off for the holidays.

My first flight, on a two-propeller plane, took place when I left St. Louis to go home for Christmas that year. I was so excited about the prospect of seeing my family again that I didn't pay much attention to the flying experience itself. It was wonderful to be back in that warm and nurturing environment. I remember waking up on my first morning back, running into my parents' bedroom, and jumping into bed with them. I also remember lots of hugs, roughhousing with my three brothers, and savoring home-cooked meals, including bacon for breakfast, a particular favorite of mine.

The end of that holiday was an altogether different situation. A couple of days before I was scheduled to leave, I began to cry and said I didn't want to go back to school. Mother explained that I had to go. We looked at the calendar and counted the number of sleeps until I could come home again. I said I understood and stopped crying. But the next morning, I began crying all over again.

In the middle of the night before my departure, I woke up, went into my parents' bedroom, and cried some more. When morning came, I tried hard to convince my parents to let me stay. They of course said it was best for me to go.

At the airport, I hugged my three brothers and both of my parents. I cried, my mother cried, and she and I hugged and cried together. My brothers tried to make jokes and did crazy things to get me to laugh. It didn't work. My father asked, "Do you have your ticket?"

"Yes," I said.

"Go on, then," he said.

I couldn't hold back the moment any longer. I walked from the gate to the ramp. I wore a sign on a string around my neck with my name and destination on it. On the plane, a stewardess (they weren't called flight attendants back then) said, "Oh, what a cute little boy you are. But why are you crying?"—as if the mere question would make me stop, think, and change my mind about the tears. She led me to a seat by the window, which I pressed my face against. I continued to cry as I watched my family wave at me.

I felt the vibrations of the baggage handlers shifting suitcases, the shuffling of the passengers, and the running of the stewardesses as they helped people find their seats. I felt the door close and the cabin pressure change. I watched the handlers pull the ramp away from the plane. I felt the engines warming up. I waved almost hysterically at my family, crying even harder, trying to prolong the moment as long as possible. The plane shuddered slightly and then began to move toward the runway. I felt the wheels travel over bumps on the concrete—*thump, thump, thump.*

By the time we reached the end of the runway, I was so tired from crying that I was almost dizzy. I felt the engines come up to speed. *Now it's too late to get off the plane*, I thought. *I'm stuck! I have to go on.*

The plane moved forward, faster and faster. I felt it lift off the ground. I looked back at the airport where my family stood. It grew smaller and smaller. Soon we entered the clouds. When we leveled off, I knew I was irrevocably on my way away from family and toward school. The trauma of leaving was over. I was so tired that I fell asleep.

Before every trip back to school for the next ten years, the pattern was largely the same. The planes changed, from two propellers to four, and then to jets. But the emotional upheaval remained the same. It wasn't that I hated school. I just missed my family. What made it all bearable was the knowledge that after a few more sleeps, I would again have the chance to be with the people who loved me so deeply.

2

TURNING THE PAGE

Whenever you read a good book, somewhere in the world a door opens to allow in more light.

Vera Nazarian

At the end of my first year at CID, my mother and Dunbar came to visit for a few days before we went home together for the summer. Mother wanted to observe Mrs. Olmstead's class so that she could continue to work with me during the summer, emphasizing what the teacher wanted me to retain. For some reason, my mother and Dunbar, who were staying at a motel, decided to leave me at the dormitory for the night of their visit. They probably didn't want to interfere with my daily schedule.

When they were getting ready to return to the motel for the night, I was so upset about staying in the dorm that I unleashed my outrage verbally. "I want go to motel with you tonight," I said, pointing to my chest, then to my mother and Dunbar, and then outside.

"We'll see you in the morning and in a few days, we will go home," Mother said.

"Not fair for Dunbar and David home, school, home, school, home," I said, using my index finger to point back and forth to home and school. "I go far away. I stay school, school, school, school. Why me? Not fair!"

Mother started to cry a bit. "We want the best education for you," she said. "We are sorry."

I just didn't understand why I couldn't stay with the family as my brothers did. Although I had now been living for several months in a school for deaf children, I still didn't comprehend the word "deaf" and how that concept related to me. Imagining hearing—something I had

43

never experienced—was simply beyond the intellectual powers of a six-year-old. With that central concept missing, much about my life and my separation from my family remained a mystery to me.

My first summer after CID went swiftly, and all too soon it was time for me to return to school. I was none too happy when my mother took me shopping for new clothes at the end of that summer. We had done the same thing the year before for the same reason, but then I hadn't comprehended the fact that I was going to be away from home. Now the meaning sank in and saddened me. For the next nine years, the pattern was the same: the two weeks before the departure for school in September were always hectic. My mother and I went to stores to buy clothes and other items. Then she started what seemed like a ridiculous ritual—sewing a name tag with my name printed on it into every piece of clothing.

That second year, Dunbar and my mother drove me to St. Louis. After arriving at school and taking the suitcase and footlocker up to the dormitory, we returned to the car for our final farewell. I cried and resisted the attempt to take me back into the main school building. My poor mother started crying also and had to stay in the car. Dunbar, picking me up in his arms, carried me into the school while I kicked and fought him. When we got inside I was embarrassed to be seen being carried, so I stopped fighting. Relieved, Dunbar took me by the hand up the stairs to the dormitory. We hugged and he left. I was relieved to see Rusty's parents also deliver a teary child. We consoled each other. That first-day classroom was full of subdued children, all tired from crying.

Mrs. Olmstead was my teacher again that year, and to my relief Rusty and Rochelle were in my class again. Mrs. Olmstead tried to make us forget our homesickness by drawing our attention to things we could look forward to. That second year, though the classroom activities were similar, our vocabularies expanded and we communicated more than ever. We wrote more and the teacher gave us many more paper activities. We received instructions such as: "Please color the second car blue. Circle the yellow balloon. Show me something soft. Draw a picture of a cat under the table."

Now that we were learning to read, the high point of our classroom days was getting a letter from home and sharing it with the class. Mrs. Olmstead usually helped us read the letters and generated conversations between us about what was happening at home.

My mother wrote often, and Rochelle got letters from home almost as frequently as I did. Sadly, Rusty received almost no mail from his parents, perhaps one letter every three or four weeks. Rusty got upset every time mail came without a letter for him. Even when he received mail, there wasn't much information about what was happening at home, which was also a big disappointment for him.

Mrs. Olmstead was always concerned about making all of us feel good about ourselves. Since Rusty was so much a part of my life, she asked my mother to write to him from time to time. I remember several times watching Rusty read letters that had my mother's familiar handwriting. I wasn't jealous, because I cherished Rusty as my best friend. Mrs. Olmstead tried to persuade Rusty's parents to write him more often but to no avail. It turned out that Rusty's parents were having marital problems, which may explain why they wrote so infrequently.

Letters from my parents usually included pictures or drawings, as well as cutouts from newspapers and magazines. These were important stimuli for developing my communication skills in both expressive and receptive language. Mrs. Olmstead showed great interest in everything we got from home, but she didn't appear to be trespassing. We were always glad to share our mail with her, for she always had things to say to increase our self-esteem and pride in our families. As I see it now, she had a genius for turning situations into opportunities to use and expand our language and reading skills.

Being away at school, we cherished photographs of our family members and snapshots of our pets and home life. We spent lots of time discussing these photographs. They were visually comforting and helped us illustrate the stories we told of our homes. These simple treasures were vital in helping a group of lonely children adjust to a life removed from family.

During that second year, we also focused on short sentences, penmanship, and writing words on paper with a pencil. Mrs. Olmstead introduced us to spelling tests, which were a favorite for me throughout my years there. CID added a new wrinkle to the old spelling bee because it involved lipreading as well. When a teacher said a word, we had to lipread it before we could spell it on paper. We had hundreds of spelling tests during our years, which meant that CID students have always been good spellers. The fact that we were deaf and had to concentrate on several levels that a hearing person needn't bother with added to our learning. Since we couldn't rely on the sound of the word to guess a spelling, we had to read it and study it. Conversely, we ran into trouble if Mrs. Olmstead used a word that we had never seen on lips before.

We spent hours reading. We were asked to read aloud sentences from the blackboard and from books opened for us to read together. Print was attractive to me from the beginning, and Mrs. Olmstead didn't have to do much to encourage me to read. For a deaf person, reading can be a special window into the world of communication.

Oddly enough, reading is an activity that is normally difficult to teach deaf children and an exercise that some schools fail to pursue adequately, as my parents discovered in their first visits to schools for the deaf. I attribute much of my natural interest in literature to my family and Mrs. Olmstead's enthusiasm for it. There is nothing like the power of a book to enhance vocabulary and open new vistas.

3

THE YEAR OF TERROR

The ache for home lives in all of us. The safe place where we can go as we are and not be questioned.

Maya Angelou

My third year at Central Institute for the Deaf turned into the Year of Terror. Rusty and I, now age seven, moved to the second-level dormitory. Our time of relative security and peace with Mrs. Morton, the housemother, was over. In the new dorm, we found ourselves in close contact with a boy who turned out to be the troublemaker of the school. Even more disturbing was finding ourselves in the care of a sterner and less congenial housemother, Mrs. Hilton.

Housemothers at CID were paid poorly. They were mostly poorly educated women who knew little or nothing about deafness. The school could have been more careful about the women they hired. After all, housemothers had to supply surrogate motherly love and make the children feel at home, thus the name "housemother." Mrs. Morton, though she lacked the desire to understand her deaf charges, was at least congenial.

Mrs. Hilton was another story. Rusty and I had Mrs. Hilton for two years, and our friendship suffered by her presence in our lives. We didn't have the time to enjoy each other's company as before. We were too busy watching out for our own tails, making sure that Don, the dorm troublemaker, and Mrs. Hilton didn't run us down. Don tended to get into fights, and as is true of many underpaid and underprivileged overseers, Mrs. Hilton tended to punish all of us instead of the real troublemaker. Don was nearly always the aggressor and didn't care if the conflict was tied to him or not, but for some reason Mrs. Hilton lumped all of us together as culprits.

The most common outcome of fights was a bloody ear from the hard earmolds of our hearing aids. Almost everyone wore at least one hearing aid, even me. Being boxed on the ear caused the earmold to lacerate the tender outer ear. Although not for this reason, I'm sure, they now make earmolds out of a softer material.

Don came from a well-to-do family, and because they had spoiled him, he was very demanding toward everyone else. Paradoxically, he was also the center of envy because his folks often sent him boxes of toys and sweets. He was usually well-stocked and began to use the toys and sweets to reward and punish the rest of us as he liked. We all came to fear him and the power he had over us. Mrs. Hilton remained blind to all of this and didn't take the trouble to correct the problem.

Keith was another boy in our dormitory to be dreaded. He was a frustrated soul, and being much stronger than the rest of us, he established himself as a bully over the next few years. We learned bit by bit that his mother was raising him alone. He made up stories about his father, who existed only in his imagination. He often threatened that his father would come after us if we were not nice to him or if we didn't do what he wanted. When he beat one of us up, he threatened further terror later on if we reported it to Mrs. Hilton, a fact she never believed. When I think about it today, it reminds me of a Mafia movie where the authorities never believe the threat exists and therefore never provide the protection needed. We couldn't report Keith or he would get someone else to strike back, and his "hit men" always lied convincingly, saying he had nothing to do with it.

Many of us developed what I'd call survival behavior. We were always on the lookout and never trusted anyone in the dormitory. It was a pretty stressful environment for boys of seven and eight to live in. The combination of conflicts made me feel so homesick that I occasionally crawled into Rusty's bed at night to talk with him. We talked without voices by reading lips from the light of the exit signs and outside street lights. It occurs to me that all kids, from time to time, could make good use of silent speech along with gestures and body language.

If it weren't for letters from my family, I would have fared much worse during those years. I suppose any child in a boarding school would be confronted by the same fears, alienations, and conflicts. Being able to hear may not have made it any better or worse, but my being in that school was a direct result of my being deaf. In some ways, having to go to CID brought me closer to my family and insulated me from day-to-day problems that family life creates. I did learn much and I appreciate the time I spent there. But if I were asked today whether I would rather have spent my childhood at home and perhaps learned a little less as a result, the choice would be difficult.

We weren't completely passive in our misery in the dorm. In fact, we did manage to pull off one ingenious, if sad, caper of revenge. In the dormitory was a slow-witted boy named Ricky. For some reason, he was Mrs. Hilton's favorite. Many of us couldn't abide his always running to her for protection and love, which she never showed to us. Some of us decided to do something about it. We taught Ricky what we called "the dirty sign"—the flipping of the middle finger. We told him to say, "I love you! I love you!" then flip his finger. We praised and drilled him for quite a while and then encouraged him to try it on Mrs. Hilton. We all scattered to different places in the dormitory, while keeping our eyes on Ricky as he went up to Mrs. Hilton. We watched in ecstasy as he did it perfectly.

Mrs. Hilton was so shocked that she took out her favorite device, her whip, and began physically admonishing him. Physical punishment was commonplace in residential schools in those days. Poor Ricky didn't understand the meaning of it and retreated to his bed, dumbfounded. The rest of us roared with laughter, but Mrs. Hilton took no notice of this or did not connect us with the incident—another indication of her lack of awareness. Can you imagine how obvious a group of giggling boys would have been?

The next day Ricky hugged Mrs. Hilton as usual, and, as always, we were disgusted with his behavior. So we explained to him that he must have flipped his finger too fast and startled the housemother. We repeated the drill. Amazingly, we convinced him to try again. We scattered and again watched the scene between Ricky and Mrs. Hilton. She was so shocked that she whipped him doubly hard this time. Again, the housemother proved insensitive. How could she overlook the mirth scattered throughout the room? Poor Ricky was crestfallen. He did not play with, listen to, or talk to us for several days. To this day, I feel bad about the incident and hope Ricky understands now that we were just kids being kids.

That third year we also acquired a new classroom teacher, Mrs. Lunde. Rusty and I began to look back fondly at the two wonderful years with Mrs. Olmstead, whose warmth and trust we had enjoyed without full appreciation. Mrs. Lunde taught us that sign language was a horrible practice that we would never be permitted to indulge in. The idea she conveyed was that people who signed were poorly educated, low class, and to be pitied and avoided. This was a particularly harsh interpretation of CID's no-signing policy but by no means an uncommon one. Throughout the world of deaf education at that time, signers were looked down upon. Mrs. Lunde would not even tolerate our homemade gestures and signs. Speech was our daily communication mode.

During my first two years at CID, I had not experienced any disciplinary problems in the classroom or dormitory. Now there were big problems in paradise. Both Mrs. Lunde and Mrs. Hilton were frequently in conflict with the students. Who created all this? All I can say is that it didn't exist the year before. One thing was certain: those two adults sure increased my homesickness. Suddenly I *hated* school!

Mrs. Lunde was not a natural teacher. Her impatience often overwhelmed us, as I think we overwhelmed her. Sometimes she was so impatient that she picked one of us up and shook the offender as if to loosen and detach what bothered her. All of us were terrified of her. We tried too hard to please her, making it even worse. The naturalness of communication slowly drained out of us and was replaced by awkwardness. Suddenly, whenever I was unable to figure out what she wanted from me, I would lose my ability to communicate. I'm sure other students reacted the same. Force is an ineffective teaching technique. Understanding and compassion may seem slow, but at least they don't scare the education out of a child.

All year long, Mrs. Lunde punished us whenever we used gestures or signs. A month before school was out for the summer, she brought a pair of boxing gloves and threatened us with them: if we dared to use a gesture or a sign, we would have to wear the boxing gloves. Within a few hours a boy named Bob was wearing them. It was an awful experience for all of us. Bob was punished often, though his use of hands seemed minor to us. Once, during one of her rages, Mrs. Lunde put a paper bag over Bob's head and made him sit for what must have been fearful eternity to a small boy.

The use of hands is natural even among hearing children. Mrs. Lunde's overreactions served only to hamper rather than help us learn.

I didn't often feel the brunt of Mrs. Lunde's anger, as Bob did, but I suffered sharply from her lack of understanding. One such incident lives on in my memory. Every Monday at CID, all students had to write letters to their parents. The teachers helped us correct spelling and grammar before we rewrote our letters and mailed them home. If we were in the mood to write something personal or private to our parents, we could write letters on our own and send them without inspection, as long as we wrote our weekly letters for the teacher to review. Day pupils who didn't live in the dormitory were expected to find a relative willing to correspond with them, so they could participate in the Monday letter ritual.

One Monday morning, I was so homesick while rewriting my letter, which had already been corrected by Mrs. Lunde, that I decided to add to the last line: "I love you very, very, very, very, very, very..." all the way to the bottom of the back page, with just enough room for me to add, "much. Paul." When Mrs. Lunde saw the letter, she gave it back it to me with one of her terrifying facial expressions and said I had to erase all the extra "verys." Why hadn't she simply asked me to rewrite the letter on another paper? The erasing took a long time. I was unhappy at the thought that my parents would never see how much I cared for them. Years later, my mother reminded me of the episode and said she and my father were so touched by the letter with all the erased "verys." So they got the message after all!

Needless to say, the bullying by other students and the threats and angry outbursts by our teacher made for a nearly impossible learning environment. I was so homesick during the Year of Terror that I began to feel insecure. At Christmas vacation, Mother gave me her special scarf, which she wore often. Understanding my loneliness, she gave me just the right thing to carry back to school. The smell of my mother's perfume was still in the scarf. Wearing and smelling it made me feel secure. I wore the gray scarf frequently that winter. Her scent helped me through some rough times.

Looking back now, it's obvious that Mrs. Lunde disliked teaching and that she didn't even like kids. I'm sure she had no children of her own. I wonder whether she even had proper training in teaching children who are deaf. I often wish there were a mirror in front each of us, so that we could see what others see when we are unkind or untruthful. It might be uncomfortable, but I for one would rather know how bad I look to others so that I could correct myself.

4

HUMOR AND HURTS

Every survival kit should include a sense of humor.

Author unknown

My fourth year at CID, 1957–58, was a contrast to the Year of Terror. Rusty and I moved on to a wonderful new teacher, and Don and Keith moved on to terrorize another classroom. We still had Mrs. Hilton, but she was only one out of three former problems.

Miss Pearl Thomas was a kind, patient, loving, and above all, *sane* teacher. She never put bags on our heads or boxing gloves on our hands and she didn't believe that shaking a child would get the answer out of him. We talked actively again in Miss Thomas's class and went back to using natural gestures that could not have been against CID's oralism policy anyway. I don't recall ever being punished for talking with my hands in Miss Thomas's classroom. What a difference from Mrs. Lunde!

That year, like second graders everywhere, we worked to improve our handwriting, waded through language lessons, computed long columns of numbers, and sharpened lots of pencils. The emphasis at this time was more on writing than on speech. I have Miss Thomas to thank for strengthening my English skills and fostering an interest in writing, which I still have today. Her classroom had a pleasant atmosphere with many items displayed on the walls, which is important for deaf students because they depend on visual stimuli. Some items, though, we simply couldn't understand. For instance, Miss Thomas put up poetry that she cherished but that was lost on our childish minds. It probably dealt with passion or compassion, two subjects we had yet to explore.

Miss Thomas did have one passion that we could relate to—she was an ardent baseball fan. She especially liked it when our class played. We often competed in spirited games between two teams made up from all the classes—the Cardinals and the Blue Jays. When we returned to class,

Miss Thomas wrote down the scores on beautifully drawn scoreboards. Pictures of the Cardinals and Blue Jays were posted everywhere. Miss Thomas was a bird lover as well.

Parents and relatives came to visit our room often, which showed how welcome they felt in Miss Thomas's class. When my parents visited, my friends particularly appreciated my father, who liked being the center of attention and accomplished it by creating fun for everyone around him. He invented games for all of us to play in the dormitory. Many other parents remained aloof. Many had not fully accepted their own children's deafness, and the reminder triggered by all the students seemed to make them uncomfortable. With my parents, it was different. They had lived with Jonathan's deafness for so long that they were completely at ease with other deaf children.

Once, my father was in St. Louis for a conference and stayed at a hotel near CID. He came every evening of his stay to play with us in the dormitory. He drew funny pictures, told funny stories, and led us in games. In one game, we had to show our daring and exercise implicit trust in each other. We lined up in two lines, holding our hands across the lines like a human net. Then one boy stood on a chair and fell backward into the net of hands. Every boy wanted a turn at being the "fall guy" to prove his courage. It was a bold game. Mrs. Hilton kept peeking out of her room, wringing her hands and probably hoping my father would leave so she could regain control.

One other game he played was a one-time-only trick. He asked, "How many of you would like to know if you are really smart?" All of us were intrigued by this question and eagerly cooperated. He had us line up and kneel on one knee. He looked at us with a smile, then walked to the end of the line of boys and pushed the first one. Each of us fell, one by one, like dominoes. He laughed and said, "Are you really as smart as you all thought you were?"

We were a bit embarrassed, but we had a good laugh at ourselves. The laughter was what mattered; many of my school friends missed out on the lighter side of social life because their hearing family or friends didn't know how to communicate with them. My father knew how to play with us so that we caught on to the games and jokes with no problem. He brought his long experiences with deafness not only into the dormitory but also, with Miss Thomas's enthusiastic permission, into the classroom. On one trip, my parents brought Happy, our family dog, with them. Miss Thomas invited Happy to visit us in the class. It turned out to be the most exciting event we'd had in a long time. A dog in a class! How marvelously unconventional!

Miss Thomas had a gift for spontaneity in addition to her great talent for teaching. She also knew we needed guidance on how to live in the world outside, so she impressed on us again and again the importance of social etiquettes and moralities. But not even the best of teachers can prepare her children for all the complexities and disappointments of real life, and being deaf made things just that much harsher. One of my first disappointments in the outside world came at a little store near CID where students went to buy candy, ice cream, and other treats. One day my parents sent me a five-dollar bill. I was excited and I knew I would go far with such a princely sum.

First, of course, I went to the store and picked out something worth about fifty cents. I handed the store owner my five-dollar bill. He must have been nervous around deaf children; he probably didn't feel comfortable communicating with us. As change, he gave me three $1 bills, a $10 bill, and some loose change. I was excited at the opportunity to be honest and to return his money to him. But the more I tried to get his attention, the more uncomfortable he became. "Go away, go away!" he said.

Finally, I spoke as loudly and clearly as my awkward voice could manage: "Look, look. You gave me this for five dollars." Despite himself, he saw his mistake, took the $10 bill back, and gave me a $1 bill in return. But instead of praising me for my honesty, he waved his hands as if to brush me away. I was *so* disappointed. I had hoped for some kind reward for being honest, but he didn't even say thank you. He didn't appear grateful at all. Rather, he seemed annoyed by what had happened. It was yet another difficult lesson in my young life.

September 1958 found me on an overnight train back to St. Louis to begin my fifth year at CID. I rode with Barney, a classmate whose grandfather was a train conductor. We had special passes to ride the train. The trip was an exciting adventure for me, so special that I even dispensed with my beginning-of-term crying ritual when I parted from my parents at the train station. Barney and I arrived on the morning of the first day of class. I was taken to my classroom, where I met a new teacher, Miss Sara Hugh Smith.

A basic key to developing good communication skills is the quality of instruction. Most of the teachers at CID were well trained and highly qualified to teach speech, but their effectiveness depended on our ability to lipread them. By age nine or ten, the students at CID knew most of the sounds needed for speech. At that point the teacher's responsibility was to help us refine those sounds into speech that could be understood by hearing people. She needed to assist us in speaking more clearly and using the sounds in different combinations with other vowels and consonants to create spontaneous speech.

Try as I might, I could not lipread our new teacher. Some of the other students had no trouble following her, but every time she spoke I had to look around the room for clues from the other students as to what she said. Whenever it was my turn for a speech lesson, I was stuck because I couldn't understand her instructions. What was worse, I couldn't speechread her corrections of what *I* said.

I thought at first that something was wrong with my eyes or maybe even my brain. Miss Smith didn't seem to speak like anyone I had ever met. It was a long, frustrating, self-effacing struggle before I finally learned that she was from England and spoke a different English than I was used to. To this day I believe it was a mistake to have hired a teacher who spoke with an accent and whose ear was tuned to British, not American, English. Miss Smith was not in touch with the subtleties of American idioms and slang. My sudden uncertainty in reading Miss Smith's speech sent me into a panic. I thought I had forgotten over the summer everything I had struggled for years to learn.

Somehow, I survived the class and even learned to understand and communicate well with Miss Smith. As with any adversity, it strengthened me. It helped me adapt later in life when I ran into all kinds of accents. Can you imagine lipreading someone from Alabama if you're from New England or someone from Boston if you're from the Deep South?

As time went on, my classmates and I grew to like Miss Smith. I especially remember her storytelling and the writing assignments she gave us. The school had a small library, but Miss Smith decided we needed to be exposed to the local public library system. She was finally able to convince our housemothers to take us there one afternoon after school. This was a great event for me. I was happily overwhelmed by the huge number of books available in the library. The librarians had been forewarned of our visit by Miss Smith, and the individual attention they gave us reinforced my delight in the library. From that time on, I looked forward to going to the local library every two or three weeks to drop off books and pick up new ones. One of the first books I checked out was *How to Be Popular*, which taught that listening to others was critical and could make or break any relationship.

During storytelling and story writing that year, we let our creative juices flow. I sent some of my stories to Dunbar, who was doing graduate work in Germany then. He wrote back several encouraging letters, which fueled my enthusiasm for writing, so I wrote more stories.

We not only wrote stories but also told stories nonstop to each other. I was talkative, which often got me in trouble with Miss Smith, especially when it was during class on subjects not pertaining to our classwork. All of us loved to tell humorous stories, hamming them up with wild facial expressions and gestures. The laughter these inspired disrupted Miss Smith often and also must have annoyed her, because she couldn't follow our line of humor. What was comical to us was not what we had said but how we said it and the gestures and facial expressions we used to enhance our stories.

Since we were not able to detect humor in voices, we relied heavily on faces and body language. We invented many funny gestures and body characteristics to describe other people, classmates, and teachers. We were terrific mimics and could capture people's personalities. Sometimes we needed only one or two gestures to identify a person. Everyone knew who we meant—everyone but poor Miss Smith, that is. She always had trouble figuring out what was so hilarious!

During that 1958–59 school year, I had a new housemother, Mrs. Hampley. She had a problem. Although she tried hard to be loving and kind and set up an affectionate bond with her dorm children, no one wanted to hug her or return her physical affection. Mrs. Hampley was plagued with overpowering body odor. I could never figure out why no one ever conveyed to her the need to bathe and utilize perfume. Of course I never had the nerve myself. We often joked about having her fumigated.

Although we all had our difficulties with Mrs. Hampley, our big problem was Keith, the resident bully. He was strong and getting stronger every day. The threat of violence was with us constantly. He inspired fear in many of us. I for one was certainly under his power.

Keith was fascinated with drawing pictures of nude women. When he was thus employed, the rest of us huddled around, watching with interest and giving him advice. We all had wild ideas of how a woman looked. We thought, for example, that her breasts grew out from just below her underarm and that a bra was used to draw them forward and keep them in place on her chest. We took great care, of course, to see that the drawings were destroyed or well-hidden from the housemother's prying eyes.

But one day on returning from class I found Mrs. Hampley waiting anxiously for me. She asked me to come to her room, which was right off the dormitory. There she showed me one of the drawings I recognized to be Keith's. "Why did you draw this?" she demanded. "Why did you hide it?"

"I didn't draw it," I protested. "I didn't hide it!"

She refused to believe me. She dragged me to my locker to show where she'd found it. I happened to have there a picture of Jesus Christ pasted on a slab of wood. I picked it up and shouted at her, "I am telling the truth! I didn't draw it! I didn't put it in my locker!" I held out the picture of Christ at her as if I were warding off Dracula with a cross.

This made her even angrier. She raced to her room for a wooden paddle, which was not, I might add, intended to be used with a canoe. When she returned, she demonstrated its intended use on various parts of my body. Throughout the demonstration, I held out the picture of Jesus, trying to keep this heathen monster off me. She only paddled harder for it. Soon her paddle broke, but she continued, now whacking me on the outside of the forearm with its broken end. Only the sight of my blood stopped her. She didn't take me to the infirmary, I suppose out of fear that I would reveal the beating. I had to wash and nurse my own arm.

I'm sure Keith was the culprit. Why did he put the picture in my locker? Was it revenge for something I'd done to displease him or was it purely for the joy of seeing me get into trouble? Whichever was true, he got what he wanted, and I had a secret and a scar to carry for a long, long time.

5

EXPECTING THE BEST

Challenge is a dragon with a gift in its mouth. Tame the dragon and the gift is yours.

Noela Evans

One day during the early part of July 1959, I was at home watching television. My mother was busy working in the kitchen. For years, my parents had helped me understand what was happening on the TV by repeating what was being said in paraphrased forms. They had done that for Jonathan and me as a matter of course. No one was translating for me at that moment. I was in the room by myself.

For the previous five years, I had attended Central Institute for the Deaf and used the word "deaf" to describe myself and others at the school. But I didn't understand its meaning. The fact that I was born deaf contributed to my ignorance about the word. I had nothing to compare my deafness with. During all those years of socializing and doing things with hearing people, I didn't really understand that I was different. I knew at some level that I was deaf, Jonathan was deaf, and my parents and other brothers were hearing. But these were labels with no real meaning to me.

Then came that summer day at home. I observed people on the TV talking with their backs turned to others. I saw people talking without looking at anyone in the face. Their lips were moving, words seemed to be floating everywhere, and somehow the people on the show understood it all. I'd seen it before without really paying attention. Now I wondered at this marvel of communication. *How did they do that?*

In an instant, I was overwhelmed by a transforming insight. The people on TV were *hearing!* They were talking back and forth without depending on their eyes! I watched carefully and suddenly I knew. I couldn't hear! They could! They were picking up things through their ears!

At that moment, all the words and phrases that had always been part of my life—*deaf, hearing, learning to talk, learning to lipread, speech, hearing aids*—began to sink into my head clearly and meaningfully for the first time. Suddenly, I saw what my life had been all about.

I ran into the kitchen. "Mother," I said, "I am deaf!"

"Yes," she answered.

"Why did God make me deaf?" I asked. I began to cry. Mother started crying too. I told her through my tears what I now understood: "I'm deaf. Dunbar is hearing. David is hearing. Jonathan is deaf. Dad is hearing and you are hearing."

Now I saw the whole picture clearly—only now, even though I had lived with the word "deaf" for ten years. I saw that going to CID made sense. Suddenly, I realized why my parents always said it was best for me to go there and why I had to leave home to return to the school, even though it was painful for me and my family. They had no choice; I had no choice. It had never been their fault that they had to send me away. My parents made me feel my deafness was no one's fault. I didn't blame them or anybody, but I had no choices. This was simply the way it was.

At least now it all made sense. The vital piece to the puzzle had fallen into place.

When the time came for me to return to CID that September, despite my new awakening, I cried and went through the same pattern I'd been through during the past five years. I finally knew the reason I had to leave my family, but it still didn't make it any easier.

I was ten years old that sixth year. I found myself in a dormitory with a new housemother, Mrs. Pelant. The good news was that Rusty, my best friend, was back again. The better news was that Don and Keith were nowhere to be seen. The best news was that the new housemother was to become my favorite housemother of all.

We all loved Mrs. Pelant. That year of living in the dormitory with her was so peaceful. No one bullied anyone and Mrs. Pelant was always fair to us. She was probably the sanest housemother we had. Although she had little education in deafness, she did well in her relationships with deaf children. She was a natural talker and communicated well.

Mrs. Pelant pointed out that we represented a variety of religions—Catholic, Jewish, Protestant. She did this in a respectful, affirming manner, reminding us to celebrate our own religion's holidays while also honoring the days that were important to other students. She understood how to encourage respect among us, an approach that was both sensitive and unusual.

During that happy year, Rusty and I were inseparable because we also had the same teacher. Miss Margaret Gossin turned out to be strict but a lot of fun. Her great sense of humor stimulated our intellectual growth. Miss Gossin was black, though we didn't know it then because her skin was fair. I realize now that she must have been an extraordinary person to hold such a job at that time. In those pre-civil rights days, it was not unusual to see black women in the CID dining room—but a black teacher in an expensive, all-white private school? That was amazing!

Miss Gossin expected the best from us, and we responded to her high expectations. The challenge of such a capable teacher also kept Keith the bully at bay. He was in our class but in another dormitory, and we all felt safer with Miss Gossin as our mentor and protector.

During that year, besides our normal work on language, vocabulary, and communication skills, we had many serious discussions with Miss Gossin on issues that tested our ability to defend our opinions. We discussed political, social, and moral issues. I was fortunate to have had previous experience with that at home. Such exercises in advanced forms of communication are important to children in general but to deaf children in particular. All too often, parents and teachers of deaf children feel that they can't grasp such concepts, and so the children's education is confined to the day-to-day mundane. Because these children are not challenged, they will not progress into more intellectual thought. These challenges are what increase children's confidence in their abilities and enable them to advance in society.

Miss Gossin often took our class out to restaurants, which was unusual and exciting for us. Each of us ordered our own meals from a waitress, either using our speech or pointing to difficult words to pronounce on the menu. At the end of the meal, each of us had to figure out exactly what change our waitress was supposed to give to Miss Gossin. For us, this was a bold step toward participating in hearing society, but our teacher knew what she was doing. Although we lacked confidence at first, after a few experiences of eating out and being forced to ask for things on our own, we learned how easy it was. The waitress was usually able to figure out what we wanted. In class, we practiced lipreading the most common questions a waitress would ask. We also studied the words we would likely find on the menu. Miss Gossin had a genius for helping us apply what we learned to real situations.

Miss Gossin also took us out to movies. Afterward, we discussed them. She once told us that adult movies were more depressing than children's movies. We wondered why, and through our discussion we determined that adult movies dealt with reality while children's cinema more often featured fantasy. The different types of movies introduced me to variations of life in general.

After each discussion, we had to write down what we had talked about. It was often a struggle to put our feelings into words. To describe a flower with all its complexities of shape, color, and smell is simpler than describing fear, hatred, or love. Miss Gossin even asked our parents to pose difficult questions in their letters to us so we would learn to wrestle with our answers and write more complex sentences.

Certain teachers at CID embarrassed or humiliated students about their mistakes. Although they were probably trying to encourage my best possible speech, I didn't always appreciate the pressure from my teachers. Too often, they didn't allow me to take pleasure in my successes and rest on a plateau for a while before asking me to tackle another problem.

That was never Miss Gossin, though. She brought humor and charm to our lessons. During the year with Miss Gossin, I played, laughed, and worked. I don't remember which I relished more. Miss Gossin also pulled me aside for serious talks, especially when she thought the quality of my classwork didn't match her expectations of me. At the time, I was content to put in the same effort as my classmates, but Miss Gossin pushed me and another student, Susan, to do more. She took me seriously and told my parents I was college material, though she admonished me many times when I was careless and lazy in my work. She would cry out, "You know better than that!" I would usually then find some foolish mistakes on one of my papers.

The trick for all parents and teachers is to find the right balance. It is a lifelong dance and not an easy one, but with careful attention, it can be done well. Miss Gossin had found the right balance between challenging her students to learn and grow, avoiding lower expectations because they were deaf, and resisting the urge to apply too much pressure, which would discourage the students' progress. Perhaps because of this, when a charity group or private firm that donated to the school invited our principal to bring pupils for a speech demonstration, Miss Gossin often chose Rusty and me. These were my first experiences demonstrating my speech and my nature as a ham to a large audience. It was fun to be with Dr. Lane, our principal, and Miss Gossin. Both seemed more relaxed away from the school setting. We spoke in front of many people and answered many questions.

Although I didn't know it at the time, it was the beginning of my career as a public speaker and an educator in the field of deafness.

PART THREE

THE TIMES
THEY WERE A-CHANGIN'

I

THE UGLY SIDE

Preconceived notions are the locks on the door to wisdom.

Merry Browne

For ten years, I lived in two worlds: the strict, routine-bound realm of school, where dealing with homesickness and surviving dorm life were my primary concerns, and the flexible world of home, where interaction between family members was as distinctive as the individuals themselves. My mother formed the foundation at home, while at different periods of my life my father and each of my brothers influenced my development. Looking back on those early years, I see how I learned about the world at large through my father and brothers while Mother maintained family stability.

That world at large intruded on our family in a dramatic way when I was eight years old. Soon after I began my schooling at Central Institute for the Deaf, my father accepted a position as pastor of a Presbyterian church in the same town where Jonathan attended school: Little Rock, Arkansas. In many ways, the South was a wonderful place in which to grow up. The people were proud of their heritage and traditions. Most we knew were well-mannered and polite and frequently warm and friendly. But in the 1950s, the American South also had an ugly side.

On the morning of September 4, 1957, our family—minus Dunbar, who was attending university in Germany—sat around our breakfast table. I hadn't yet left home to start my fourth year at CID. As always, we ate oatmeal. As always, my father, wearing pajamas and a bathrobe, pulled out his Bible. He read to us each day, straight through the Bible over the days and weeks and months. On this morning, however, my father altered the sequence. He turned to the Psalms and read aloud, "The Lord is my shepherd, I shall not want." His voice cracked. "Though

I walk through the valley of the shadow of death, I will fear no evil; for Thou art with me."

The night before, my father had received a momentous phone call from Daisy Bates, co-owner of the local black newspaper and head of the Arkansas chapter of the National Association for the Advancement of Colored People (NAACP). A federal court had ordered that Little Rock's Central High School be integrated that year. For the first time, black students would legally walk the halls with white students at the school. Nine students who had earned excellent grades in their black-only schools had been selected to take this historic step.

Many citizens and political leaders in Arkansas had other ideas, however. Governor Orval Faubus, citing "evidence of disorder and threats of disorder," had instructed the Arkansas National Guard to prevent the black students from entering Central High on September 3. Fearing harm, the "Little Rock Nine," as they later became known, didn't even try.

Later that day, a federal judge ordered integration to begin the next day. But the word from angry whites was that if the teenagers attempted to enroll, they would be murdered. The Ku Klux Klan promised "bloodshed if necessary."[1] The school superintendent told the black students' parents to keep their children at home to prevent a riot because there would be no police protection. Only two years earlier, Emmett Till, a black fourteen-year-old visiting his family in neighboring Mississippi, had been kidnapped, beaten, shot to death, and dumped in a river. The situation in Little Rock felt like a powder keg awaiting a match.

When Daisy Bates called on the evening of September 3, she had a simple yet profound request: Would my father gather a group of white ministers to accompany the black students to Central High in the morning? She knew my father was president of the Greater Little Rock Ministerial Association, an organization dedicated to promoting the public's interest in all churches and denominations. She also knew that my father was a humanitarian in favor of civil rights and that public support from the white community would draw attention to any injustice.

My father agreed to make calls and meet the students in the morning but said he didn't know if he would go with them. He phoned a dozen church leaders. Only one local minister said he would join my father.

After our breakfast, my father drove to meet the students. My brother David, twenty-one years old and six foot one, went with him. David wanted to protect my father. My dad didn't argue.

Seven of the eventual "Nine" students, along with another girl who thought she wanted to join them in the attempt to enroll at Central (she later changed her mind), were gathered at a street corner a few blocks from the school. My father spoke to the teens, praising them for their faith and courage. They planned to begin walking to the school at 8:10 a.m. At 8:09 a.m., a black man asked if my father was going to walk with them.

"I don't know," my father said.

"Reverend Ogden, isn't it about time you made up your mind?"

At that moment, a strange feeling came over my father. He later recalled, "I felt: This is right; this is what I should do. There was not the slightest doubt but that I should do it. I ought to do it. And I felt this was the will of God for me. Every bit of fear just drained out."

"All right," my father said. "We will go with you."

My father began walking toward the mob gathered at the school, followed by the students, David, two visiting white pastors, and two black pastors. The local minister faded into the crowd.

Dunbar wrote the following description of the mob's reaction in his book *My Father Said Yes*:

> People down the street spotted the little group. They surged forward. They picked up their pace: heavy-necked burly men in short-sleeved shirts and hats; some younger with crew cuts and polo shirts; and hard-jawed, hair-sprayed, thick-armed women in dresses. Some of the guys laughed, smoked a cigarette, on a rowdy late-summer morning's adventure. Some pointed. "Look, there are the niggers. Get 'em."[2]

The mob did not attack, however. It may have been the presence of my father in his light summer suit, leading the tiny band. It may have been the presence of the National Guard soldiers, in uniforms and helmets and carrying rifles.

My father led the students up the steps at the front of the school, where a horizontal line of soldiers blocked their path. The mob closed in around my father and the students. Two soldiers parted a space, and Lt. Col. Marion Johnson, commander of the Guard troops, stepped forward.

My father spoke first, in a loud voice so all could hear, "Are you here to see to it that these children enter this school or to prevent them from entering?"

"The school is off-limits to these people," Johnson said, pointing with a nightstick at the closest of the teens.

"Does that mean that these children cannot be admitted to school?"

"Yes. That is what it means."

One of the two black pastors spoke up. "We understood from Governor Faubus that the soldiers are here to keep the peace, for law and order."

"During the night my orders were changed by the governor," Johnson said.[3]

And that was that. Faubus had decided to defy the federal courts a second time. Although tense and worried, my father led the children away from the mob without incident.

As an eight-year-old, I understood very little of this. Hatred based on race was a foreign concept to me. But when I saw my father on TV that evening, I knew something big was happening. I wanted to be on TV too, so I asked my father if he would take me to the school. The next day, a Thursday, he did. White students sat in their classrooms; the Nine stayed home. Soldiers lined the periphery of the grounds. We walked on the school grounds and examined the jeeps, half-tracks, and stacked rifles. My father explained some of what had happened the day before, pointing to this spot and that, repeating what was said.

On September 23, 1957, thanks to a diversion and a police escort, the small group of black students successfully entered Central High through a rear door. By late in the morning, however, police could no longer keep the angry crowd away from the school, and they drove the Nine home. That same morning, a black journalist from Memphis was attacked by the mob. He died three years later from his injuries. It wasn't until the end of September 1957, when President Eisenhower issued an executive order placing the National Guard under federal command and ordered a thousand US troops to Little Rock, that the Little Rock Nine were allowed to attend classes at Central.

Most people in Little Rock opposed my father's role in this watershed moment of the civil rights movement. Our phone lines were tapped and we received hate mail, obscene phone calls, and even bomb and acid-throwing threats. Friends advised us not to sleep in the front rooms of our house in case a bomb was thrown through a street window, so we all slept in the back of the house.

My father started Thursday morning prayer meetings for the parents of the students, as the students' families had been threatened. Attendance by both white and black community members rose. One man who attended and extended his support was an emerging civil rights leader, Dr. Martin Luther King, Jr. Many national reporters and civil rights figures ended up in our living room because it was the only safe and friendly place for black people and white people to meet in a city torn by racial mistrust.

At the end of that first year of the crisis, one of the nine black students, Ernest Green, graduated from Central High School. Daisy Bates asked my father to take Dr. King to the graduation exercises at Central. Ernest Green's family sat in the bleachers. The only other black face in the football stadium belonged to Dr. King, who sat with my father. Both my father and Dr. King were treated roughly by the police at the graduation. They asked my father, "What are you doing with this black man? Where do you think you're going?" At one point they grabbed my father's arm and spun him around. But he refused to leave his guest.

My father's pastorship at Central Presbyterian Church was a casualty of his convictions. From the day he walked with those black students to Central High School, he began to lose control of his church. Gradually, many people left his congregation, though others who supported my father's beliefs joined. Ministers, rabbis, priests, and people from other churches attended the Thursday morning prayer meetings. But even though my father had the support of many of his parishioners, the opposition was strong and determined.

In the summer of 1958, church deacons came to my father and told him he had six weeks to find another church. That's about as close as the Presbyterian Church comes to firing a minister. But a historic victory had been won. I knew my father had made a noble and sacrificial effort. I was proud of him.

It wasn't long before my father was asked to pastor the First Presbyterian Church in Huntington, West Virginia. We moved there in early fall 1958. For my mother, the best part of moving to Huntington was the relief at being able to answer the phone and hear friendly voices again. She no longer had to worry about hostile and obscene calls or about bombs or acid. Much weight had been lifted from my parents' shoulders.

Most of the danger of that time went over my head. I didn't recognize the intense feelings people had until my return to classes at CID. While at school one day, I saw an article about my father and the Little Rock crisis in *Time* magazine. I was so proud that I began showing it to others at the school. But a teacher suddenly snatched it away and told me not to discuss it, saying it was a closed subject. I learned that not everyone regarded my father as a hero.

While he was in Little Rock and after, my father continued to support the civil rights movement. He responded when people asked for favors, such as the night a black family's car broke down in an area that was unsafe for nonwhites. He drove out and towed them and their car home. He also accepted invitations to speak at other churches, synagogues, universities, and more, where he advocated for the rights of African Americans. He continued to host black families and leaders at our home. And in September 1958, after Martin Luther King, Jr., was stabbed at a book-signing event in New York, my father went to the city to tape an interview with CBS and a talk for the Voice of America and to visit his friend in a Harlem hospital.

As I look back on those events after all these years, I appreciate my father's actions more than ever. He took a stand that he knew would cost him personally and professionally, one that might even endanger his family. Yet he felt so strongly about doing what was right and supporting the disadvantaged that he did it anyway. Only now do I see the deep impact those times had on me. They exposed me to passionate and opposing opinions of other adults and left me much more sensitive to issues of culture and race. Perhaps most important, they taught me that every human being deserves respect and dignity and that some things are worth fighting for, no matter the cost.

In the spring of 1959, on a sunny and humid afternoon, I was at Busch Stadium watching a St. Louis Cardinals baseball game with the boys from my dormitory. The teenage sister of one of the boys at our school was visiting from Alabama. She was at the game too, sitting in the row behind me. Someone must have pointed me out to her. She'd read about my father and what he'd done to support the Little Rock Nine.

I turned around and noticed her looking at me. Her face was twisted, her brows furrowed, her lips turned down. "You're a nigger lover. You should be sitting over there with the colored people," she said to me, pointing to the outfield bleachers. "Those people smell. You belong over there, not with us."

I was shocked and puzzled. Why was she angry? What did she have against black people? Perhaps I am especially sensitive to the ugliness of discrimination because I have felt it myself as a deaf person. Avoiding, separating, fearing, and hating people because of their skin color—or because of their inability to hear—made no sense to me then. It still makes no sense to me today.

NOTES

1. This quote comes from my brother Dunbar's book, *My Father Said Yes* (Nashville, TN: Vanderbilt University Press, 2008), 21.

2. Ogden, *My Father Said Yes*, 28.

3. Ogden, *My Father Said Yes*, 29.

2

COMMUNICATION CHOICES

To effectively communicate, we must realize that we are all different in the way we perceive the world and use this understanding as a guide to our communication with others.

Anthony Robbins

My start at Central Institute for the Deaf coincided with Jonathan's enrollment at Arkansas School for the Deaf, where signing was the primary mode of communication. My parents asked Jonathan not to use signs with me so that I would conform with CID's policies. He respected their request. We continued to talk with each other using lip-reading, speech, gestures, and body language. When I was very young, I didn't comprehend that there was such a thing as formal sign language and that Jonathan used it with his deaf friends.

Years later, my parents told me how shocked they were to learn there was a Jonathan unknown to them. They knew him as a quiet, even timid boy. Then one day, when they had to pick him up at school, they found Jonathan sitting with his deaf friends and signing a hundred miles per hour. He was vivacious and lively. He had never been like that at home. They knew immediately that they had done the right thing by letting him go to a signing school. For Jonathan, sign language became the door to social interaction. For my family it became the living symbol of a basic fact about deafness: although Jonathan and I were deaf, we were not without language. We simply learned different ways to express ourselves, ways that suited our different personalities.

Far too often, in a family with more than one deaf child, the deaf members stay together and apart from the rest of the family in a kind of communication bondage. But for Jonathan and me, who used different modes of communication, this was not true. I spent about the same amount of time with him as with the other members of my family. Still, we did share a great sensitivity to others' nonverbal expression, and in some ways, he worked with me in deepening this sensitivity.

In my early years, I became extremely sensitive to Jonathan. He maintained strong eye contact with me. People don't realize that their eye movements, most of which are outside their conscious control, communicate messages of excitement, arousal, pleasure, grief, sorrow, and so on. The shades of meaning conveyed by the eyes can be extremely subtle.

At the age of five or six, I found myself understanding Jonathan's feelings by looking at his eyes. When Jonathan disapproved of my behavior, he reprimanded me with his eyes without his knowing it, and I felt punished or scolded. Although the eyes of everyone in my family were an important source of information, I found Jonathan's more powerful, more penetrating, and more expressive. From time to time I felt more vulnerable to him than others. He taught me, more than anyone, how profoundly informative visual stimuli can be.

Once, when I was about twelve, Jonathan took me to the airport to meet our parents on an incoming flight. While waiting for the plane, we sat across from a row of telephone booths, all occupied. "Look," Jonathan said, "what can you tell about those men?" We scanned the line of men talking on the phones and speculated on which were enjoying their conversations and which were not, which were talking with people they liked or loved, which were conversing with strangers or business associates, which were nervous about what they were saying, and which were talking naturally. We also guessed at which were lying and which were telling the truth. We were fascinated by what we saw. I felt almost as though we were eavesdropping on their conversations.

Often, Jonathan and I were left out of a conversation with hearing strangers while our parents were busy talking with them. At those times, Jonathan would comment on the discussion. He would say things like, "This person's body is saying 'Okay' but his gestures are saying 'No'" or "His gestures are saying 'You did well' but his eyes are saying 'You weren't good enough.'" Jonathan made me more aware of people whose messages were mixed. I began paying more attention to my parents' interactions with hearing people. For me, trying to tell whether a person was sincere was like a guessing game. It kept me intrigued. After the "game" I would ask my mother to fill me in on details of the conversation to learn whether my initial suspicions were well-founded.

The longer Jonathan was at Arkansas School for the Deaf, the more I sensed his disdain for and distrust of hearing people outside of the family. Little by little, I understood that he felt hearing people were not worth the effort it took to communicate with them. Compared to his deaf friends at school, they struck him as cold and boring. His friends had many bad experiences with hearing people, and Jonathan himself experienced some of the discrimination they described to him. Since he agreed with his friends, he began adopting their attitudes. He became ever more deeply entrenched in the signing world—and loved it.

One day at home I found an alphabet card that contained pictures of hand shapes for the letters of the alphabet. I was about eight or nine. I went to Jonathan and fingerspelled a few words to him. He was furious and chased me, trying to get the card. It was like a game until he caught me and took the card away. He may have been worried about my parents' reaction, for he was always faithful to their request that he use no sign language with me. But he also may have just been selectively proud and protective of his own private world of signing.

One summer Jonathan had nothing to do, so my parents encouraged him to work at a lakeside vacation camp. He worked hard all summer doing odd jobs and earning his own money. When we visited him he proudly showed us the camp and all his different tasks. Jonathan was learning that he was capable of being independent.

After that experience, my parents encouraged Jonathan to go to a religious camp for deaf people, sponsored by the Church of Christ. He was eighteen. At the camp there were many deaf people from all over the Midwest and from other Church of Christ congregations. One camper was Dorothy Louise Wright, a shy girl from Texas. Dorothy and Jonathan fell in love immediately. Everyone at the camp called them "the love birds."

When Jonathan returned from camp my family was stunned when he suddenly became interested in letter writing. Writing had never been one of his favorite activities. But he wrote to Dorothy almost every day. He was a different person, obviously transformed by his new feelings.

When Dorothy visited, I loved to watch the two of them talk in sign language. Dorothy was terribly shy, and though she had enough residual hearing to play the piano, she almost never used her voice. That came from her school training. My family was happy for Jonathan but sad that none of us could communicate with Dorothy. We didn't know any sign language and Dorothy had no speech. When Dorothy signed, she didn't form words on her lips. It was impossible to lipread her, and she didn't even want to talk.

Just as the world around us was adapting to important and dramatic change, so too was my own family. When Jonathan graduated from Arkansas School for the Deaf in 1959, he wanted to go to the Southern School of Graphic Arts in Nashville to learn the printing trade. He planned to become a printer and work for a newspaper company. Clearly, it was his intention to marry Dorothy, but he felt he had to get a job first. Here, however, he came up against my father.

My father felt that Jonathan had the intelligence to go to college, so he talked him into applying to Gallaudet, the liberal arts college for the deaf in Washington, DC. To attend Gallaudet, a student had to first pass entrance examinations. Jonathan did well on these exams, but he hesitated about going to Gallaudet. My father came from a family where everyone went to college. To him it was unthinkable for anyone in his family not to receive a college degree. But Jonathan was not interested in college at all. Breaking a family tradition was the least of his concerns. Still, my father put pressure on the deaf school to encourage Jonathan to go to Gallaudet. He himself talked long and hard to Jonathan about it. Finally, Jonathan agreed to give Gallaudet a try.

After one semester, Jonathan was bored with his studies and didn't want to return. He kept thinking about printing at the Southern School of Graphic Arts, and about Dorothy. My father was disappointed but satisfied that Jonathan had at least tried Gallaudet College for one semester and had earned Bs in his courses. My father felt better knowing Jonathan could have finished college if he had wanted to.

Now that Jonathan was free, the wedding was on! My mother—who had prayed that Jonathan would marry a deaf woman rather than wind up in a difficult "mixed" marriage—was sure Dorothy was the right girl for him. The only problem was the left-out feeling that stemmed from the language barrier. The marriage ceremony highlighted this issue in a sad way, for it was conducted in sign language by a deaf minister. My father, as a minister, was disappointed that he was not allowed to perform the ceremony or play an important role in it. I think we all felt the wedding confirmed Jonathan and Dorothy's membership in that "other world," far away from us. I wish we had thought of including a sign language interpreter.

Now Jonathan and Dorothy together lived in the deaf world. The only way to get there seemed to be through the knowledge of sign language. I didn't feel a part of their world at all, though I was as deaf as Jonathan. My instinct was to include everyone, hearing and deaf— anything else felt unacceptable. I decided at the wedding that I would never separate myself or my future wife from my family in that way.

It wasn't until years later that I realized there was another side to the coin: when hearing people with deaf signing family members do not learn sign language, they do just as much to isolate themselves from those close to them. When my family realized that Jonathan was not cut out to be an oralist and supported his choice of Arkansas School for the Deaf, they should have learned sign language so they could better communicate with him.

3

LESSONS ON LIFE AND DEATH

Anything that is worth teaching can be presented in many different ways. These multiple ways can make use of our multiple intelligences.

Howard Gardner

My mother had the knack of making the world seem interesting no matter what was happening around our family at the time. For example, in a restaurant, she might say that a waitress had a strong accent, that someone in the kitchen dropped and broke dishes, that someone was arguing at the cash register about the amount of the bill. She might fill in even more details if she knew them, telling us who owned the restaurant, how business was going, and that the owner always hired family members when they turned sixteen.

My father had a different approach. He taught his boys about life by devising lessons and delivering long, serious lectures. My father and my mother differed in that she tended to be down to earth while he looked at the world through more aloof, even critical, eyes. My father worked hard to convey the meaning, the moral, and the overall picture of what was around us.

When I was about twelve and our family was on one of our many summer trips, we explored the Civil War battleground at Gettysburg. My father showed me the battlefield and explained details of how the Union and Confederate soldiers had clashed. Gettysburg is a large area, and we drove around to different memorials and points of the conflict. When we discovered a helicopter that took tourists over the battlegrounds, I became infected with the idea of having a view of the whole scene from above. My father agreed enthusiastically. In the air, my father gestured with animation toward different parts of the battlefield, interpreting the pilot's explanations. He did a beautiful job of repeating everything the pilot said. It made the historic war much more real to me. I started to understand that wars were not always the well-organized affairs I had viewed in the movies and on television.

Visual examples are the key to communication with a deaf child. From above, I could *see* the battlefield and *envision* the fight. My imagination was fired by a living picture. From that living picture, I started to pick up abstractions such as "hero," "conflict," "North and South," and "right and wrong." The helicopter ride was one of my most memorable experiences with my father.

It also seemed to symbolize my father's way of showing me the world—from up above. All my life, he tried to tell me what the world was like and how it was to be perceived. He wanted to elevate me to a position above, so that I could look down and view what was happening below with people, nations, events, and life in general. While my father was working hard to give me the broad overview, my mother was down on earth in the nitty-gritty of everything.

Both perspectives greatly influenced my understanding of life. I appreciated the day-to-day details that my mother provided, information I was unable to gather from listening in on conversations around me. And I was also grateful for my father's "elevated" and often visual viewpoint, which gave meaning to what I was seeing and experiencing.

Neither approach prepared our family, however, for the tragedy to come. Although good education and active communication skills may help sharpen people's awareness of what goes on around them, my family and I were to learn that some things in life can't be foreseen, averted, or understood. In his way, this is the important life lesson that my brother David taught me. I was aware that my brother had problems, but I was not to know the severity of them for many years. Perhaps David's mischievous side was because of these problems or a way to compensate for them.

In many ways, David was the most sensitive person in our family. It may be the reason he escaped into the world of pranks and may also be one of the reasons he decided to escape this world.

It was June 1960, shortly after the incident where David tossed a crocodile into a pond at the zoo, that he left our home in Huntington, telling my parents he was driving to visit his girlfriend in Tennessee. Three days later a pair of police officers came to our door. They spoke to my parents, who started to cry.

"What's going on?" I asked my mother.

"David's happy now," she said through tears. "He's in heaven."

"You mean he's dead?" I said. I was numb. I couldn't believe it.

I wanted to know what had happened. I kept asking my parents about it, but the answer was always the same: "We don't know." Later, I found out that David had been killed by a shotgun.

On our way to Rogersville, Tennessee, to claim David's body, we visited a rest stop. In the restroom, I again asked my father about what had happened to my brother. "We don't know," he said. "Maybe he was cleaning his gun and the gun went off."

"Did somebody kill him? Did somebody come in and shoot him?"

"We don't know."

With no definitive answers, I grew more and more frantic. My mind filled with wild possibilities. "If someone shot him, we should all get the police and catch the bad person," I said. "We should put him in jail."

My father did not want to talk about it. "We'll have to wait and see," he said. Later, I asked to read the obituary. "We haven't received one yet," was my father's reply.

Dunbar was studying for his PhD at Yale and planned to meet us in Springfield, Ohio, for David's funeral. Jonathan was away at printing school in Nashville, so my parents and I drove from Rogersville to get him. I asked if I could be the one to tell Jonathan and my parents agreed. He was surprised to see us. We told him to sit down.

"David was on his way to see his girlfriend," I said. "He was cleaning a gun and it went off."

A strange expression crossed Jonathan's face. He didn't say anything for a while. Then, quietly, he began to cry. He packed a suitcase and we drove to Springfield. At my grandmother's house the night before the service, I woke up in the bedroom I was sharing with Jonathan and saw that he was gone. I went to my parents' bedroom and found my entire family there, talking. I felt excluded and sensed that everyone was withholding information from me.

At breakfast the next morning, I finally erupted. In an angry and loud voice, I said, "Where is the obituary? I know it's in the newspaper. I want to read it!"

At last, my mother produced the paper and handed it to me. The article said that David had taken his own life. *Oh, now I understand,* I thought. *This explains everything.* I knew David had suffered from terrible headaches after he'd hit his head in a car accident years before. He also, like my father, dealt with depression. He committed suicide because he was in great physical and emotional pain.

Now I also understood why Jonathan seemed to hide his feelings from me when I'd broken the news to him. He and David had always been close. He'd realized immediately that David's death was a suicide.

David's pain was gone, but it continued for my family and me. In their grief, my parents could not bring themselves to tell me what David had done. I'm sure they felt that hiding the truth would protect me somehow. The result, however, was additional anguish and confusion for me. My grief was intensified because I didn't understand, and because I sensed others knew what had happened yet would not tell me. Deaf children often get lost in emotional situations because the constant explanations they need to replace incidental hearing are forgotten in the turmoil.

During David's funeral service, I was aware of a strange restlessness in the audience. The minister was unknown to us, and instead of giving us comfort, he preached that David was lost and even suggested that perhaps there had not been much hope for him in his life. My father was furious. Jonathan and I, used to reading people's body language, felt the tension and anger in the audience. Going to the cemetery and leaving David there was difficult for me. No more David meant no more teasing, laughing, dancing, and storytelling.

David had written letters to his close friends and each family member the night before he died. My parents gave me the paper he left especially for me. It was a beautiful, page-long letter saying how he hoped I would have a good life and that he knew I would grow up to be a fine person. He also wrote that he hoped I would not suffer like he had.

David meant for his letters to soften the blow of his death. All I can say is that they didn't serve that purpose very well. It was impossible for any of us to sit down and read those letters without breaking into tears. Years later, after seeing the many things that David's suicide did to my family—creating guilt and sorrow—I concluded that suicide gives pain to everyone it touches. Only the one who dies manages to escape.

4

THE UNIVERSITY OF LIFE

Teaching kids to count is fine, but teaching them what counts is best.

Bob Talbert

After David's death, Dunbar again became the focal point of the family to me. I was eleven years old, just teetering on the brink of adolescence. It was natural that my oldest sibling should emerge as my guide to the ways of the world. Life was suddenly important, and Dunbar was earnest about life.

Dunbar always treated me as if I were an intelligent being. He talked to me seriously, asked me questions, and seemed genuinely interested in my opinion. I remember his attempts to engage me in serious conversation as far back as when I was three years old. This differed from my other brothers' communication styles—Jonathan was direct, economical, and to the point, whereas David had been playful, teasing, and full of fantasy. With my father still preoccupied with the civil rights movement and my mother taking care of the practical world, Dunbar's probing style was just what I needed at this stage of my life. David's death had shaken me into realizing that life was serious and required hard work. I started seeing Dunbar as someone upon whom I could model myself.

When I first started going to Central Institute for the Deaf, Dunbar wrote me letters from college, where he was studying English literature. His first letter was full of drawings showing how much he and I were alike in the fact that we lived away from home and went to school. I was always proud of the letters he wrote me, though in the beginning I didn't always understand what I read.

In the fall of 1956, Dunbar went to Germany for three years on a scholarship. While he was there, he married a German girl named

Annegret. In the summer of 1959, Dunbar brought his wife home to America. The family went to New York City to greet the arrival of their ship. I was ten.

I was fascinated with the idea that there were other languages besides the one I was trying desperately to master. I was intrigued by the German language and spent many hours watching Annegret and Dunbar speak it. I immediately liked Annegret's straightforwardness.

Dunbar had coached Annegret on how to communicate with Jonathan and me, and she caught on easily. She already spoke English well so it was a simple transition. It's my experience that hearing people who have themselves had to struggle to learn a new language and have traveled in other countries are more likely to understand the problems of being deaf and be better communicators with deaf people.

Annegret was one of the few people who didn't waste words in talking to us—a big help, since we couldn't hear her inflections to tell us what was important. We learned to watch her face carefully when she talked because she always had something important to say. Perhaps because of her German accent, Annegret enunciated much more clearly than anyone else in the family. I could lipread her easily. It was odd that her accent would make her speech clearer, while at CID, Miss Smith's English accent had thrown me into a state of confusion.

Maybe communication really has more to do with personality than anything else. In any communication, a person must *want* to understand and be understood or else the conversation fails. The more effort you put into a conversation, the more you get out of it. Communication works best when you use other senses to speak in addition to your mouth. Lipreading, for example, involves intuition. If you know the situation and the person you're talking to, you can almost guess what they're going to say.

When I would appear with a new hat, for instance, I knew Annegret would always say something like, "Where did you buy that hat?" Maybe I couldn't read "buy" on her lips, but I'd "know" and could respond. Some people seem to be born with a strong ability to intuit (at least in part) what someone is saying or about to say. Some people are also able to read the body and face of others easily. Annegret is one of those people. I also was blessed with some of those same gifts. That's why it was so much easier for me to understand family members than to understand strangers. I knew my family, and vice versa, they knew my face, my sounds, my interests, my mind.

I grew up around Annegret. Since she was the only child in her family, I became a little brother to her. We liked each other immensely. Annegret treated me as an adult and discussed things with me frankly.

After returning to the States, Dunbar began graduate studies at Yale. Every summer my parents and I visited him and Annegret in New Haven. These were happy vacations for all of us. It was during these times that Dunbar and I really got to know each other again. Dunbar and I talked more and more as I grew older and more mature. I grew from a little boy into a teenager with many thoughts and ideas percolating in my head. It was wonderful for me to be in an academic environment, and Dunbar proudly introduced me to many of his college friends.

Dunbar had a way of making it easy for me to follow conversations. He made a point of enunciating clearly while talking to his friends so that I could follow him better. He also asked from time to time if I understood or agreed with him. When his friends spoke to him, he summarized the conversation as if he were confirming the points being made, but it was really for my benefit. Many of his friends altered their speech and enunciated so that I could follow them too.

Dunbar was an animated talker and incorporated gestures and signs into his speech—again, for my benefit. I loved the attention my brother gave me and the fact that he was proud of me. He never acted as if I were a burden. Just as when he was a teenager, I was again the sidekick who accompanied him everywhere. I was fascinated with his friends, who always had interesting things to say. Often when our conversations were over, Dunbar filled me in on details I'd missed.

While Dunbar was at Yale, I began receiving letters from a surprising source—Jezebel, his Siamese cat. Jezebel's letters, written with considerable "help" from Dunbar, always made me laugh. She told me how she was always trying to get Dunbar's attention by meowing or by jumping onto the table when he was working and walking over his papers and that Dunbar always rudely pushed her off. She also described the time she was accidentally shut inside the closet all day, with no food or water. She was "furious," but the description of her dilemma was hilarious. She always signed her letters with an inked paw print.

In December 1961, Dunbar and Annegret came to my parents' home for Christmas. They gave me a large box. When I opened it, I was surprised to find another gift-wrapped box inside. This, they said, was for Jonathan. My gift was inside someone else's box. This trick went on from person to person in the family, and finally to my mother, who found in her small box a baby rattle. At first, we were puzzled, but my mother caught on to the joke. A baby was on the way.

Soon after Dunbar graduated from Yale, Stephanie was born. Dunbar had been offered a teaching position in the theater department at the University of California, Berkeley. He asked me to help him move to Berkeley while our parents stayed in New Haven with Annegret and Stephanie for a few weeks. We stuffed a television set, file cabinet, clothes, utensils, books—their whole life—into a 1959 Volkswagen bug. We filled every nook and cranny. I was thrilled that Dunbar had asked me to accompany him on the coast to coast drive. I was thirteen years old. It was to be, for me, a focused and invaluable lesson in the ways of the outside world, away from my isolated school and insulated family life. By the time we reached Berkeley, I would pass, under Dunbar's watchful direction, into adulthood.

I had responsibilities on the trip. I kept written records of monies spent on gas, food, and other items since the University of California would reimburse Dunbar for moving expenses. I played navigator,

Dunbar and Paul arrive in San Francisco.

reading the maps and giving directions to Dunbar. I also learned to take pictures with his 35 mm Argus camera. Every time Dunbar moved into the left lane to pass another car on the road, I looked on the right side and signaled when it was okay to pull back over. The car was so full it was impossible for Dunbar to see out my side.

At the beginning of the trip, Dunbar said "Write" when he wanted me to record how much a turnpike toll was. He said it again and I told him I'd done it. Then he kept on saying it. Finally, Dunbar realized that the words "write" and "right" were identical on the lips. What he was saying after we'd paid the toll was "Right," directing me to check the right side of the car so he could change lanes. From that point, he usually used sentences such as "Please write it down" and "Please check the right side," so I'd know exactly what he meant. Or, if he was in a hurry, he pointed to the glove compartment and said "Write" or to the window on my side and said "Right."

This may sound like a simple problem with a simple solution, but it shows Dunbar's sensitivity to the subtle problems of deafness. Many people never think about rephrasing their messages to a deaf person when the message doesn't get through the first time. Instead, they keep repeating the same wording with growing frustration and higher volume. Too often, I have seen an angered and frustrated hearing person literally shouting the same message repeatedly at a deaf person who, of course, registers the same bewildered look no matter how loud it's repeated.

During our long trip, I kept Dunbar awake by asking questions. After a short while I got so I could lipread him from the side, since he couldn't always turn his head while driving. His answers were often long and involved. I was interested to learn that Dunbar hadn't taken his studies seriously while at Davidson College but that he had worked hard at Yale because he valued reading and research. I think talks on that trip were responsible for my later plunge into studies and my improved grades. Dunbar nurtured in me the desire to make something of my life while also stressing that one should contribute to others along the road to self-accomplishment. These thoughts were new to me. They were like seeds planted in the fertile soil of my heart.

Not all our discussions were serious. Dunbar loved to talk about people. I asked endless questions about his friends and professors, whom I had met in New Haven. He told me scandalous things about the faculty that made my eyes grow wide with surprise, and he shared wild stories of college life that both repulsed and attracted me. I was privileged to have a hearing person tell me many things that deaf children rarely learn. Communicating with a deaf person proves so difficult for most hearing people that they rarely venture into the realm of gossip, complex social commentary, or "frivolous" stories.

My parents learned from their early experiences with Jonathan that professionals often advise parents to treat their deaf child no differently from a hearing child. This is sound advice for challenging deaf children to do their best, but often the opposite approach is needed too. Subtleties arising from deafness are easily overlooked unless one takes special care. My parents learned that deaf children do, in fact, differ significantly from hearing children in the ways they receive and transmit messages. Because the means of communication differ and the alternative methods of communicating with deaf children demand more energy, deaf children are often shortchanged when it comes to casual information that hearing children pick up seemingly "out of the air."

Hearing children absorb everything they hear, long before they learn to talk. That's why they seem to come equipped with "family knowledge"—beliefs, customs, opinions, and understanding held in common by family members—even though their parents may put little conscious effort into instilling such knowledge. But most deaf children have no access to the casual conversation, dinner table talk, bedtime question sessions, and other auditory activities in which such family information is exchanged. For this reason, deaf children tend to grow up more isolated than hearing children, and they often seem more pragmatic and deal more in terms of black and white than do hearing peers.

My family knew that Jonathan and I learned an enormous amount through body language and all the unconscious subtleties of nonverbal communication. Yet our parents also realized they had to point out, describe, and explain every aspect of our family experiences, never assuming we would pick it up automatically.

Dunbar knew this too, and at this time in my life he stepped into the role of interpreter. He made everything that happened in our lives, society, and the world more available to me. He had a way of making everything so interesting that I kept asking questions until we had exhausted the subject at hand. My parents were my interpreters in the areas of family relationships, rules of conduct, courtesies, moral standards, and many aspects of basic information. My father tended to delve into human nature and its tendencies in politics and social injustice. Both of my parents were well educated and well read, so I could talk to them about many things I read or learned about in literature. But Dunbar was different from my parents in one special way. He was fascinated by interpersonal relationships. He loved talking about what made people tick and how they behaved in relation to one another.

Our conversations about his friends might have seemed like gossip to some, but he always went beyond the who, when, and what and into the *why* of people's behavior. He gave me simple insights into human nature that went far beyond the common generalities my father made about "man." In our cross-country talks, Dunbar introduced me to new dimensions of human nature—ones that many of my deaf acquaintances never came to know well.

Another advantage to Dunbar's three-thousand-mile University of Life was that it was packed with practical experiences that I very much needed. One night I persuaded him to stop in Logan, Utah, at the home of a CID classmate. I was fond of Susan, one of the brightest friends I had. Her father was a professor of ornithology. Her parents were a lively couple, and Dunbar enjoyed them.

While there, Dunbar and I went into the bathroom to wash up before supper. I urinated into the toilet bowl. Suddenly, with alarm, my brother said to me, "Shhhhhh, they can hear you, it sounds like Niagara Falls right here in the bathroom!"

I had never been so embarrassed in my life. I was thirteen, self-conscious, and trying hard to make a good impression on Susan's family. At that moment, I learned one of life's most important lessons: if you're trying to impress someone, always urinate against the side of the bowl and not into the water.

Dunbar taught me a great deal about becoming an independent person. In later years, I traveled with him and the rest of the family to Europe. Everywhere we went, he encouraged me to spread my wings and fly—and *think*—on my own. But nothing he taught me showed more sensitivity to deafness or concern for my future as a self-reliant man than that all-important lesson in Susan's bathroom.

PART FOUR

PREPARING FOR A HEARING WORLD

I

THE STRUGGLE FOR INDEPENDENCE

The greatest gifts you can give your children are the roots of responsibility and the wings of independence.

Nishan Panwar

The death of my brother David and the closeness it brought with Dunbar matured me greatly. By the fall of 1960, when I entered my seventh year at Central Institute for the Deaf, I had started to become a serious person. When David died, I started thinking more about life. His death hit me hard but also helped me make positive decisions. I couldn't play forever. I started to follow Dunbar's lead and pay better attention to my studies.

I was heading into the final stretch at CID. At the end of the Advanced Section in four years' time, I would leave the familiarity of the deaf school to test my English skills in a public school in my hometown. I was going to be "mainstreamed." At age fifteen, I would finish my schooling alongside hearing peers.

When I got back to CID, I felt like I was leading a double life. The teachers loved me, but the housemothers saw me as a troublemaker. I had gained confidence and was better able to express my opinions and oppose the status quo. My sharp tongue expressed a new independence of mind. My newfound personality seemed to both attract and repel my new housemother, Miss Cora Lacy. As a result, we spent much time arguing, discussing, and explaining, all important interchanges in which I sharpened my English skills—often at my housemother's expense. I was more fluent with the English language, thus more articulate in getting my points across.

Romance was at the root of some of those conflicts. I had fallen in love with Nancy, one of the older girls. She was a pretty brunette with an expressive face. Unfortunately, she did not have too much affection for me. One day Nancy hurt my feelings and then wrote a note to apologize. She handed me the note in the dining room.

Miss Lacy saw the transaction and followed me back to the dormitory. She asked to see the note, but I laughed and said it was none of her business. The remark infuriated her. She warned that she would send for Mr. Maltse, the dormitory supervisor, and have him take the note from me. I said that would be fine with me, so she stormed off to call him.

I didn't know what to do next. My friend Erik suggested I tear the note into tiny pieces and give her the pieces in a box. I followed his suggestion and wrote Miss Lacy a note that said, "Here are the pieces in this box. If you really want to read the note, you'll have to put the pieces together first!"

Miss Lacy was furious when I presented her with the box. Mr. Maltse soon showed up in my room, carrying the box. He told me I had to work on the pieces until the note was glued back together again. I protested that the note was personal and its contents were nobody else's business. Mr. Maltse grabbed me and said I was to do as he said. He handed me Scotch tape and said, "You work on it for as long as it takes to get it back together."

What was I going to do? To the dubious rescue came Dave, another of the boys in my dorm, who said, "No problem!" He brushed the pieces of my note off the table and into his hand, opened the window, and threw them into the wind. We then witnessed a beautiful scene, as my incriminating evidence fell like snowflakes to the ground. An hour later, Miss Lacy came up to my room to check on my progress. I sat at the table with a Cheshire cat grin. She looked around for the note, and I told her that it was gone for good. She became furious and left.

Soon, to my amazement, Mr. Maltse reappeared and demanded to know what had happened to the pieces. I was getting deeper and deeper into trouble through the "help" of my friends, but I warmed to the challenge. I told him a bird had flown in the window, taken the note, and scattered it. He didn't like that answer one bit. He began shaking me and demanding to know who the "bird" was. I decided to remain loyal to my friend. Mr. Maltse kept shaking me, and I kept saying, "A bird threw it out!"

"Who?"

"A bird."

"Who?"

"A bird."

It went on like this for quite a while until Mr. Maltse suddenly got a relieved look on his face, turned, and left. He returned with Robert, another dorm friend, in tow. He began interrogating Robert, asking why he'd thrown the pieces of note out the window. I of course protested that I hadn't said anything about Robert. Mr. Maltse slapped me and called me a liar.

I was shocked. How had this thing gotten so far out of control? I defended myself and Robert: "I am not a liar. I did not say, 'Robert.' I said, 'A bird.'"

Mr. Maltse was adamant. "No, you told me Robert! Now you're lying." He continued to slap me around. Mr. Maltse had mistaken "a bird" for "Robert." Somehow, despite all my speech practice, in a crucial situation I had been misunderstood even by a person used to interpreting the speech of people who are deaf. This was infuriating and frightening. Would my oral skills fail me like this when I left CID for the hearing world? It was a disturbing question I had to ponder during the subsequent three Saturdays I spent writing "I will obey Miss Lacy. I will obey Miss Lacy," thousands and thousands of times.

A contradictory mix of self-doubt and self-assurance was common among us boys as we emerged from childhood. We began to take seriously our sense of right and wrong, as well as our right to privacy. Robert began to suspect that Miss Lacy was reading our mail. He was upset and felt she had no business doing this, so he called a council of war. We parleyed about the problem. Many of us expressed concern. We knew there was a federal law against reading other people's mail.

Robert suggested we take drastic measures and wrote a letter. "Dear Miss Lacy: You are wrong to read this letter. You have no business reading other people's mail. If you had not read this letter you wouldn't know that we all think you are fat, old, and nasty . . . Sincerely yours, Robert."

Robert folded the letter, put it in an envelope, and addressed it to himself. He didn't seal it but folded it inside tightly so that someone would have to work to open it. He put the letter in the top drawer of his dresser where he usually kept mail. We couldn't wait until the next day.

When we got back from school that next afternoon, we all walked into the dormitory together. One by one we passed by Miss Lacy's room and took a quick look inside. It was obvious from her facial expression and the way she sat clutching the arms of her chair that she was *furious*. We ran to Robert's room and looked in the top drawer. The letter was gone! We had her. She *had* opened Robert's letter! We jumped for joy.

Miss Lacy knew she'd been outsmarted. She couldn't report the incident because it would prove she had been reading our letters. She did get her revenge by being harsher with us for a time, but she never mentioned the episode. We reveled in every minute of her discomfort. We had triumphed over injustice.

2

LANGUAGE, LANGUAGE, LANGUAGE

Language forces us to perceive the world as man presents it to us.

Julia Penelope

Although our curriculum became more diverse as we matured, language, language, and more language was what the CID Advanced Section was all about. The objective was to prepare us to function without faltering at a mainstream high school. That's what we'd been working toward all along, but now the urgency increased. Our teachers' instruction on communication skills was relentless.

Even so, our deaf-to-deaf communication differed sharply from that of our deaf-to-hearing exchanges. When deaf students spoke together, they faced each other so that they could lipread fully. It didn't matter how bad the student's speech was. Lip movement and being able to see the lips was what counted. Some CID students could communicate well with their peers but not with hearing people. They knew how to blow up the consonants and vowels in words so that they were more visible on their lips, but conversely, they had poor voice or speech quality. Two deaf students might speak easily without even uttering a sound, just by mouthing the words. But when time came to talk to a hearing person who didn't know how to lipread—which would be the case when we mainstreamed—deaf students would have to use their best speech and work hard to make themselves understood.

I found myself shifting back and forth between using good speech with my hearing friends and using clear lip movement with deaf friends. My teachers reprimanded me for doing so. They wanted us to speak clearly and enunciate well at the same time. This was not easy to do despite nine years of training.

One reason for the difference was the tremendous range of students at CID. Some wouldn't have been there but for their parents' insistence. Some students' vocabularies and exposure to books and ideas were minimal. At the other end of the spectrum were bright students with large vocabularies and inquiring minds. There was also a full range of hearing loss. Some students had residual hearing that could be boosted with hearing aids. Some, like me, had none. Given this spectrum, we students tended to adjust our speech with each other to the lowest common denominator, exaggerating our enunciation and never worrying about the speech quality when we talked among ourselves. Gestures and facial expressions always played a major role.

Many of the gestures we used were signs that had originated with former CID students whose vocabulary of gestures survived after them. We also made up our own signs and used a few we picked up from deaf signers we met at the park or in other public places. Our vocabulary of gestures was not as large as that of the spoken word, but it helped us expand our communication in different ways.

One of the signs we used was to wave across the room to get each other's attention. Sometimes, when the other person remained unaware of the signal, the wave would advance from hands to arms and become more animated. Often this was distracting to others, and they eventually got the person's attention for you. If the person I wanted to talk to was close by, I used my eyes, face, or index finger to attract his attention. If I wanted a more discrete exchange, I employed my eyes or face more subtly. Although hearing people use these gestures too, the CID students were more attuned to each nuance. A raised eyebrow or slight tilt of the head could communicate volumes. Our hand waves and other gestures grew more restrained as we got older. Still, when we were mad, regardless of our age, we still waved vigorously to get someone's attention. Our teachers encouraged us to use our voices, and some of the students could hear their names when called. But for others like me, who had no residual hearing whatsoever despite many tedious (and infuriating) hours spent supposedly developing listening skills, there was no hope of ever hearing another's call.

A determined person can force his words on another hearing person no matter how unwilling the latter is to receive them, but deaf people can refuse to "listen" by simply turning their eyes away. This sometimes leads to drastic measures. At CID, when a student refused to listen to (look at) another, the ignored person sometimes punched the ignorer in the upper arm until he gave in. If the stubborn nonlistener continued to look away, the ignored would shake the other's shoulders. And if this still didn't work, the by now frustrated speaker would wrestle with the other's head to bring it around to face his own lips. There was not much the "talker" could do, though, if the would-be recipient closed his eyes. This was a common practice among us. It was so easy to close off the rest of the world by closing our eyes. No one could reach us then. Occasionally, though, a speaker was so adamant that he even tried to pry open the other person's eyes.

Another common gesture was pointing the index finger under your chin while saying something important to another deaf person. This was a habit picked up in class, when our teachers did it to emphasize key words.

Many of our gestures bore little obvious relation to their meaning. One example was forming an "O" with the thumb and index finger, the other three fingers extended outward, and placing this hand sign to the chest to accompany the word "polite." This meant it was actually not nice or polite to behave this way. This gesture was a warning: "Watch out, it's not nice to do that."

Another common gesture was tapping the index finger under the chin a few times when we used the conditional clause to mean "if," such as "If we go now, we must eat early." We used the gesture with the "if we go now" part of the sentence. The gesture made it clear to others that the sentence was conditional. Yet another was sliding the side of the index finger across the chin just below the mouth, to indicate that someone was lying (I learned years later that this is the sign for "liar" in American Sign Language). When one shook his head vigorously in the negative, he meant that person didn't lie. A favorite of mine was brushing the tip of the nose upward with the index finger to indicate that someone was a snob or stuck up, and this is also close to the sign used in American Sign Language.

We had another group of signs of a completely different type. These were nicknames drawn from characteristics peculiar to the people being referred to. Ricky, the boy who'd been Mrs. Hilton's favorite, loved going to the barbershop for a haircut. He always had his hair cut so short that there was nothing left on his head. He used to rub the back of his head with the palm of his hand to indicate it was time for another haircut. Soon many of us started to rub the backs of our heads to refer to Ricky. We did this if we were looking for him, if we wanted to talk to him, or if we were trying to get his attention. When he left the school after a few years, the famous gesture of rubbing the back of the head gradually died out. It was kept alive for a while when we used it to mean it was time for a short haircut, but when the fad for longer haircuts came in, the "Ricky" gesture eventually disappeared.

Many of our gestures were unique among the students of CID and not recognizable at other oral schools. In fact, students at each school established their own set of gestures. They remind me of tribal language. We recognized graduates of CID according to the gestures they used or the specific mannerisms they had, even if we hadn't met them before. In a way, these physical characteristics became the regional "accents" of those who heard with their eyes.

Gestures were discouraged in the classroom, however. In the advanced section, as in the nursery and primary sections, all teaching was done by spoken word. Students were expected to lipread the teachers, listen to their voices through the amplification system (despite the fact that some could not hear a thing), and understand every syllable being uttered in class by the teachers and other classmates. When some of us didn't understand words the first time, the teachers repeated the sentences, each time in a slightly different way until even the poorest lipreader grasped the point.

For me, most of the teachers were fairly easy to understand. I always loved the challenge when they gave us new words and increased the complexity of language. I usually did well, and when my teachers repeated major points in their instruction, I often drifted off, daydreaming with my eyes on the teachers' faces as if I were still listening. I even learned to lipread and repeat back a sentence without really understanding what was being said. Given our emphasis on comprehension at CID, I always felt guilty about pretending to understand.

I once explained all this to Dunbar. He told me that hearing people did the same. This was a big surprise to me—I thought only I took the easy way out. We discussed this at length, and Dunbar told me that hearing people often tuned others out, usually because communication was less important to them. I came to realize that deaf people valued communication more highly than hearing people because they had to work much harder to achieve it.

At this time in my education I began to put together the pieces about the similarities and differences between being deaf and being hearing. One of my discoveries was that hearing people pick up nuances in a person's voice to determine the person's real attitudes, much as deaf people pick up nuances in the face. It seemed the degree to which anyone did this depended on individual personality.

Much of the education at CID involved identifying and discussing specific points of information. The biggest problem at any school for the deaf is that many children have a narrow scope of general information. This is partially because their families seldom communicate to them, compounded by the fact that their vocabularies are too limited to allow them to browse through newspapers and other reading materials to absorb incidental information. The teachers at CID attempted to compensate for this by discussing minute points about current events and national affairs. For the students with limited exposure to ideas and information at home, a residential school education was a lifesaver. Without proper input from families, many children, deaf and hearing, suffer from information starvation. The greater a child's vocabulary and language skills, the easier it is for him or her to advance in everyday discourse with other people and therefore advance in life.

However, as our teachers knew, there is much more to learning a language than simply expanding vocabulary. The secret to acquiring language is to learn the basic structures—grammar, syntax, morphology, pragmatics. This is a tremendously complicated task. Hearing children have the advantage of learning language unconsciously by constantly hearing it, absorbing it, and repeating it like little parrots. For deaf children, parroting is also necessary, but for obvious reasons much more tedious.

Deaf children have to learn the principles one at a time and study the way they work by interacting with adults or others who really know how to communicate. Without this sort of directed communication, there can be little language growth or development. The English language is so complicated that it can't be learned directly from books. It needs to be broken down, learned word by word and principle by principle, and practiced under the guidance of teachers who know what their deaf students should concentrate on.

To get a good education, you need good educators. Most of the teachers at CID were special people with a grasp of what was expected of them. As a rule, they were personable (as opposed to most of the house-mothers, whose jobs were to be disciplinarians). Some of the teachers were exceptionally amiable, most communicated with enthusiasm, and others had good instincts. A few were well-rounded and possessed all the elements. I believe there are born teachers, just as there are born learners. Teach as hard as you will, some students will simply never succeed in a classroom. Teach as hard as they can, some teachers are never successful in the classroom. But if you put the right teacher with pupils ready to learn, communication and education will grow exponentially.

Class size is important to any subject, but it is never more crucial than in teaching deaf students. Sometimes at CID we were fortunate to be in classrooms with only four to six students. This gave us the opportunity to know our teachers better and to develop personal relationships with them. We got plenty of individual attention, and the small-group atmosphere allowed the teachers to show us how conversation worked. The dynamics of conversation—how the ball is tossed from one participant to another—should be obvious. But individuals tend to be self-centered and often force their words into a conversation. Even if you can hear, it is hard to communicate when two or more people are talking at once. For deaf people, it is essential that the speakers take turns, since a deaf person can lipread only one person at a time. For these reasons, conversation had to be carefully taught.

To prepare us for the outside world, teachers sometimes invited hearing visitors into our conversations and classroom discussions. We were comfortable with visitors provided they weren't afraid of us, but they were often affected by our deafness and imperfect speech. Still, even that was a learning experience, because we would have to cope with other people's fears and prejudices in the hearing world.

Being a good conversationalist and knowing language principles were not the only important elements of a good teacher of deaf children. Our best teachers were often the ones who loved to have fun with us and who interacted with us as people. They showed respect for us and for our feelings. Learning the English language without hearing is a monumental task. It requires confidence in oneself and understanding from others.

3

ROLE MODELS

Setting an example is not the main means of influencing another; it is the only means.

Albert Einstein

I was eleven years old when I started in CID's advanced section, in fall 1960. We boys were feeling the flush of independence and relished the rare opportunity to escape the confines of our school. We occasionally dined at restaurants, most notably the eatery owned by baseball star Stan Musial, where Stan greeted us and signed his pictures for us. And we went to movies.

We saw a movie in a theater every Sunday night. There were no captions, of course. I often wondered whether the school authorities ever considered how much of the movies we could follow. Did they think we would benefit from viewing and not hearing movies? Did they believe we would understand the plot through osmosis? Were they just plain ignorant about what we could follow or didn't they care? It was a huge puzzle for me.

We learned over the years to follow the stories on the screen with little or no help from our adult mentors, but it took a lot of practice. The more action in a movie, the more we understood it and, of course, the more we liked it. When the movie was heavy with dialogue, we needed help from a hearing interpreter but rarely got it. If we did, the explanation was usually so brief that we missed the subtleties. Much of this was due, naturally, to the fact that it's difficult (and embarrassing) to translate in a dark and quiet theater. What we saw on the screen was always so much more complicated than the version our interpreter gave us. It made us wonder about our interpreters' understanding of deafness. Did they think we didn't notice that something beyond us was going on?

When I was in the advanced section and we watched TV, I tried to encourage the housemothers and other adults who watched with us to interpret for us in the same way my family had interpreted shows for Jonathan and me at home. I realize now I must not have verbalized well enough how much we were missing. I could have told them it was impossible for us to understand everything on TV and perhaps challenged them to watch with the sound off themselves.

Sadly, those adults weren't as attuned to our speech as our regular teachers were. Many subtle points of our communication were lost on them. Because we were trained lipreaders, by the time we reached the Advanced Section, we could understand people who were not trained to lipread better than they could understand us. At the time we didn't know that this was the case. It took me a long time to understand that hearing people had difficulty with my deaf speech and still longer to realize that even many of our adult caretakers at CID had trouble following what we said.

Although we did get out once in a while, we students were mostly isolated at CID. Fortunately, the authorities there did try to bring the outside world to us. The institute director, Dr. Richard Silverman, established a two-year program with Washington University in St. Louis. Each year, twenty Washington students who were training to become teachers of deaf children came to CID to study. Some of these students even lived in the dorms at CID. Dr. Silverman made a similar arrangement for a handful of male dental students at Washington to come to CID. Both groups of these adult students spent a few hours every day taking care of us in exchange for room and board.

For me and my classmates, this was an invaluable link to the real world. These young college students had meals with us in the dining hall and joined us after school hours at the nearby Forest Park, where we played a variety of sports. We had so many fascinating conversations with the college students. We exchanged a lot of teasing and humor between us and learned what life was like for them. Some of us who couldn't afford to go home for short holidays such as Easter or Thanksgiving were invited to join the college students and their families. One year, Ann Gilcrest, a training teacher, took me to her family home in Indiana for Thanksgiving. Another time, student Joan Sher invited me to her hometown of Rock Island, Illinois. I fell in love with her family; they were easy to talk with.

Paul and student teacher, Joan Sher.

Dr. Silverman's idea was brilliant. During our time with the college students, we were immersed in a world of speaking and lipreading. It was a great way to practice what we were learning.

I have managed to stay in touch with some of these former college students, including Joan. My wife and I meet with her every year in Palm Springs at a film festival. In addition, a few years ago, I ran into two professionals in the field of deafness who had been student teachers during my first two years at CID. In front of a group of my peers, they recalled with great pleasure (and to my great embarrassment) that they had bathed me at CID. I realize that this early social contact with hearing students was useful in saving my classmates and me from social isolation.

Ellen was one of these student teachers who had an important influence on me. She was a liberal, even radical, thinker who experienced many conflicts with the CID administration. Ellen didn't like what she saw in the dormitory lives of the children. She disliked the residential institution environment. She felt empathy for the kids and became unpopular with many of the housemothers for voicing her opinions.

Ellen's most serious conflict with the school authorities arose when she befriended our first black student teacher, a young man named Douglas. Everyone else on the staff seemed to avoid contact with him, because he was black. But Ellen offered him friendship, causing quite an uproar, particularly among the housemothers. In their ignorance and also due to the times, they were shocked that a white girl would show interest in a black man.

Ellen's stand made me feel a special bond with her. After all, I had been raised in the tolerant atmosphere of a liberal family and lived through a dramatic chapter of the civil rights movement. I had also experienced my own confrontations with a few individuals at CID about the rights of black people. Many people associated with CID weren't exactly sympathetic to my family's views. And of course, there had been the visiting sister of a CID student who called me a "nigger lover" at the Cardinals baseball game. The day after that incident, I went to Mrs. Daniels, my reading teacher and the CID ethics expert. She was a fantastic person to talk with and always treated the students as equals. We had a long discussion. She said that I had acted properly and that she was proud of me for my restraint. On that day, I was indeed the son of my father.

Soon, other problems arose about Douglas using our dorm bathroom and eating in the dining hall. I had several heart-wrenching talks with Mrs. Daniels in which I complained bitterly about racism at the school. She spoke quietly about how the biggest problem was public ignorance and suggested that time was the best healer for racial tension. Mrs. Daniels asked me to pray for everyone. I felt comforted at the thought that there were at least some people with my sympathies at CID. Mrs. Daniels, Miss Gossin, and a few others let me know of their admiration for my father's involvement in the civil rights movement— but there were others who definitely did not.

Ellen finally decided to leave CID and return to Antioch College after her bitter experience with the housemothers. But by then we had established a special friendship. She told me a lot about Antioch College and even lent me the college's catalog. She said I was the kind of person who would thrive on the freedom, creativity, and cooperative work-study plan offered at Antioch. I didn't realize it then, but she had planted an important seed in my mind. If the student teachers were meant to open vistas to us unworldly boys at CID, Ellen certainly had done her job with me.

Equally important to our education was the influence of other deaf adults at CID. In the fall of 1960, the institute hired Sally, an alumnus of CID, to teach physical education and home economics. She had received her bachelor of arts degree from Blue Mountain College in Mississippi. She was one of the best lipreaders I'd ever met. We loved her bubbly personality and the attention she gave us.

Sally was direct and frank and talked to us on our level—a welcome change from the hearing staff, who sometimes seemed condescending. She showed us real life—for example, telling us about how she was doing with her boyfriend, or about a problem between a teacher and the principal, or about a conflict between a teacher and a student's parents. Some might call that gossip, but to us it was an invaluable window into interpersonal relationships.

Sally also showed us how to be more compassionate toward fellow students. When she learned that the mother and father of one of the students were going through a divorce, she took on a motherly role toward that student. She told us what was happening, allowing us to sympathize as well. That fact that she trusted us with such sensitive information was a boost to our self-esteem.

Today, Sally says that we students were naive, that we'd lived sheltered lives because we spent so much time away from home and had gaps in our education about the world. In many ways that is true. One day, some of the girls approached Sally and said that their teacher was pregnant. They knew it because she'd started to wear maternity clothes in class. The girls wondered if the baby would be born any day. Sally explained to them that pregnancy is a nine-month process—the girls had no idea.

That conversation got Sally in trouble with a supervisor, an old maid type who told Sally it was *her* duty to talk about such things with the girls, not Sally's. Fortunately for the girls, Sally continued to answer their questions. She simply asked them to keep their conversations confidential.

Sally naturally had more interaction with the girls at CID than with us boys. Fortunately, a new and important influence entered our closed circle. Rich Meyer was a 1953 graduate of CID who had mainstreamed into a hearing high school after graduation. He came back to volunteer at CID in 1961 after graduating from college. For most of us boys, it was our first opportunity for extended personal interaction with someone like us. Rich was *not* a hearing teacher, *not* a disciplinary housemother, *not* someone outside our silent world. He was a bright, interested, *deaf* adult.

Rich volunteered his time because he knew personally the problems we encountered because of being deaf, the kind of interaction we needed, and how to share it with us. He took a personal interest in each of us and enjoyed our company. Rich graduated from Culver Stockton College in Canton, Missouri, with a bachelor of science degree in biology. He'd just started working as a pathology technician at the Washington University School of Medicine, only a few miles away from our dormitory.

The boys at CID craved the company of this intelligent new person. Rich could relate to us on our level and was willing to carry on conversations with us for hour upon hour, often with a cigar in his mouth. He was exceedingly patient with our lack of experience with the outside world. Rich dutifully answered hundreds of questions about everything from the quality of American cars and issues involving politics and world events to dating, sex, and the responsibilities of marriage.

We were relieved and exhilarated to see that one of "us" was active and successful in the outside world, for that was the whole objective of our long, hard work at CID. School officials had invited two deaf adults to tell us about their experience at a mainstream high school. These two said that they had no problems making friends or adjusting to life in the hearing world. My CID friends and I now call this "The Big Lie." These two adults wouldn't admit that life in the hearing world can be hard or that some hearing people are not always nice to those of us who are deaf. Rich, on the other hand, was realistic. He admitted to us that mainstreaming wasn't always easy and that we would interact with some obnoxious people. Yet Rich had succeeded in that world. We gobbled up this living, breathing proof that it could be done.

It's a shame that CID took so long to expose us to deaf adults who could serve as role models. But I'm certainly glad they did so while I was still at the school. The time when I would leave CID and enter the hearing mainstream was fast approaching.

One day Miss Lacy overheard some of us asking Rich questions about sex and reported it to the principal. Shortly thereafter, the principal decided it was time for us to have a sex education class. To give us the "lecture," our principal employed Mr. McBette, a hearing man who worked as an audiologist. Mr. McBette was nice enough, but he was definitely not the right person for this particular job. He didn't have the skills to communicate properly with us, and this was a subject that required more than the usual amount of skill and tact. Mr. McBette started by explaining to us that we were growing up, that we were becoming men, and that it was time we learned about "the birds and the bees." He was off on the wrong foot there. Our bodies had already told us we were becoming men and we had definitely progressed beyond the birds and the bees.

Mr. McBette brought a movie to do the difficult part for him, but here we again faced a familiar problem. The movie didn't have captions and we didn't understand one word of it. We couldn't figure out any of the vague drawings the movie used as explanations. We sat and watched with uncomprehending eyes and minds and rapidly increasing frustration.

After the movie, Mr. McBette was nervous and awkward as he searched for words. We were all terribly embarrassed and smiled and nodded, pretending to understand. When he asked if we had any questions, we replied, "No, no, none at all," to which he showed a great deal of relief. He finally said, "I am very glad you enjoyed the film so much," and left us. That was the extent of our sex education from the CID administration. But it definitely was not the end of our sex education *at* CID. The next time we saw Rich, we pumped him for information. What a relief it was to have someone who could answer us—not with unintelligible movies or embarrassed platitudes but from life experiences!

During the 1962–63 academic year, another deaf adult, also an alumnus of CID, entered our lives. Rich spent his time with us on a volunteer basis. But Paul Taylor was hired part-time as an assistant to Miss Lacy in exchange for room and board at our new residence hall. Paul had just graduated from Georgia Institute of Technology with a bachelor of science degree in chemical engineering and was starting a master's degree at Washington University in St. Louis. He was extremely intelligent and fun to be with. His enthusiasm infected all of us. While Rich was more of a listener, Paul was an extrovert who loved to show and tell us about life. He gave the school authorities many headaches, especially Miss Lacy and the principal, Dr. Lane—he was a bit too much for them. They tried to dampen his enthusiasm and extinguish some of the excitement he poured into our lives.

Paul once asked a group of us boys, "How many of you would like to learn a little math?" Mathematics study at CID tended to be pretty

boring, but we knew Paul would make it interesting, so we enthusiastically said we wanted to learn. That Saturday, after breakfast, Paul
took us into a classroom. "How can we measure how fast water drains
from a bathtub?" he asked. We soon found out, using a formula Paul
knew from his engineering study. Then we learned formulas for how
to measure the draining speed if the water was hot or cold. It led to a
long discussion. For us, it was practical and fun. Paul had a knack for
bringing a dull subject to life.

Sally and Paul were popular with all of us. Then Sally began to fall
in love with Paul. She ended her relationship with her boyfriend and
started dating Paul. When Sally and Paul began spending more time
together, we had a chance to associate with the CID girls more. That
was a healthy development since we were ready and willing and becoming mature enough to benefit from the social interaction. Had it not
been for Rich, Paul, and Sally, my introduction to the world of boy-girl
relations would have suffered years of postponement.

We learned other lessons from our new mentors as well. One day
Paul took all of us to the movie *Lawrence of Arabia*. It was a long show
and we missed most of the story. Paul often explained a movie before
we saw it and talked with us again afterward to answer further questions. But with *Lawrence of Arabia*, he too was at a loss. Because so
many of the actors spoke with a British accent, he didn't follow much
of it either.

We got into a wonderful discussion about the limitations of lipreading, which was a truth we'd sought for a long time. Here was a deaf role
model confirming what we'd often suspected. During the discussion,
one of us brought up how unfair it was to have to pay for something we
did not understand. We were in the mood to rebel and said we ought
to ask for a refund. Much to our delight, Paul agreed. He tried to persuade the theater manager to refund our money. Although the manager
refused, he did give us a handbook summarizing the story.

Seeing Paul's assertiveness was very rewarding. Sally also stood up
for what she wanted, which was wonderful exposure for us. To see the
two of them meeting and interacting with hearing people gave us a
realistic picture of what to expect when we grew up.

We also considered revolutionary the fact that Paul admitted he
didn't understand something. We were often dishonest in communicating with hearing people, pretending to understand when we didn't

really understand at all. It was common to feign comprehension when a situation proved to be volatile or embarrassing for us. But that only made matters worse. I worried about this habit and felt dishonest every time I did it. It was a no-win situation and often separated us further from the world we were trying so hard to become a part of.

But here was a deaf adult *admitting* to a hearing stranger that he did not understand! He was a hero to us for doing so. We saw from Paul's actions that not understanding was simply not understanding. It was not the end of the world.

Paul and Sally began a romance that quickly blossomed. They announced their engagement and were married in the summer of 1963. During my last year at CID I didn't see them as much as I had the year before. They did, however, invite some of us over to their house for visits. It was good for us to see a deaf couple living together successfully. In light of my future marriage to a deaf mate, it must have had an effect on me.

Sally stayed at CID as the physical education and home economics teacher. Paul continued his master's degree studies at Washington University while also working full time at McDonnell Douglas Corporation as an engineer and programmer. These people—Rich, Sally, Paul, and a few others—were perfect role models for us when we needed them. Their honesty and strength brought us what we needed to prepare ourselves for entering the real world.

When CID officials brought other deaf adults to visit us in the classroom, we got to talk to them for periods of a few hours or so. We always asked what it was like to be in a hearing school and to be part of the hearing society. They always answered, "No problem! Things are going fine!" We pushed for more specific information: "Do you sometimes have trouble communicating with hearing people?" "No." "Can you lipread everything your friends say?" "Yes." "Do they understand your speech well?" "Yes." "Do they sometimes ask you to repeat?" "No." Well, we concluded, perhaps these visitors were very well-trained and very successful at what they did.

It didn't occur to me until years later that these visitors were fooling themselves with "The Big Lie" or perhaps were trying to be supportive by telling such falsehoods. For us, seeing Paul admit that he didn't understand *Lawrence of Arabia* was worth a million happy-go-lucky "No problems!"

One memorable evening in 1964, we encountered role models of a different sort. Every Sunday night, the boys in the residential hall a block down the street congregated with us in front of the black and white television in the dormitory to watch *Disney*, *Bonanza*, and other programs. We'd talk about the programs for the next few days.

But on Sunday, February 9, we saw something that changed our lives. We happened to be watching the *Ed Sullivan Show* when the Beatles made their record-breaking, first live American appearance. Although I couldn't hear their music, some of the other students with residual hearing could. But all of us delighted in watching their lively body language, their happy faces, and the screaming fans.

Five minutes into their performance, Miss Lacy marched into the television room to tell us how "immoral," how "evil," how "awful" the Beatles were. We feared she would turn off the television. Some of us voiced our disagreement while keeping our eyes on the show, hoping we could prevent her from ruining our evening. Even though Miss Lacy continued to pace around and wring her hands, somehow the TV stayed on.

For the next few days, everyone talked about the Beatles. It was the beginning of their "invasion." We loved their cool look and the response they generated. It seemed that the older people were, the more shocking they found the Beatles and the more they denounced the band. The younger teachers and college students thought they were great. For us, liking the Beatles was a chance to rebel and align with the younger generation. Some of the college students gave us copies of lyrics to their songs, which helped us appreciate them even more.

I got permission to interview people about the Beatles for our student paper, *CID News*. I never forgot the reaction of Elli Blumenthal, a student teacher. When I asked what she thought of the Beatles, she screamed, "EEEEEEEEEEEE!" I was puzzled by this bizarre response until it dawned on me that she was imitating the fans' reaction.

We students were looking for a symbol of our desire to protest and rebel. Voilà, we'd found it. Miss Lacy and other school authorities never understood how a world-famous music group could turn on a bunch of deaf kids.

4

ADVENTURES IN SCOUTING

Progress always involves risks. You can't steal second base and keep your foot on first.

Frederick B. Wilcox

In 1961 I joined the Boy Scouts. The Scouts was like a breath of fresh air in our lives. There were no families, dorm mothers, or school administrators to contend with, only deliriously happy kids and fun-loving Scout leaders. Some of the Scoutmasters, including Bill Sheldon, Bill Blank, and Rich Meyer, were even deaf! The whole experience couldn't have differed more from life at CID.

Camping trips were the highlight of Scouting life. Two or three times a year we filled our backpacks and assembled in front of the main school building. All the non-Scout children were envious. I remember, in my early years, watching the Scouts and wishing I was old enough to join them. I dreamed of the fun they would have on those wondrous weekends.

When I finally became a Scout and went on camping trips myself, the fun part turned out to be very different from what I'd imagined. It wasn't the great outdoors or cookouts or sleeping in tents that I treasured but getting together in one of the tents to have serious discussions—about sex!

At night, one could walk around among the tents and instantly tell which contained deaf Scouts and which contained hearing Scouts. From the tents of the former group came the glow of flashlights, while the other tents were dark. Our flashlights were bright and powerful— we kept them working well because we depended so much on them to talk at night about our favorite subject. From outside the deaf tents you could see the flashlights moving around the tent as each talker held one under his chin so that others could lipread him. An obvious advantage for us was that anyone walking by heard no words to give away the subject, whereas if you listened at the hearing tents you would soon collect incriminating evidence.

On camping trips, we got the opportunity to visit and communicate out of reach of CID authorities. Those of us from the dorms were fascinated with the lives of the few Scouts who were day students at CID. They lived at home and had more freedom to explore some aspects of life. They would bring pictures of women, dirty jokes in print, and—most treasured of all—stories of what was happening in their homes. Day students sometimes related to us their parents' marital problems. They went into detail recounting parents' fights, arguments, affairs—all juicy stuff we were dying to know. We looked forward to each camping trip for the "next chapter" of the story. These were as gripping as any soap opera to us—and some went on for several seasons before being "canceled" by a divorce or the family moving away. I am sure these parents would've died if they'd realized how much we knew about their sex lives and marital problems!

The day students had more access to normal family life than the rest of us did. After all, we went home only during holidays, when our families put on their best behavior for us. The day students had more real knowledge about their families than most of the residential boys did about theirs. One boy mentioned his parents' recent fight. He was warmly invited to our next nightly talk, where we interrogated him about every detail of his family life. He told us that his parents drank at a party and started arguing. The mother began flirting with another man and the father picked a fight with him. The father then locked his wife in the bedroom and later threw her bodily out of the house. It was definitely a soap opera.

We discussed the matter seriously, asking hypothetical questions such as, "What if there had been no drinking? What if the parents had been more loyal to each other?" It was incredible how much we learned about sex and social intercourse during those Scouting nights. Robert Baden-Powell, founder of the Scouts, may not have approved, but what more wholesome place to learn such things than with the Boy Scouts!

When we first started these discussions, we were young and immature, but as the years went by we became more sophisticated in our topics. To keep the tradition alive, we passed our hard-learned information on to younger Scouts we approved of as "intellectual" peers.

My Scouting experience had more conventional aspects to it as well. Every spring, CID's Boy Scout Troop 132 participated in a contest with the nineteen other troops in the St. Louis district. On a Saturday, we all gathered to compete in outdoor skills—building fires, compass reading, and message sending by flags. We competed on equal footing with hearing patrol groups of the other troops. Our troop had four patrol groups, all headed by deaf patrol leaders.

A boy named Bernard was the leader of my patrol group. He told us how badly he had been beaten the year before in a similar contest and resolved not to let it happen again. I knew what he meant: during my first two years of Scouting, the deaf patrols scored a humiliating one hundred fifty out of a possible one thousand. I think many of the boys in my patrol were bright, but we were not exactly the ideal Scout as portrayed in fables or pictured on the Scouting manual. We were not really outdoor people. We liked to talk, not sweat. We liked good food. We liked to pad our sleeping bags with leaves to sleep in comfort. So, with Bernard, we spent Friday night thinking about how we could win a little respect from the other troops.

For the fire-building contest, we put a few pieces of wood in a can of kerosene and left them overnight. In the morning, we dried them in the sun. We were confident when the time came for us to demonstrate how fast we could build a fire, which then had to burn through a string held two feet above the ground. The judge used a stopwatch to time how long it took us to build a fire. He was stunned when we did ours in something like two minutes. The second-best mark was three and a half minutes. Everyone admired our performance. Thank goodness no one smelled the flames.

Another difficult part of the contest was sending Morse code messages with flags. My patrol group hadn't studied the Morse Code very well, choosing instead to play cards, so we had to enlist help again. The judges put half of us at the far end of the field, about fifty yards away, and gave us a few sentences to transmit to the other half of our troop with our flags. Someone thought to bring a pair of binoculars, which seemed an innocent enough item to the judges. But instead of reading the flag signals, we used the binoculars to lipread the person using the flag. As the flagger enunciated the messages clearly for us, we just wrote down the sentences. The judges were impressed with the accuracy of the message, and again we scored high.

We had no trouble with the compass and first aid tests; we scored well without having to cheat. But then we had to measure some trees by using logic. One of us pretended not to understand what was expected and began a conversation with the judge, knowing he would need to concentrate to understand the deaf speech. While the talking was going on, some of us crowded around the judge and snuck a peek at the answers on his paper. Then we pretended to measure with our hands and figure the heights. When we turned in our scores, we made sure that they were not 100 percent accurate but close enough. The judge was thrilled with our answers.

The most difficult competition was running a distance as a group within a timed period. We bombed on that one. We had no way to outsmart their stopwatches. At the end of the day, when the final scores were announced, we felt guilty. We were relieved we hadn't come out at the top of all the patrols but instead won top honors within Troop 132. In the end, we didn't feel too proud about our success, but no one ever discovered our dishonesty. It did teach some of us the price of cheating—self-disgust.

The next year, when I was thirteen years old, I was chosen to be a patrol leader. I decided to direct the patrol toward more laudable achievements and we cleaned up our tarnished image, taking an approach very different from that of Bernard the year before.

During my last year at CID, 1963–64, I was elected senior patrol leader of Troop 132. I had the opportunity, for the first time, to speak in front of groups of people. This was a novel experience and it gave me so much confidence that some of my classmates accused me of being conceited. I definitely was becoming more outgoing and self-assured, but then I was also becoming a teenager.

At the same time as my election to senior patrol leader, I attended another prestigious induction. The Order of the Arrow was an exclusive organization—a secret "Indian" brotherhood for special Scouts. The year before, and for the first time in the history of CID's Boy Scout Troop 132, one of our deaf Scouts was chosen to join the Order of the Arrow. This was my close friend Erik, who had served as senior patrol leader before I was elected. My troop chose me to be the second troop member to join the Order of the Arrow.

Before I could be inducted, I had to survive a series of grueling trials devised to test the nominee's worthiness. The scene of the ordeal was a camp outside St. Louis for all the Order of the Arrow members in the district. The trials were intense. To pass I had to sweat, starve, sleep alone in the woods, and perform other tasks.

For the first time in my years of Scouting, I honestly had to work. During the proceedings, we were allowed almost no food and were not supposed to talk for twenty-four hours. The no talking proved to be the most difficult part for me, a natural talker. I practically had to cement my mouth shut. It was a frustrating experience.

All the leaders of the Order of the Arrow dressed like Indians and went through rituals supposedly typical of those performed by early Native Americans. I didn't understand or follow any of these. I was the only deaf person there and almost no one knew I was deaf.

At the end of the ritual, we were taken by "American Indians" (Scout leaders dressed as Native Americans) to different parts of the woods to spend the night alone. Each prospective inductee brought a sleeping bag. We were not allowed to bring anything else—no compass, flashlight, tent, or other luxuries. The "Indians," carrying fire torches, took us on a long walk through the woods to make sure we didn't know where we were. The task was for each of us to find our way back the next morning.

I was excited about the challenge but more than a little apprehensive about having no padding for my sleeping bag. One by one the Indians showed us where we were to spend the night. When my turn came, I thought I'd be somewhere near the other Scouts. I was wrong—no one was anywhere in sight. I watched the torches of the Indians slowly disappear into the forest as they left me to the darkness. I prayed no snakes or wild animals would pay me a call during the night. I got a stick and scraped away the rocks, dirt clods, and twigs from an area where I could sleep. I was almost successful.

I had no idea what time it was. I finally became resigned to being alone and began to look at my surroundings. I was overwhelmed by the beauty of the stars. I had never seen so many of them before. I realized it had been a long time since I had been that far from the city and away from the bright lights. I finally understood what people meant when they said that one could not really see the stars unless they were away from civilization. That night I was sorry I had never bothered to learn astronomy. I spent a lot of time admiring the stars, then drifted off and alternated between sleep and wakefulness for the rest of the night.

Every time I woke up I noticed how the stars had moved. Soon I became aware that they were traveling in a pattern, a big wheel circling around a central star. This was a stunning discovery for me. I had stumbled upon a major element of astronomy all by myself. I no longer felt that the Earth was the center of the universe but that our little globe was just a small part of a magnificent plan.

When morning came, I was surprised to see how deep into the woods I was. I figured out from the sun's position where the headquarters was and walked back, thus proving that I was a worthy survivor of the weekend. That night they held another ritual inducting those who had succeeded into the Order of the Arrow. Although I didn't understand all the words the Indians said, I was proud to be a part of the ceremony and to have succeeded in joining the elite fraternity. I had participated in the hearing world and been acknowledged by it. This was a milestone in my life, but I still had a long way to go before I would gain complete acceptance in that world.

5

NEW SKILLS AND OLD BLOCKS

Pleasures are transient; honors are immortal.

Greek proverb

During our years in the Advanced Section, we never heard anyone tell us that being deaf would limit us. In fact, the teachers rarely spoke of deafness and what it meant to be deaf. They focused on making us feel good about ourselves and on showing us our potential. We never heard anyone say, "You can't do it because you're deaf." That was a relief, because by then it was time for us to start thinking about our future.

At first I dreamed of becoming a mathematician. This changed to thoughts of being a veterinarian. I remember Joan, a student teacher, telling me that this was a great idea. She introduced me to her future husband, Paul Sher, who was then in a medical school. The idea that he was studying to be a doctor struck me as wonderful. They both made me proud of my choice to study animal medicine. Other classmates picked extraordinary careers such as business, education, sports, agriculture, engineering, and the like. One student was serious about becoming a professional bowler and golfer because he was very good in those two sports. He almost made it.

The more I thought about veterinary medicine, the more I realized how much science I would have to take. I also worried about operating on an animal without being able to listen to its heartbeat. So I switched back to mathematics, where I could pursue my interest in the physical sciences and do research in theoretical mathematics.

I'm grateful to our teachers for their support of our aspirations and dreams. Mrs. Daniels, for one, always said, "Go as far as you can in life!" I took her encouragement literally. Not until we found ourselves in our prospective hearing high schools did we have to face the true meaning

CID graduation.

of deafness and grapple with its reality and its obstruction to our chosen goals.

In spring 1964, the night before our graduation from CID, students and their parents celebrated with a meal at Stan Musial's restaurant. The parents ate together and the graduates ate at a separate table. My whole family had come to St. Louis for the graduation. Dunbar flew in from California, Jonathan and Dorothy came by train, and my parents drove from home, now Charleston, West Virginia. I was more thrilled with their presence than with graduation itself. I was a bit conceited in my belief that I had the best, most loving, and most understanding family present.

Steve, one of my classmates, would be going to an exclusive prep school for boys near his hometown. All the rest of the class was headed for public schools. I was envious of Steve because of my family's emphasis on education. Steve's parents asked me why I didn't consider going to the prep school with Steve. I liked the idea and brought it up with my parents in the middle of all the excitement. At dinner, Steve's parents also tried to influence my parents. My father was firm in his decision that I should go to a regular public school at home. He was not open to the idea of the prep school at all.

It wasn't until after dinner, when we were back at my family's motel, that my parents explained how eagerly they had awaited the day I could live at home. We would see each other every day! They could participate in my schoolwork and my free time. I realized then that they had missed me very much. They had given two of their children to CID for twenty-one years, and now they were looking forward to me living with them full time. Suddenly I saw how wonderful it would be—no more traumatic parting, no more housemothers, no more living in a closed society. Instantly, I dropped the idea of a prep school and let myself revel in the idea of living with my family after ten years of boarding school.

The next day, after all the songs had been sung, the speeches made, and the diplomas passed out, I still had one more episode to live out with my housemother, Miss Lacy. It had to do with a trip to the basement to pick up a piece of history.

CID was on a street called Kingshighway Boulevard. It had been built over an old road dating back to the late 1700s or early 1800s, when French colonists were in the St. Louis area. The French road was built using red granite blocks. I was fascinated with the history of the street, so when it was torn up for expansion I managed to spirit away two granite blocks for safekeeping. I wanted to take them home. Several weeks before graduation, I put the blocks in my school locker. When Miss Lacy saw them, she ordered me to "throw those filthy blocks out."

I refused, saying, "They are a piece of history. I must keep them. I want to take them home."

Miss Lacy persisted and reported it to the principal, Dr. Lane, who then called me into her office for the "last" time. She reminded me for the umpteenth time that I had to respect and obey Miss Lacy. We discussed it for long and heated moments and she finally agreed to let me keep the blocks if I put them somewhere in a dark corner of the basement. I was ecstatic. As I took them to the basement, I did so with the knowledge that I had finally won a long overdue victory over Miss Lacy. When I retrieved them on graduation day, it was like receiving a different kind of diploma.

As I had anticipated, my family was thrilled with the blocks and the history behind them. It was so typical of the kinds of things we did. We put the blocks in the family car and they went all the way to California on our vacation before we took them home. Those blocks are still on my bookshelf in my study; they are among my favorite treasures. To me, they are more than just a bit of St. Louis history. They represent my years of toil at CID, for learning the English language without hearing is no less difficult than mining granite from a quarry. My triumph that graduation day was to be able to carry my new, hard-earned language skills *and* my ancient blocks away with me into the mainstream world.

PART FIVE

A NEW LIFE AT LINCOLN

1

INTO THE MAINSTREAM

Don't be afraid to take a big step if one is indicated. You can't cross a chasm in two small jumps.

David Lloyd George

In September 1964 I started my tenure at Lincoln Junior High School in Charleston, West Virginia, a public school near my parents' home. I was fifteen years old and entering ninth grade. Ten long years at Central Institute for the Deaf had prepared me for this day. I now had a foundation in the English language designed to help me to succeed in classes with hearing students. The dream I had worked toward all those years was finally about to be realized.

During the months before my big move, however, I endured much debate and misgivings about whether I should attend a public, hearing school and live with my parents. My parents were their usual supportive selves. It was obvious that Dunbar was thrilled with my decision. But Jonathan felt differently. He was worried. He believed I would be happier with other deaf students and would get a better education if I didn't have to deal with communication problems while going to school. He suggested I opt for a state school for the deaf and forget the idea of public schools. He reminded me how much he had enjoyed Arkansas School for the Deaf.

But I had already made up my mind to go to Lincoln Junior High. I felt I had to give it a try since all my CID friends were going to public schools in their hometowns. I didn't want to be the only one who didn't. Besides, I felt ready to take on the challenge, partly because my family said I was capable but mostly because the CID faculty had assured me I could excel in whatever I chose to do. I explained again and again to Jonathan how all my CID friends across the country were trying out public schools and that I felt the need to do the same. Otherwise, I would regret not having tried.

Jonathan remained convinced, however, that I was going to be miserable and that I would never have hearing friends. "What if your social life is empty and you learn nothing at that school?" he said. "Wouldn't it be better to be sure you learn something, be *sure* you'll have friends?"

I shrugged off his fears. It was true that I couldn't picture what it would be like at Lincoln until I got there. All I knew was that the CID faculty said I could do it, the guest speakers who were deaf said I could do it, and my parents said I could do it. And best of all, I would be living at home with my parents all year around.

A few days before school started, my father and I went to Lincoln to meet with my teachers and explain my deafness to them. Before going, we decided which subjects I would take. After checking the requirements for graduation from high school, we picked civics, algebra, English, and a health class. Which foreign language I should take was a problem at first. I considered German, as Dunbar and Annegret would appreciate my knowing the language, but the school didn't offer it. Finally, I decided on Latin, since I wouldn't have to speak or lipread it as in French and Spanish. Latin was only a written language requirement. The thought of more speech lessons turned me off.

I remember well the day of our visit to the teachers because I had no idea what to expect. This was what I had been preparing for all these years. Now that it was here, I realized I was stepping off the end of my world into a new one.

My father and I went to a Mrs. Greenwood's class. This was to be my homeroom. Mrs. Greenwood was nice and friendly. We explained that I had a profound hearing loss, that I read lips, and that I spoke differently than hearing people but well enough to be understood. I added that I needed to sit in the front of the room so I could have a good view of the teacher's lips and whatever was happening in the classroom. Mrs. Greenwood asked me to pick a seat, so I chose the one right in front of her desk, in the second row. She assured me that we would get along splendidly.

Next, we went to the English teacher's room. Mrs. Carp was also friendly and receptive to our explanations. "I will be happy to work with you," she said. "You can sit at that desk because I usually stand in front of it." She explained that she sometimes went to the blackboard at the side of the classroom and that she often walked between two desks. She agreed to reserve the desk for me and added, "I will try to remember to keep my face turned toward you so you won't miss what I have to say. I know that some teachers tend to keep their faces away from the students' faces, but I won't do that to you." She impressed me as being sensitive and assertive.

Next, we visited the Latin teacher, Miss Jones. She was affable and agreed to everything we suggested. She didn't say much but made us feel that there would be no problems. She taped a paper with my name on it to the desk I picked, which embarrassed me a little.

Miss Waggy was the algebra teacher. She suffered from a serious curvature of the spine. She was short, with a large hump on her back. She was quiet as we explained everything to her. When we were through, she said, "I will be happy to work with Paul, and I look forward to having him in my class." My father and I later agreed we weren't sure how receptive she really was, but we would wait and see.

Finally, we talked to the civics teacher, Mr. Chase, who was most unfriendly. Without any eye contact with me, he told my father that I didn't belong in the school at all. I belonged, he said, at the residential state school for the deaf, two hundred miles away from home. He treated me as if I were a problem to be ignored.

Mr. Chase spoke fast. I didn't understand a word, but I could tell from my father's body language that he was upset. When we left the room, my father calmly told me not to worry. He called the principal later and requested that I be assigned to a different civics class. There was no problem and I got Mrs. Burdette, whom I would meet on the first day of school.

One day before school started, all the students were supposed to go to Lincoln to buy textbooks for their classes. Mrs. Beckman, a family friend from my father's church, had a granddaughter who was also going into the ninth grade. I had always been fond of Bernice, the granddaughter, and we had become friends during my holidays, so I went with Bernice and Mrs. Beckman to the school to buy the books.

Before I left, Mother said, "Paul, I'd like you to buy two copies of everything." I tried to brush her off, saying, "No, Mother, that won't be necessary." But she insisted. "Please, Paul. I'll be able to help you in case you fall behind in your classes or have trouble with a subject." I protested. I didn't want people to know that she was taking my classes too. But I finally gave in to her insistence that it was good insurance.

When I went to the textbook room and told them that I needed two of everything on my list, the textbook clerk asked out loud, "Why two?" I said, "I just need them," and gave her a big smile, hoping she would quietly proceed with the paperwork. But to my horror, Mrs. Beckman piped in, "Paul's mother needs them so she can tutor him in case he gets behind with his schoolwork."

I felt humiliated and blushed vividly. I had wanted to express my independence and had hoped to make it through high school without having to depend on anyone else. The textbook clerk gave me a warm smile. "Oh, that's a very good idea," she said. She then proceeded to babble on about it while giving me my two copies of everything. I felt impatient with her. Above all, I didn't want Bernice to think I was a mama's boy.

In front of Bernice, I tried to explain to Mrs. Beckman that it might seem as if my mother was controlling my life, but she only wanted to be involved because I had been away from home for so long. I doubt that Mrs. Beckman listened or understood, but Bernice did. She told me not to worry about it. "You're already independent," she said. This time I beamed with the vivid color of pride.

2

MY TEACHERS

If a child can't learn the way we teach, maybe we should teach the way they learn.

Ignacio "Nacho" Estrada

Finally, the big day arrived. I was nervous. I didn't know what to expect. I felt like a racehorse waiting to blast out of the starting gate. Adrenaline was pumping through my system. Since Lincoln Junior High was close to my home, I walked to school. I carried the battered briefcase that Jonathan used when he went to Arkansas School for the Deaf. With every step I felt his love, wisdom, and support, even if we did not agree that it was the right course for me.

The hallways at Lincoln seemed to overflow with students. What a contrast to the first visit I had made with my father. This time I couldn't even see the walls. I saw nothing but students—all vocal, hearing boys and girls. They were talking, joking, laughing, flirting, shouting. And I was to be a part of all this! How would it all work out?

I found my homeroom with Mrs. Greenwood and sat at my chosen desk. On that day, the homeroom period was longer than usual, as we had to iron out the bugs in our schedules and get our locker assignments. There were many announcements over the loudspeaker from the principal's office. I didn't know what to do about these announcements except to smile sheepishly and look around for clues. Mrs. Greenwood kept saying that there was nothing important for me to know. *How in hell*, I asked myself, *would she know what's important and what's not important for me?*

In the homeroom, I saw a friendly face sitting in the first row on the left side of the teacher's desk. He kept looking at me. I knew he was a "foreigner" also. He asked me what my name was and soon we were in conversation. We tried to talk but found it difficult with all the background noise so we resorted to writing notes to each other. His name was Carlos Molores. We found out that we lived only three blocks from each other and agreed to walk home together after school.

I liked Carlos immediately. He was friendly and very much his own person. He showed no reservations about talking to a deaf person in our conversations, which flowed freely from the start. It helped that his communication style included many gestures and varying facial expressions. To show emphasis, Carlos didn't just raise his voice. He punctuated words by throwing up his hands or pointing his finger. We became fast friends.

Soon we broke up to go to our classes. For me it was Latin with Miss Jones. There was the paper with my name on it taped to the desk. I raced in, peeled it off, crumpled it up, and threw it into the trash. I didn't want anyone to see the desk with my name on it. No one else had an assigned seat and I didn't want anyone to think I was getting different treatment. To most adolescents, being set apart or having grown-ups call attention to you is a curse. But to me, the "deaf boy" in the class, it was even more of a trauma.

I was surprised at how easy it was to lipread Miss Jones. She seemed to exaggerate her lips—not because of me but because that was her natural way of speaking to the class. I got the impression that she was almost euphoric on that first day of school. She seemed genuinely glad to see everyone. She introduced me to the class, explaining that I was profoundly deaf but that I read lips and that I spoke fairly well. I didn't feel comfortable being held up before the class as someone different, but everyone in the class seemed friendly and receptive to the situation. Some of the students even came up to say hello and welcome me aboard.

In Miss Waggy's algebra class, I took the chair near her desk with the armrest I wanted. Then Miss Waggy had the rest of the class sit in alphabetical order, leaving me sitting at my chosen place. Because she didn't explain my deafness, some of the students were puzzled when Miss Waggy chose me from the rest of the class to sit at that chair. This time I was interjected into the classroom without any explanation, and the feeling was equally strange.

Miss Waggy started right off talking about what to expect in her class. My heart sank. I couldn't read her lips. She didn't move them much and didn't enunciate at all. I knew I would just have to wait and see how things turned out. Miss Waggy was also rather cool and straightforward, with little or no animation or personality. Two out of three.

I was eager to see what Mrs. Burdette, the unknown civics teacher, was going to be like. The next period, I introduced myself to her and asked permission to sit at the front of the class. She agreed to it, but by her attitude I could see she had no confidence in my ability to survive. She was just resigned to the fact that I was going to be there. She began speaking about what we were to learn in civics. I soon realized I could have given the same information in five minutes that took her a full half hour.

After lunch I went to Mrs. Carp's English class. The moment I walked into the room, I knew everyone was terrified of her. The other students had been at the school in seventh and eighth grade, so they knew who she was and what she demanded from her class. They were all frozen in their seats. When Mrs. Carp saw me, she told the person sitting at my chosen spot to move elsewhere so I could take my seat.

Mrs. Carp outlined the English class activities clearly and I was pleased with how easy it was to understand most of her speech. Her strict nature dictated that she speak forcefully, which made it easier for me to read her lips. Everyone in the class was attentive in her presence. It turned out we had a lot of homework, reading, and papers to write. Even so, from the first day to year's end, I held a great deal of respect for Mrs. Carp. I didn't really mind all the work or her no-nonsense nature, though some students resented every minute of their time with her.

Mrs. Carp always wrote the next assignment on the blackboard at the end of class period. It was a perfect way to ensure that I didn't miss anything expected of me, which was easy to do if the teacher wasn't altogether clear. I asked other teachers to do the same, and they all agreed to do so for the rest of the school year. However, some teachers were not as organized as others, and it was hard for them to remember. This was especially true of Mrs. Burdette, who was never clear in her expectations of us.

After Mrs. Carp's class, I had a study hall period with Mrs. Hunt, a friendly teacher in her late twenties. On the first day, we didn't talk much, but later in the school year a real friendship blossomed.

The last class for the day was health with Mr. Stern, a popular physical education teacher. I didn't understand a word he said and never bothered trying to talk to him much. I sat halfway from the front with Carlos Molores beside me. From time to time, Carlos explained what was happening. He showed me different things in our textbook to let me know exactly what Mr. Stern was covering at that moment. It turned out that Mr. Stern lectured straight from the book all the way through the school year, deviating only to discuss his favorite subject, our school sports teams.

At the end of each school day, we returned to our homerooms. That was my schedule every day.

I have already said that deaf children must be treated as normal human beings yet with special care; they must be both challenged and protected. It is a contradiction and may sound like preferential treatment, yet these same attitudes should be applied to hearing children as well. Each child is fragile or vulnerable in different ways. To be raised and educated properly, a child should be challenged and protected in proportion to his needs. This is much to ask of parents, let alone teachers, who have fifteen to thirty pupils in their class. If you add a deaf child to that class, of course the effort required of the teacher is multiplied. Some teachers are equal to the task, but others who are already challenged just to keep up with the hearing children will fall short. Each of my teachers at Lincoln had his or her own personality, abilities, and limitations.

Homeroom teacher Mrs. Greenwood meant well, but the worst thing you can do to a deaf child is isolate him from information. Miss Jones showed too much preferential treatment, while Miss Waggy didn't explain to the class why I was different. Mrs. Burdette showed no faith in me and Mrs. Carp gave no quarter to anyone. Mr. Stern should have been on the gridiron and in study hall, while Mrs. Hunt became a friend. I did learn from this array of teachers, although with some it was from omission.

At the end of that first day, Carlos and I left school together for home. We talked about school. As we talked he understood more and more of my speech. I appreciated how easy it was to lipread him. We struggled a little for the next few days, but within a few weeks all barriers to our communication were gone. I was thrilled. I had my first hearing friend at school, and it had taken such a short time.

Carlos had lived an interesting life. He came to the United States from Cuba during a group escape attempt, but his parents were caught and kept in Cuba. An older couple in Charleston knew his parents from their travels in Cuba and agreed to take care of Carlos as long as it was necessary. No one knew when or if his parents would ever join him. When Carlos started the seventh grade at Lincoln, his English was practically nonexistent. After two years, his English was nearly flawless. He was extremely bright and absorbed everything he read and heard.

When Carlos and I met, he understood my situation. His experiences as a foreigner had taught him what it was like to be a stranger and made him more empathetic to me than many others would have been. His struggle to understand a foreign language and to be understood made it easier for him to be patient with my struggle.

I thought Carlos and I might stop being friends when we discovered differences between us. Instead, our friendship grew stronger throughout our high school years.

3

SURVIVING SCHOOLWORK

We have been told over and over about the importance of bonding to our children. Rarely do we hear about the skill of letting go.

Joan Sheingold Ditzion

I found Latin an exciting and challenging subject. I was always thrilled to discover an English word that had its root in Latin. My father got into the game of listening for words in my Latin vocabulary. When he recognized one, he'd teach me the English derivatives, which meant I was learning new English words as well. It was important that I enlarge my vocabulary to keep up with my expanding academic experience, and this was a perfect way to do so.

I liked Latin class because it was easy for me and I didn't mind memorizing. Miss Jones was cheerful and outgoing, just the opposite of the stereotypical Latin teacher. She was good about adopting Mrs. Carp's idea of jotting down assignments and expectations on the blackboard. Once in a while, when there was no homework, she wrote on the board "Vacation!" or "Take a break from Latin."

In Latin class, we had to memorize many, many word endings. I started to write these on index cards, but my mother came up with the brilliant idea of writing the endings for different categories on a roll of paper. She then tacked the twelve-inch-wide strips of paper on the walls in my bedroom. In a month the bedroom walls were covered with Latin. I was able to look up and memorize right above my desk and bed. What dreams I must have had—no posters of movie stars for me! My bedroom looked more like that of a Latin scholar than of a ninth-grade student. I began doing very well in Latin.

It was a different story in algebra. During the second week, Miss Waggy realized I was having trouble. At CID, the students who weren't good lipreaders, speakers, and listeners struggled, but since these were among my strengths, I flourished. Our teachers in English, reading, and history were generally quite good. On the other hand, for whatever reason, our instruction in math and science tended to be substandard. At Lincoln, Miss Waggy determined that I was two years behind. I hadn't done any preparatory math work for three or four years at CID. I was shocked when she said I should be taking a seventh-grade math class.

After a few days of discussions, Miss Waggy encouraged me to pursue independent study in class and after school. I was not very happy at first, but I realized she was right and that I had to work hard to make up for what I had missed at CID. Miss Waggy had confidence in me, but my parents began to worry about all the extra work I was doing. In the end, I persuaded them that I could handle the work. Miss Waggy turned out to be a very special person. Perhaps she was empathetic with my deafness because she had her own physical issue, her back.

Over time, Miss Waggy became sensitive to my needs. When she began to talk while facing the blackboard, she would suddenly freeze, turn to me, and start all over. In my outside studies, we worked hard together. I was fast and made up the two years of math in four months, which pleased her immensely. She knew I would eventually catch up to the rest of the class with my algebra, and I did.

In civics, it was difficult for me to follow Mrs. Burdette. She was always rambling on about things not covered in our textbooks. At first, I was apprehensive about what I was missing. She had the habit of using her fists and hands during the rambling, which signaled to me that what she was saying was important. I started asking a new friend who sat next to me, Tom McQuain, whether I was missing anything important. He got into the habit of sharing his notes with me, which was a lifesaver. Mrs. Burdette encouraged Tom to do this, because she was clearly uncomfortable with my asking so many questions. It was obvious that she had a mental block against my speech. Many times, Tom and others in the class had to help her understand me.

As time went on, Tom often had occasion to write down his favorite expression: "You are not missing anything. She is beating around the bush." Sometimes I had trouble believing him, because Mrs. Burdette seemed to be saying something profound, emphasized by a shaking fist or gesture in the air. But Tom made sure I knew what to study for tests—if I missed *that* information my grades would suffer.

One day, I realized to my dismay that Tom was sick and not in class. I depended so much on him that I was afraid I'd miss something important. I asked around the class for another note taker. Mary, a friendly girl, agreed. She wrote down everything Mrs. Burdette said, including the unimportant stuff. Mary didn't have Tom's knack of sorting out the trash. I couldn't believe all the garbage that showed up in Mary's notes. Much of it was nothing more than Mrs. Burdette's conservative political comments about her favorite presidential candidate, Barry Goldwater.

For the first time, I realized how much of what Mrs. Burdette said was a waste of time. I was disgusted with the whole thing. Yet I thanked Mary many times for doing it and she continued to do it from time to time when Tom was absent. Every time I showed Mary's notes to Tom, he broke up with laughter. I was very grateful to have Tom as my ears. He went on to become a senior staff attorney for the West Virginia Supreme Court of Appeals, and he says that "working for me" led to his thirty-five-year career in state courts.

In English, Mrs. Carp gave us an overwhelming amount of work, but she encouraged me by advising, "Getting started is an important step in the right direction. Once you get started, you've finished half of the project." That was good advice. I used that advice for the next four years in high school. Mrs. Carp scared everyone to death, but I wasn't afraid of her because I knew she supported and understood me. She was impressed with my work and had confidence in my ability to improve. She knew how important it was for me to enlarge my vocabulary and expand my writing skills.

At the beginning of that first semester at Lincoln, my mother asked me many questions about my homework assignments. Using her own copies of my textbooks, she did the same homework and then checked my answers. She never told me correct answers; she only showed me my mistakes. I then double-checked and corrected the mistakes. She tried to do this for each of my classes, with the exception of algebra. As time went on, I became a little irritated. I felt she was mothering me too much. At the same time, I knew she wanted me to do well.

Part of the reason for my mother's heavy involvement was that she was a natural teacher. She took much pleasure in educating and raising her two younger brothers and then her three sons before I was born. My mother and father both felt that all parents ought to play a major role in contributing to their children's lives. In addition, with me, it was an adventure for her.

I loved to talk and my parents were able to communicate with me about almost anything. Whenever I mentioned something that had come up at school, they were ready to jump in and discuss it. Still, I wasn't crazy about having my mother check my homework and monitor every step of my schoolwork. I was eager to prove my independence. But at the same time, I didn't want to tell her to bug off. All parents and children face this challenge, of course. It can be hard for parents to know when to step in and help and when to hold back and let children work things out for themselves. The trick is to gradually release the reins so that by the time the children are ready to graduate from high school, they are able to function on their own.

One day just before Christmas, my mother came down with a bad case of the flu and had to be in bed for two weeks. She fell behind in her studies and stopped checking my homework. I was sorry she was sick but glad she had to bow out, for I was eager to convince her and myself that I didn't need all the help she was giving me. She soon realized I was doing well enough without her help. From that point on, she stopped doing the homework altogether. It was another small victory in my march toward independence.

4

DANCE MOVES

Never allow yourself to be made a victim. Accept no one's definition of your life, but define yourself.

Harvey Fierstein

With my schoolwork under control, I began to take an interest in a social life. Every Friday night, Carlos and I went to the school dance. I had learned to dance and socialize at Central Institute for the Deaf. With Carlos around, it was easy to make friends. We fooled around, flirted with the girls, and danced. It was great fun.

At one of the dances I noticed one of the attractive cheerleaders and decided to ask her to dance. When I greeted her and asked her if she'd dance with me, she froze, looked at me, and said, "I don't want to dance with a deaf person!"

I was devastated. I left the dance immediately and went home. I cried. I was crushed. Never had I been rejected so bluntly. Through my tears, I told my parents I would never go back to school. I was through.

My father listened quietly and then asked, "Do you know the girl?"

"No," I said. "I've only seen her around."

"Why do you want to dance with her and not someone else?"

"She's the one I wanted to dance with. She's pretty."

"You are telling me that you want to quit everything because of one girl? Guys get 'no's from girls all the time. Still, the same guys will get 'yes's from others. Don't expect everyone to say yes to you."

"But she is pretty and I really wanted to dance with her!"

"But there are many other pretty girls."

"But I wanted to dance with that one."

"Do you really know her and what kind of person she is?"

"I don't know her at all but I'd like to get to know her."

136

"Are you going to forget everything at that school because of that girl?"

I felt a little silly for threatening to quit school. But at the same time, I didn't like the feeling of being rejected. My father went on: "There will always be people who won't have anything to do with you because of your deafness. You will always meet people like that. You can't throw away your future over one girl you don't know at all. People who reject you because of your deafness have their own problem: insecurity. You don't need to associate with people who are ignorant and insecure. She must be very ignorant. There are many more people who would love to dance with you. I think you should go back to the dance."

This was typical of the way my parents or Dunbar responded when my deafness led to a conflict. They refused to let me feel sorry for myself and explained that the cause was a problem with the other person. The parents of some of my deaf friends took it personally when a friend or acquaintance said something negative about their deaf child. They felt injured, almost a victim. My parents never adopted this attitude themselves and steered me away from it as well. It left me feeling more confident about myself and who I was.

In this case, I knew my father was right. I agreed with him and went back to the dance. No one but Carlos knew I had been gone for an hour. He told me he had looked for me and asked where I was. I explained a little but said I'd tell him later. And we danced on.

A few weeks later, we had an impromptu dance contest. As couples danced, other dancers stopped to watch the best ones. At the end, the best duo received an ovation.

I happened to be coupled with one of the best dancers in school. As we danced, other students began forming a circle around us. They watched and cheered us on. I remember thinking, "I wonder if the pretty cheerleader is watching with envy."

At the end of the dance, Carlos ran up to me. "I don't believe it, Paul," he said, jumping up and down. "You really dance the best. Now everyone will want to dance with you!" Carlos tended toward the dramatic, a trait I loved in him. Not only was he fun, but his exuberance made it easier to communicate with him.

Some of my friends asked how a profoundly deaf person could dance at all, let alone maintain the rhythm that is essential to dancing. So I told them the secret: deaf people can feel the vibrations of the music through the floor. All one needs is a sense of what to do with that rhythm. I also have to give credit to CID for all the dance lessons, dance nights, and even proms we enjoyed there. Many of my friends at CID were fantastic dancers.

The big problem I experienced at the Lincoln dances (and later in high school) was speaking to other people with loud music in the background, which drowned out our voices. I had the advantage in being able to lipread, as you can imagine, but I had to learn to talk louder so *I* could be heard. I was never comfortable talking so loud. It took a lot of energy, so I began to enunciate more and use more gestures. Sometimes I stopped using my voice altogether. In this way, many of my hearing friends learned to lipread, often without even realizing it. After my triumph on the dance floor, it seemed many students tried harder to understand me. (I would like to be able to say that the story ended with the cheerleader and me having a passionate childhood romance, but things turn out that way only in fiction.)

Due to our chaperon, the aptly cast Mrs. Burdette, those dances would have made a great comedy skit. It was hilarious watching her wield her long blackboard pointer as she marched between the dancing couples, prying apart the ones she deemed to be too tightly wrapped around each other. On Monday morning, she was back in class, raving about Goldwater.

One day, halfway through that first semester, Carlos suggested that I run for the student council. I thought it was a great idea. My parents agreed. Being on the student council would give me more opportunities to make new friends and meet people. It would also improve my self-confidence and public speaking. But my real reason for running for the council was to see if I could really do it. I was driven by the feeling that I had to prove to others that I was as capable as anyone at the school. In the back of my mind, I was always comparing myself with everyone else.

The biggest obstacle was Mrs. Burdette, who was the adviser to the student council. She was in charge of the council meetings, even though she gave the president, vice president, and three committee seats de facto freedom to run them. Even without her blackboard pointer, she still had the leverage to approve or disapprove everything the council did. I decided to run for the president's position and turned in my application. Mrs. Burdette flatly rejected it, saying I could never do the job because of my speech. Some of the main duties of the student council president were to lead the pledge to the flag and school prayer, as well as read announcements over the public-address system.

Carlos was more upset than I was about Mrs. Burdette's decision. I thought it made sense, but then she turned down my application for the vice president position for the same reason. She tried to convince me that when the president was absent, the vice president had to make the public announcements. She told me my speech was just not clear enough for everyone to understand. I was disappointed but I halfway agreed with her.

When I look back, I see that I might have worked out a plan for someone else to read my speeches into the public-address system or to interpret for me at student meetings. But my confidence in my position in the hearing world was by no means 100 percent. I had been in school for only one semester, so I thought I would wait and see. I didn't want to jump into anything too fast. In the end, Mrs. Burdette advised me to run for one of the three committee seats. I accepted that. I didn't really want to have to speak a lot during the meetings anyway. Whereas at CID I had been a great talker, here I was going to have to start out as a listener.

I had fun campaigning. I had no trouble smiling, shaking hands, and patting everyone on the back. My friends and I put up posters and even hung a sign around the statue of Lincoln that read, "Student government of the students, for the students, and by the students."

I swept the election, much to Carlos's pleasure and amazement, with 95 percent of the vote. I was a little disappointed when the excitement of the campaign and the election were over. I liked getting involved with people through the student council. I didn't feel left out at all, because I understood nearly everything that was happening in the student council meetings, even though I didn't get it word for word. It's true that Mrs. Burdette treated me like a deficient. But the other four students on the council always gave me my fair share of responsibilities.

The best part of the student council was meeting in the principal's office every morning to participate in the announcements, the pledge to the flag, and the school prayer on the public-address system. I was right there lipreading everything and was able to read from the paper what the speakers were reading aloud. That was a contrast from sitting in my homeroom every morning, not able to hear the loudspeakers at all!

I wondered what Mr. Chase, who thought I belonged at a school for the deaf, thought when I was elected overwhelmingly to the council. I wondered what he thought of my straight As as well.

5

COMMUNICATION CHALLENGES

In the whole round of human affairs little is so fatal to peace as misunderstanding.

Margaret Elizabeth Sangster

Overall, the students at Lincoln supported my being there. Many, it seemed, were affected by the friendly nature and ready smile that I employed as a tool to help overcome my deafness. In October, my second month at school, the student body even voted me most popular boy of the month. I was surprised and even thought it was some sort of sick joke. I said to my parents, "How can one thousand students know me well enough in one month to judge objectively?" I couldn't believe they would pick me for the honor when I had only a few close friends. But I was overlooking my high profile as the only deaf student. It was the same as being Dunbar's mascot when I was younger.

It is usually flattering when people pay attention to you, but I have to say that the difference between positive and prejudiced treatment is sometimes difficult to distinguish. Sometimes a deaf person feels as embarrassed by one as by the other. Carlos and Tom were thrilled with the vote and kept telling me to think of it as proof I had been accepted into the student body. Tom looked at it as a wonderful way of breaking down barriers and Carlos thought it was great because he appreciated adoration. He wanted the same honor someday for himself but never made it.

I kept telling Carlos that I didn't communicate with everyone in the same way I communicated with him. "With other students," I said, "all I did was say, 'Hi.' And on that basis alone they decided I was the most popular student." He kept saying that they liked what they saw, not what they knew. Finally, I agreed to be a good sport and accept the honor. I thanked them and smiled a lot, as usual. But privately, I felt as though my conversations with most of the students were superficial.

I concluded that communication was not as treasured a commodity at Lincoln as it had been at CID and was at my home. I learned two things early on about the hearing world: one, that adolescents were more concerned with the image of a person than the content; and two, that most hearing people didn't appreciate the art of speaking as deaf people do. At my new school, as everywhere in hearing society, communication was taken for granted. It was just a normal part of life and was not to be valued more highly than, say, grades, possessions, knowledge, wisdom, love, or friendship.

I just couldn't comprehend this. It was such a different attitude from what I had grown up with. For the Lincoln students, communication was nothing but small talk. I felt that most of the conversations they held were below my level. I didn't realize until much later that some of the difference had to do with maturity. I was one year older than everyone in my class and more mature for my age because of the boarding school struggles and my family environment. Being the baby, I grew up fast to keep up with my older brothers.

Carlos was a wonderful friend. With his help, I was able to breach many barriers with other students. Carlos was my "advance man." Whenever we met new friends, Carlos would say, "All you have to do is look Paul in the face. If you talk slowly, he can lipread you, and if you listen a little more carefully, you will understand him." Carlos understood my speech perfectly and helped me get a head start in communicating with others. If I'd had to do it alone, without Carlos, things would have been much harder for me at Lincoln. Many students didn't know how to handle enunciating, talking slowly, gesturing openly, showing facial expressions, and lipreading. They were intimidated by my deafness and my speech. But Carlos helped put them at ease and gave me a chance to develop friendships.

Still, I couldn't understand everyone I met, not by a longshot. Speaking styles and vocabularies were different, and each person was a new lipreading challenge. People often used words I had read but not seen on lips before. To keep my lipreading skills up with my expanding reading and social vocabulary, I reluctantly began private lipreading lessons, which I continued throughout my high school years. I didn't want the extra work, but I recognized the importance of doing it.

A strange method of social selection began to form. I found myself preferring the company of students who were easy to lipread rather than those who were difficult to understand. It was a painful struggle to try to make friends with students who otherwise were warm, friendly, and wonderful but whose speech I couldn't understand. It was even more painful to have to choose friends or girlfriends based on that criteria.

I couldn't read some lips at all, and some people never could understand my speech, even after weeks of trial and error. With others, it took only a few days before we were exchanging ideas with ease. I remember one boy with whom I tried to talk. Our conversations always ended up with paper and pencil. After four years together in school, he finally asked me why all my other friends could understand me but he could not. I wrote back that perhaps he had a mental block against my speech. He disagreed, saying he thought he was willing enough to listen. Even so, speech never worked between us despite our efforts.

Even among students I talked with easily, I often felt dissatisfied with the quality of the conversation. I complained about this to my parents and Carlos. They explained that I was geared to heavier conversations and said I might need to lower my expectations. But my education had prepared me for serious conversations. I didn't know how to make small talk. If I couldn't understand a group of students talking, I always felt as if I were missing something important. I became envious of them. My imagination convinced me that they were discussing vital matters.

My study hall teacher, Mrs. Hunt, and I always had good conversations. She interpreted the announcements from the loudspeakers for me, something no other teachers attempted to do. I grew fond of her and looked forward to study hall and the chance to talk about all the interesting things happening at school.

One of the things we discussed was social chitchat. I complained that when I couldn't understand a group of students and I asked them to explain, they often told me it wasn't important. I just couldn't accept that hearing people talked for hours on end about nothing.

Mrs. Hunt was sensitive to my frustrations, so one day she had me sit by her desk. She had a piece of paper and pretended we were discussing the paper. She wrote down all the conversations going on in the study hall—yes, we eavesdropped on the other students. And I couldn't believe it! It was all gossip, all nonsense. That afternoon gave me an important insight into human nature.

From time to time my parents volunteered to take groups of my friends to football games and other social functions. I always missed out on the laughter and conversation in the backseat of the car, so I asked my father or mother to listen and store up all the conversations. When they told me later what had been said, I was amazed that people wasted their breath on such drivel. I realized that I was lucky to have close friends like Carlos and Tom. They were more mature than most of the others and had wonderful, interesting things to say.

On reflection, my surprise at the empty-headed conversations of my fellow students made sense. At CID we discussed important topics, issues, and ideas in order to promote our English development. We learned to pay a great deal of attention to everything being said. We were reprimanded if we ignored someone or let someone talk without listening to them. Concentration was necessary; not a minute was wasted. We treasured every word as important and valuable. Of course, we also engaged in small talk and often teased each other, but the emphasis was on local and national news, politics, and other issues that had implications for our lives.

At Lincoln, I brought a different attitude toward conversation than most other students. I was more serious, more idealistic, and more mature. Many students used their communication skills simply to enjoy themselves and make friends. Everything they did or said seemed superficial, light, even ridiculous.

Yet I wanted to be friends with everyone. I hadn't been taught how to strike up a casual conversation. I thought, *What do I say to a stranger? Once a conversation starts, how do people manage to keep it going for so long without a purpose other than social interplay? What is discussed when people stand around in groups? How can I break into a group of people, join cliques, and introduce myself?* I was never sure of what to say.

I had no way of answering these questions except by trial and error. I was a proud person who didn't want to make social blunders, so it wasn't easy for me to experiment. I knew that deafness and isolation at CID from the hearing world had prevented me from learning about small talk. It was not hearing that I missed as much as *overhearing*, eavesdropping, and talking about the "weather," so to speak.

Many times I wondered, *Why didn't CID tell us the negatives? Why didn't they warn us of the few oddballs who would be intolerant of our deafness? Why didn't they tell us our speech would not always be intelligible to everyone? Why didn't they tell us that sometimes, in order to be accepted in hearing society, we would be expected to talk nonsense?*

My lack of hearing had made communication so important to me that I completely overlooked the fact it could be used as a social as well as an educational tool. It was a new concept for me. My few special friends—Carlos, Tom, Mrs. Hunt, and others—helped me solve this puzzle of communication. They were my stepping-stones to understanding the new world I was entering.

Even in the familiar world of my family, communication sometimes remained a challenge. It was so nice to go home at the end of each school day—a new experience for me. Over the previous decade, when I went home from CID for the holidays, my family had showered me with attention. Now things returned to a normal state. Every evening at suppertime, my parents and I talked about our daytime experiences, ideas, and what was going on in the world. I realized what I had missed all those years away from home. I felt like I was getting to know my parents. I was now experiencing their daily lives. I knew who they were. I saw them get upset, cry, laugh, and rejoice. All of this opened my eyes.

At dinner one night, my father started talking about how much he missed David and then about how awful he'd felt about leaving Jonathan, a little five-year-old, at CID that first time. He became very emotional. Then he turned to the time I almost rejected him. I had no idea what he was talking about.

He told me how when I was seven and in my second year at CID, he and Mother had arrived at the school to take me home for the summer. When I saw them at Forest Park where I was playing, he said I had hesitated to run to them. He described my expression. To him my face had said, "Why should you come back for me when you don't really love me?" Tears began rolling down my father's cheeks as he described the moment. He felt that my expression showed that I had never forgiven them for leaving me at CID.

I was dumbfounded on hearing this story and seeing my father cry. I remembered vividly the day he described. What had really happened was entirely different from what my father had perceived. My parents had written me saying that they were coming on a certain day to take me home for the summer. The principal of the school confirmed the date of their arrival. Eagerly, I looked forward to that day and I counted the number of "sleeps" until they would arrive.

The day before they were supposed to come, I was playing at the park. Suddenly, I saw my parents. Apparently, they had decided to come a day early. I couldn't believe what I saw! There was my father walking toward me with his arms open wide. I kept staring, trying to be sure it was them. When they got close, I recognized them and ran into my father's open arms.

"Yes," my mother confirmed when I had finished the story, "we did arrive early that year." Soon all of us were crying and commiserating at how easy it was to misunderstand or misinterpret.

I felt awful that my father had carried that burden with him for so long—and for no reason, since what he believed was far from the truth. This experience made me think about the power of accurate communication and the consequences when things aren't perfectly clear. The lives of deaf people—and all people—can be filled with such muddles, even when everyone tries their hardest.

TEACHING THE HEARING

Man's mind, once stretched by a new idea, never regains its original dimensions.

Oliver Wendell Holmes

As time went on and the novelty of me being the lone deaf student at Lincoln wore off, I found I had friends and enemies just like everyone else. My popularity began to balance out as fellow students realized I was the same as any other student, with the slight exception of my way of communicating.

Carlos was right there with me, helping me along as I sorted through the students. He recognized the ones that were sincere and saw through those who cultivated me as a curiosity. Carlos teased me after some of the girls complained to him that they weren't used to the kind of attention I gave them. What they felt was that I stared at them too intently. It took a while before Carlos realized that of course I stared—I used my eyes more than other people because everything was communicated to me through my eyes. We eventually had to explain to the girls how much I depended on looking at people. Later on, I learned that many of the girls liked the looks and attention I gave them.

Eye contact was so important to me that I often stopped talking to people who took their eyes off my face. Those who understood my speech encouraged me to keep talking while they looked around at other things. But I couldn't do it. I had a mental block about talking without a pair of eyes turned directly toward my face.

Many students were fascinated with my lipreading ability. They were convinced that I understood more than I did. They started having ridiculous expectations, thinking I could lipread the teachers' secret conversations, even from across the room. Some friends—especially boys—wanted to spy on the girls and asked me to help them eavesdrop.

It was hard to convince them that I had limitations. Most of them never understood clearly that my success depended on the situation, the amount of foreknowledge I had on the topic being discussed, the lighting in the room, the distance between myself and the person I was lipreading, and how well the person enunciated. Mumbling, food, gum, or a toothpick in the mouth made things very hard. As time went on, though, my real friends came to understand even the subtlest differences about my style of communication. They appreciated my honesty in asking them to back up and repeat what I missed.

I began to notice an interesting trend. While I continued to be amazed at how much effort hearing people wasted on trivial conversation, my friends began to appreciate how valuable communication was to me—and to them. This was a revelation. It made me see that deaf people have an important lesson to teach hearing folks, a lesson that we learn throughout our lives and that hearing people might never learn at all.

As I look back on my year at Lincoln Junior High School, I have to give credit to both the students and the teachers. It was an imaginative and generous decision on the part of the teachers to allow me into their classes. The problem of having a deaf student in a class of hearing students must have seemed formidable to teachers untrained in deafness. They knew that I could not be allowed to hold up the rest of the class, yet I also couldn't be disregarded and left to flounder. They let me plunge in and waited to see what happened. I think I was lucky to find them receptive overall.

My reception by the students was exceptional as well. Judging from the experience of other deaf friends, things could have been very different. Some friends told me of negative experiences with the hearing kids at their schools, such as being teased for their "funny" speech and verbally abused because they couldn't hear the abuse.

During the summer after my year at Lincoln, three friends from CID and I got together for two weeks at my friend Steve's farm in Illinois. All of us had graduated from CID a year earlier and completed one year as the only deaf students in our respective schools. Steve had attended the private prep school for boys near his home, the one my parents had been so unreceptive to when Steve's parents encouraged me to go there. It was wonderful for all of us to get together and share notes on our experiences. We had a lot of fun—we swam, played games, read, and talked.

Before those two weeks, I wasn't 100 percent satisfied with my progress at the junior high school. I wasn't sure why. I just couldn't judge how I had done. But when the four of us got together to talk about our achievements, we were able to compare and reevaluate. Through talking with Steve and Bob, another of my friends, I learned I was doing very well. I had earned As while the others had received somewhat lower grades.

Socially, too, I seemed to be fortunate. Bob complained about not being able to make friends with other students and told us he had finally begun cultivating deaf friends from the community. That had helped sustain him until he finally developed some hearing friends. He couldn't figure out why it was so hard to make friends other than the fact that he was deaf and the other students were hearing. I now believe that there was a more specific explanation, an ignorance on his part of the rules of social chitchat.

On the other hand, another friend, Erik, was popular in his school because everyone appreciated his rugby skills. He was one of the most valuable players on the school team. Students also appreciated his sense of humor. Humor will get you friends most any time.

We also compared our coursework. I knew that my classes at Lincoln were appropriate and even a little advanced. The courses Steve took at the prep school impressed us a great deal. I was a bit envious of him at first. He told us he had a long list of books he had to read during the summer. I thought that was great, but I sensed that down deep he wasn't happy at his school. He extolled the reputation of the school too much. Steve had originally wanted to be at home with his parents and go to school in his hometown. But his parents had persuaded him that the quality of education was better at the private school, so he'd agreed to go. Steve became defensive about his school when we teased him about there not being any girls.

On this visit, I began to see things in Steve's home life I hadn't noticed before. I became aware that Steve's parents were never truly comfortable around him. Once, at mealtime, his parents were having a conversation and made no effort to draw us into it. We were curious, so Steve asked what they were talking about, and they snapped back, "It is none of your business!" The rest of us were shocked. Years later, Steve told us the sad truth: his parents never felt comfortable having him around, so they always sent him away to school—first to CID, then to the private high school, and then to college. Learning that and learning through visits to other deaf friends that this attitude and practice were common, I looked back with gratitude that my parents wanted me at home after I left CID. It was more confirmation that they loved me as I was.

PART SIX

ON MY WAY

A NEW START

Education is that whole system of human training within and without the school house walls, which molds and develops men.

W. E. B. Du Bois

I began tenth grade the next year. My whole family was amused by the name of my new school—Stonewall Jackson High School—since Dunbar and David had gone to Robert E. Lee High in Virginia. We were making a tradition of calling on Confederate generals for our education.

I didn't feel it was necessary for my father to go with me to meet the teachers this time. Many of them had already heard the word that had drifted up from the junior high that I was a hard-working, straight-A student. Two of the high school teachers knew my father and had spread the word to expect me. Also, I felt more confident this year, since many of my friends from Lincoln would be at Stonewall.

I couldn't believe how much bigger Stonewall was than Lincoln. There were about two thousand students at the high school, twice as many as at Lincoln. My first grateful discovery was that there was no public-address system for announcements. Each homeroom teacher read the memos and then I was able to read them myself. Now I could decide for myself whether something was important or not.

Mrs. Barth was my English teacher. She was a warm person and proved to be one of my strongest advocates over the next three years. She explained to the class that I was deaf, that I needed to sit in the first row, and why. She told the class that all they had to do to communicate with me was look me in the face and enunciate naturally.

Because of Mrs. Barth's matter-of-fact introduction to my speech peculiarities, I had an easy transition into her class. Under her influence, the students helped make English pleasurable and easy to follow. Two or three of the students were willing to help me with notes and to fill in important details I may have missed. Another wonderful thing about Mrs. Barth was that she was always willing to share the school gossip with me. The feeling in her English class was one of maturity. We discussed challenging issues, including the problems the school was experiencing, and we tried to find solutions.

Mrs. Barth gave us a lot of homework, and I often read and discussed the poetry and literary works with my parents. Then, when I was in class, I felt I could participate on an equal footing with the other students. If I hadn't previously talked through and understood everything I'd read, I would have gotten lost in the class discussions. The secret to lipreading successfully was to know the material in advance since I needed to learn how words I had read looked on the lips. Mrs. Barth was easy to lipread, and she educated the class to include me by facing me so I wouldn't get lost during discussions.

Unfortunately, I was far less comfortable with my Latin II teacher, Mrs. Bush. She was cold, strict, and rigid. The atmosphere of her class dampened my interest in Latin as I'm sure it did for others. She let me sit in the front row, but she didn't want me to disrupt her by asking questions during class, so she assigned Jennifer, a student, to sit next to me. I had to ask my questions of Jennifer, and she would either answer them or later ask Mrs. Bush and write down the answers. I couldn't lipread Mrs. Bush at all, so I relied heavily on Jennifer and the notes she took.

I thought of dropping the class, but I had to have one more year of Latin and Mrs. Bush was the only Latin teacher at Stonewall Jackson. I was doing the equivalent of an independent study. I didn't understand a thing that was going on in class, and Jennifer's notes weren't always that helpful.

As time went by, I sensed resentment building up in Jennifer. After all, she hadn't volunteered to take notes and help me. The teacher had appointed her, giving her no choice in the matter. I felt bad for Jennifer. She was irritated with me for being so dependent on her, but at the same time she probably thought I didn't need her help, since I did well on my tests. What she didn't realize was that being near her motivated me to work hard and do as well as she did. I admired her abilities and was sad that she never allowed us to become friends. I wondered how long it would take her to get over the resentment she had built up against me.

As the year progressed, I felt more and more like a recluse in that room. I didn't understand most of the conversations going on in the class. I missed out on all the excitement and got little or no feedback from the teacher or my fellow classmates. It was all due to an unreceptive teacher. Even so, I was surprised to see how well I did with my grades. But that didn't make up for being left out.

Halfway through the second semester of Latin II, Mrs. Bush fell ill and couldn't continue teaching. No one was told what was wrong, but the rumor was that she had cancer. I wondered if physical suffering had made her cold, aloof, and remote. Mrs. Brawley, a substitute Latin teacher, finished out the school year. For me, it was a positive change. All of a sudden, I got the attention I needed. Mrs. Brawley released Jennifer from her obligations to me, a big relief for both of us. My attitude toward Latin II changed so much that I even decided the next year to take the leap into Latin III.

I was terrified when I first arrived in Mr. Hamilton's geometry class, not of him but of the subject. Yet I soon came to love geometry and eventually was doing so well that I even tutored other students.

I had a positive experience in biology with Miss Blackwood, a young woman just out of graduate school. She accepted me immediately and I liked her very much. It wasn't always easy to follow what Miss Blackwood was saying, but she was always willing to have me stay after class to review things I missed or misunderstood. She was popular with all the students. We loved her easygoing attitude and abiding confidence in us. She asked for a volunteer to sit next to me to take notes that I could copy.

Other classmates kept me abreast of underground quiz alerts. These warnings circulated among the students, telling of upcoming tests that teachers would "pop" on us. It was a good thing I had someone to sift out the important stuff for me, because there was so much talk to sort through every day. Everyone talked about everything! To me it was like bits of fluff flying through the air, and each person had to decide which pieces to catch and use. I was spared from having to deal with the minutiae of conversations but always grateful to have someone signal me and say, "Here's something you *need* to know."

2

MAKING SENSE OF THE SOCIAL LIFE

Society is like a large piece of frozen water; and skating well is the great art of social life.

Letitia Elizabeth Landon

Having my father around was a bit like having the public library at the dinner table. All I had to do was ask a question and he would supply the information. It was great; it beat looking it up. The only problem was that my father didn't know how to keep his answers short and sweet, so I had to find ways to make him give quick replies.

My best strategy was to ask a question just before he had to leave for an appointment. Even that sometimes backfired when he came home and picked up where he'd left off. Another trick was to privately ask my mother the question. If she didn't know the answer, she asked my father. Mother had a marvelous way of making the answer even more interesting than it really was. But this strategy sometimes backfired too. If my father found out the question was originally mine, not Mother's, he would say he preferred answering me directly and I would be subjected to another lecture. All things considered, I would rather have had the long-winded replies than receive no input from my father, which is the fate of many children.

Watching my father and mother together, I grew up knowing it was possible for opposites to coexist and even live in harmony. My father was a strong liberal and a registered Democrat, while Mother was conservative and had Republican sympathies. I listened to many of their political discussions and saw how they were able to live in peace. They respected each other, and their love for each other made it possible for them to live with the "opposition." They fought fairly, never raising their voices or showing disrespect for each other. There was no hint of violence in their otherwise heated and impassioned discussions. I teased my parents, saying I would become a "Repocrat" or "Demopublican."

Just before I entered Stonewall High School, I "overheard" my father telling friends he was relieved that I was not like Jonathan with girls. When Jonathan went to Arkansas School for the Deaf, he had absolutely no interest in dating. My parents tried, without success, to encourage Jonathan to date. I heard a family story that on prom night, my father found Jonathan at home reading a comic book. Father asked Jonathan why he hadn't asked someone to the prom. Jonathan answered that he had nothing to say to girls, even though there were some in his class who had shown interest in him. Jonathan told Dad he just didn't want to get involved; he wasn't interested in any of them. Father was upset! "You can't let life go by without contacts with girls!" he said. My parents' worries about Jonathan's social life continued until the day he came home from church camp very much in love with Dorothy.

My father was glad to see me dating. He felt, as I do now, that any social activity is a form of growth and education for young people, and for a deaf child it is even more important in developing confidence. Dad was always generous with the family car and made sure I had it for dates and friends on the weekends.

At Stonewall Jackson I met a wonderful girl named Natalie. Very quickly, Natalie became part of my group of close friends along with Carlos and Tom. Natalie was cheerful, beautiful, and down to earth, with a lot of warmth to share with others. She was also bright and had a great sense of humor. Natalie was my frequent date in the tenth and eleventh grades. We communicated exceptionally well. It took Natalie a little time to get the nitty-gritty of communicating with me, but I hardly remember any of the awkwardness that usually came with a new hearing friend. Natalie had great eye contact and it seemed natural for her to look at me. Hearing students often forgot to keep their faces in my view, but Natalie always remembered.

Occasionally, during the time I dated Natalie, I dated others without telling her. One was Rosemary, a vivacious Italian girl. She also had a great sense of humor. She lived in a beautiful house in an exclusive neighborhood. The first time I went to pick Rosemary up, the whole family, including her grandmother, came out to meet me and take pictures of us. I didn't mind the fuss because we were all communicating so easily. Everyone in the family spoke with gestures and used body language. We talked for forty-five minutes before Rosemary and I finally managed to get away and head to a party.

At the party, I discovered something that quickly ended my relationship with Rosemary. After I introduced her to my friends, Rosemary promptly began conversations and effectively closed me out of them by not keeping her face within my view, even though she knew I depended on lipreading. She was a flirt, which turned me off. I felt she had deserted me. I had high expectations of communication with my dates but found I wasn't getting any help from Rosemary. My friend Tom pitched in to make sure I understood some of the conversations. And Carlos, though he was wrapped up with his date, still made sure I could read his lips throughout the evening. He did this subtly. We were such old friends that our communication had become smooth and spontaneous.

It was obvious that Carlos didn't like Rosemary and that he was a little disgusted that I had left Natalie at home. When the party was over, Rosemary and I left to go for ice cream at a local teenage hangout. Once there, she gave me her attention again, but this only served to show me her capricious nature.

I decided that for me Rosemary was too loud, flirtatious, overbearing, and most of all, insensitive to communication. I never asked her out again. I had no idea if she ever figured out what happened and I often wondered what she did with the pictures her family took of us. Although I saw Rosemary at school, I was cool and remained distant. I didn't know enough about communicating feelings at the time to be openly honest with her.

Sheepishly, I went back to Natalie. She was wonderful, witty, and always careful about communicating with me. We spent much of our time talking about ourselves, the future, and what we wanted to do later in life. I was studious and serious about everything I read, heard, or talked about, while Natalie took things a little easier and reminded me to stop and smell the roses once in a while instead of always analyzing them. It was good for me.

My serious approach reflected an internal conflict about achievement. Without realizing it, I felt a sense of duty to prove that I, a deaf person, could accomplish anything that anyone else could. Natalie made

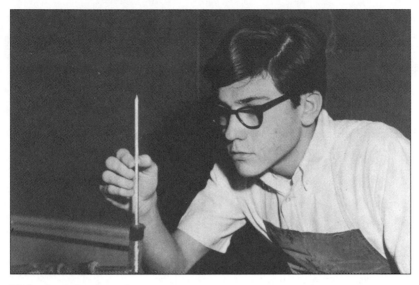

High school chemistry class.

me feel as if I were special without having to prove it all the time. Her humor and the time I spent with her helped me breathe more freely, though occasionally I got irritated with her for taking things too lightly and I reminded her that life was short.

My family loved Natalie and her warmth, and they were impressed with her intelligence and grades. But I was shy around Natalie's family because they were so quiet. Still, Natalie made it easy for us to communicate, and I gradually warmed to her family, eventually feeling at home with them. Her mother had health problems, which developed my sympathy for Natalie and her family.

My feelings were complicated, and as time went on, I found myself developing a protective attitude toward Natalie, as a big brother would have. It was not clear to me what was happening. I found myself looking for more, but I was never sure what it was. I just couldn't shake the feeling of restlessness and dissatisfaction with what I had. My eye would wander and I would date someone else. Carlos would sometimes tell me that I had hurt Natalie's feelings. Back I would go to Natalie, always glad to have her easy communication. It was my first experience with fickleness in myself.

In the spring of 1966, the second semester of our sophomore year, Carlos celebrated being reunited with his family. Cuban dictator Fidel

Castro had revised his emigration policy to allow some citizens to leave the country. Carlos's parents were among those who got out. A church sponsored their journey and helped them settle in Charleston. It had been four years since Carlos had seen his parents. So many things were happening at that time that I didn't see much of Carlos outside of school. I started drifting away from Carlos, Tom, and that group of friends.

Suddenly I wanted to be on my own, though on what terms I wasn't sure. I thought I could find more perfect friends, but at the same time I knew I was rejecting some of the best relationships I'd ever had. What I wanted, I had no idea. I was restless. I had to find out what other sorts of people were out there.

I remember how hurt Carlos was when I drifted away. He tried to find out what was bothering me. I shut the door and kept it closed, not knowing how to verbalize my feelings to him.

At the end of tenth grade I went to Europe for the summer with Dunbar and my parents. That cut me off from Natalie, Tom, and Carlos. I was so busy experiencing new vistas in places like Iceland, Luxembourg, West Germany, Austria, Italy, and Greece that I didn't even think about my old gang. I made a clean break. I was on my own.

Upon my return, I went out with Natalie from time to time, but more and more as a friend than as a sweetheart. When she tried to make our relationship more serious, I backed off. Like me, she was too young to articulate her feelings. She never confronted me or asked for an explanation.

My academic life was rich and full during my junior year—I discovered Shakespeare, I played tennis, I participated fully in the Latin club—but during the whole year I drifted from one clique to another, still looking for the ideal friends. Where were they? One group would look interesting, but when I got to know them I became restless and moved on. One was a group of cheerleaders and jocks, but I found them boring and their weekend routines shallow. With them I went to football games. They asked me to use binoculars to lipread other students for them. They encouraged me to eavesdrop on other teams in the hope that I could pass some game strategy along to them. I tried my best, though I didn't understand most of what I saw. It didn't feel right to cheat.

By the beginning of my senior year I began to appreciate my original friends. Whatever perfection I had been seeking, I never found it in other groups. I think my restlessness was an expression of independence, in this case an independence that nearly lost me my very good friends.

3

EDUCATING THE IGNORANT

A great deal of intelligence can be invested in ignorance when the need for illusion is deep.

Saul Bellow

Dunbar was a good tennis player. I hadn't played for years, but when I was in high school my brother reintroduced me to the game. A friend and good player, Scott, began giving me lessons and encouraged me to pursue tennis more seriously. In the eleventh grade, Carlos and I played as the second doubles pair on the school team. I was thrilled to be on the team and to have Carlos as my partner. Mr. Knight was our coach. Although he knew little about tennis, he was easy to communicate with. Mr. Knight was pleased with my abilities, which bolstered my ego. And Scott invited me to play with him often, so I improved.

But something I'd unknowingly brought from CID ended my tennis career. It was a fear of public performances, which had its beginnings in frequent public corrections from my teachers whenever I spoke before an audience. Not until our team competed with another high school did I realize that I was terrified of playing tennis in public.

My first doubles match was a disaster. My legs shook and I couldn't concentrate on the game. I fought just to stay calm and didn't have enough extra strength to win the match at the same time. Despite our loss, our team won its first victory of the tennis season. I was left, however, with absolutely no confidence in my ability to compete in front of a crowd. I told Scott, who was sympathetic to my problem. He'd been playing for a long time and had learned to handle the pressure. He convinced me that time would help me master the problem.

Unfortunately, he was wrong.

Mr. Knight didn't know that I had stage fright. He gave me pep talks and tried to help me work on my weaknesses. During practice the weaknesses were gone. I felt great and played well. But when my second real match came up, my fears returned. Carlos and I lost again, though again our school won overall.

When we played our third tournament with another high school, Mr. Knight stood on the other side of the court facing Carlos and me. He'd learned from the first two matches that he couldn't talk to me during a match, so he tried to signal instructions from our opponents' end. I could see him and my opponents at the same time. He walked back and forth behind the other team waving his hands, making signs, and trying to send messages. But this made things even worse, if that was possible. His attempts to communicate instructions were exactly like being interrupted and criticized while giving a speech. It brought back all the bad memories and frustration I had felt at CID when my teachers corrected me in front of the class. Naturally, we lost the match. Mr. Knight didn't know enough about tennis to be able to figure out my problem, and I never told him.

That year, our school went on to become number two in the state. Scott was ranked number one. Carlos and I lost all but one match, so I felt undeserving of the accolades and the letter I received. But I thought I might be able to overcome my problem, so I went out for tennis again the next year. We had a better qualified coach and I made the fourth singles position on the team. I played better than ever during practice and defeated all those who tried to unseat me. But after I lost the first two matches in competition with other schools, I knew I couldn't continue. It wasn't fair to my team.

My real opponent was "the audience," not the tennis player. I quit the team, realizing that my stage fright was a deep issue that would take a long time to work through. This was something more fundamental than tennis. It had to do with my performance as a deaf person in the hearing world. It was wrapped up in my consuming drive to overcompensate for my deafness. The issue surfaced often during my high school days, including in my dating life.

I had been attracted to Bernice since Lincoln Junior High School, when she and I went to buy books on that first day. I visited her from time to time, and during my second year at Stonewall Jackson I asked her to a football game. She accepted with much enthusiasm.

When I got to Bernice's house, her father said he didn't want me driving her to the game. He claimed that there were too many careless drivers on the road and said that he would take us. I felt insulted because I didn't buy his reasons. I knew that Bernice's grandmother influenced the family. Bernice had told me that her grandmother had no confidence in deaf drivers. I didn't know how to react, so I just went along with it, trying to be a good sport and not rock the boat. Later, though, I realized that it had been a mistake. I should have just told Bernice to forget it and that I'd see her at school.

The whole thing was humiliating. I was seventeen years old. I had started gaining driving experience many years before. My father had each of his boys sit in his lap while he drove as soon as we were old enough to grip the steering wheel. When I was twelve or thirteen and we were in a safe area, my father would slide over against the door and allow me to practice driving. By the time I took my driver's test a year and a half before my date with Bernice, I'd put in many hours behind the wheel and had no trouble obtaining my license. I'd been driving successfully on my own ever since. Despite my experience, and feeling like part of a herd of cattle, I went along with Bernice and her father in his car.

At the game, Tom and Carlos greeted me and asked why I had come in someone else's car. I wouldn't talk about it and pretended nothing had happened. How could I tell them I had left my car at Bernice's house and lost control of the date? It was awkward between Bernice and me at the football game. She didn't ask what was wrong and I didn't dare share my feelings with her. I was really disgusted when we got back to the car and found her father sitting there reading newspapers, waiting for us. We got into the car. Her father asked where we wanted to go next. I said nothing, so he suggested we go for an ice cream cone. I acquiesced and again swallowed my pride. After the ice cream, I was finally released to go home.

Over the next few days I unleashed my frustration and expressed my humiliation to Carlos. He couldn't believe that Bernice's father could be so rude and discriminate against me so blatantly. Carlos was so dramatic that we played out the episode again and again for my edification. I vowed never to let it happen again and decided not to ask Bernice out a second time. I never told her why. I was starting to collect quite a score of social mistakes of omission.

A few weeks later I saw Bernice out with Jack, my math and geometry archrival. My surprise turned to disgust on learning that Jack had been driving her around in his Mustang. Carlos and I commiserated about how disgusting it was that Bernice was interested in Jack and how unfair it was that her family let him drive her around while refusing me the same privilege.

We soon heard rumors that Jack had been in a serious accident after running a red light. He was ticketed and his car was badly damaged. We were thrilled by this turn of events and wondered if Bernice's family would now start driving them around in the family car when they went out on a date. We fantasized on how satisfying it would be to see Jack herded around like cattle as I had been. But we soon saw Jack driving Bernice around in a new Mustang! I decided, "To hell with them," and I forgot Bernice for good.

A month later I met another wonderful girl, Darlene. Carlos liked her and encouraged me to date her. I decided to take her to a movie. I didn't think I would make the same mistake twice. But when I got to Darlene's house, the first thing her mother said was that she didn't want me to drive Darlene around because I couldn't hear other cars. I noticed Darlene had been crying and was embarrassed about the whole thing. It was obvious that she didn't know how to handle the situation.

This time I wanted to be assertive. But how? If I said, "Forget it!" and walked out, then Darlene would be hurt, and it wasn't her fault. If I went along, I'd look like a fool again and prove for sure that I couldn't learn from experience. Damn her mother!

I decided to be the fool and save Darlene from the embarrassment. Again, I swallowed my pride and quietly went along for the ride all the way to the movie theater. When we got there, Darlene's mother said she'd return when the movie was over. Darlene persuaded her to not come back until an hour afterward. Darlene apologized for the way things had turned out and tried to convince me that her mother was worried about *any* boy driving her, not just me. I didn't believe her, though, and avoided the subject as much as possible.

After the movie, we went for ice cream. We tried to bring back the spontaneity, but we couldn't revive the sparkle that our friendship possessed at school. Again, I wrote off the relationship, calling it a terminal case.

Carlos was furious. He wanted me to get revenge. But these experiences were teaching me lessons I needed to learn about prejudice and ignorance. It isn't a simple matter to get people to give up their preconceived notions about deafness. In fact, I was a safe driver with four extremely acute senses. I'd had a lot of practice scanning the world with my eyes for information. I'd also had a terrific role model, as I had observed Jonathan drive for eleven years. Everyone at home felt he was the safest driver in our family. The Department of Motor Vehicles had licensed me as a driver. But these parents had ignored all that. They preferred to hold on to their false impressions without even questioning me about my competence as a driver. I knew that challenging their ignorance would have been painful for their daughters and probably futile as well.

Those humiliating episodes are partly responsible for my commitment to writing and educating people about deafness. I knew then that arguing wouldn't change people's minds, that the only chance to stimulate new thinking was by offering people a new perspective and giving them an opportunity to think about it. One has to think long and hard about deafness to understand its effects. These parents, I knew, would never empathize deeply enough to understand that vision can replace hearing.

Few people use their sense of hearing to drive anyway. With radios and CD players in cars and the confusion of sounds in traffic, almost no one relies on sound to make driving judgments. If you did, I think you would be making a mistake. For example, from what I've learned from hearing drivers, the horn is the most worthless item on a car. By the time a horn is used, the accident is already about to happen. In my estimation, if you don't know visually what all the cars around you are doing, you shouldn't be driving.

I became committed to educating the hearing public. At school with my student friends, I was happy to do a simple indoctrination. Time and again friends would drive by in a car and honk. I wouldn't hear the greeting, of course, and later at school a friend would say, "Why didn't you wave the other day? Are you trying to avoid me?" I would have to remind him that I didn't hear the car horn and that the trick was to wave at me.

I'd see the startled look of recognition. "Of course!" he would say. It was yet another lesson in how frequently hearing people fail to understand deafness. It was also another lesson learned by my hearing peers. Gradually my friends remembered to wave their greetings. Whenever I saw them, I waved back in response.

I confronted ignorance about deafness in a different form at the beginning of my junior year. I'd been looking forward to taking an accelerated English class from a popular teacher, Mr. Armstrong. But the day before classes were scheduled to start, another teacher pulled me aside and said, "You know, Mr. Armstrong doesn't want you in his class."

I was surprised. "All my friends are in that class," I said. "I want to be there too. It will be a good class for me."

My teacher adviser and advocate, Mrs. Barth, tried to be gentle with her explanation: "Mr. Armstrong wants to have the freedom to be able to walk around in his class during discussions, to give lectures while standing by the window." It seemed more likely to me that he was either uncomfortable with having a deaf student in his class or he didn't think I could keep up. Either way, I was crushed.

I was assigned to a different class, English Literature. I couldn't follow the class discussions, so my parents bought the textbook and I reviewed the appropriate assignments with them before each class. I began to appreciate these talks with my parents, and they relished them as well. I was essentially homeschooled for that course. We did the same thing with my senior year English course. Mr. Armstrong had done me a favor. Those sessions with my parents better prepared me for college and also made up for a little of the time I'd spent away from my family at CID.

The attitude of my mathematics teacher, Mrs. Ava Crum, could not have differed more from Mr. Armstrong's. Since I was doing well in her classes, she decided that I should finish my senior year math instruction in one semester and do an independent study in statistics during my final semester. This was in the days before advanced placement classes. Mrs. Crum convinced my parents to let her tutor me. It was a wonderful experience; I loved the one-on-one time with Mrs. Crum. She was visionary and saw my future long before I did. Her confidence and investment in me helped make up for Mr. Armstrong's rejection.

A year or two after I graduated from college, I received a letter from Mr. Armstrong. He had heard how well I was doing academically. He said he regretted not having me in his class and was sorry he had given me up. It was a small sign of progress in what would become, for me, a lifelong effort to educate the hearing world about the potential contributions deaf people can make.

4

MORE COMMUNICATION CHALLENGES

Communication works for those who work at it.

John Powell

Any deaf person must make certain adjustments. In the days before texting, communicating by telephone was one of my most unique challenges. Most teenagers love talking on the phone, and I would have been no exception. But when I was in high school, there were no telephone devices for people who were deaf. The first teletypewriter wasn't introduced until 1964, the year I graduated from CID. Even then, it took many years before they were in adequate service.

Yet with a little ingenuity, I used the telephone often. My parents and I developed a system for calling and relaying messages. When I had to talk to my parents, to either check in or let them know what was happening, I used a pay phone (which at the time were readily available). I put in a dime and dialed their number. Then I said hello a few times until I guessed it was about time somebody had picked up the phone. Next I said the phone number I was calling from and repeated it a few times to make sure it was written down. Then I gave my message—for example, "I need to be picked up at school at 7:00 p.m." or "I'll be home later than planned." I repeated the number I was calling from one more time and then hung up the phone.

If my dime appeared, it meant the line had been busy or no one was at home, so I repeated the whole process later on. But if no dime came back, it meant that someone had answered. I then waited for a reply to my call with my hand on the phone. When the phone vibrated, I knew someone was calling back.

According to the code my family and I had worked out, if the phone rang once the answer to my message was "Yes" but if it rang twice the answer was "No." If the phone rang three times, it meant "I don't know."

Finally, if the phone rang four times or more, it meant my message was not understood or not complete. I had to pick up the phone and try again. This time I'd try to speak more clearly or add details I'd left out before. This system evolved during my four years of high school and was very effective. At that time, my parents were the only ones who could understand my speech perfectly on the phone.

The system never really worked with my friends. For one thing, I needed to use a pay phone, since I depended on the dime to know if I had succeeded or not. Therefore, I couldn't really talk to them from home. Also, they had parents, family members, and others in the households who all answered the phone, which certainly would have complicated the system. Still, it might have worked out if the friend was the only one who answered the phone. Then it would have gone something like this: I call my friend and give him the phone number I'm calling from. He returns the call immediately to let me know he is there. I proceed with my message and hang up. I wait for one of the following messages in bell code: "Yes," "No," "I don't know," or "Please repeat, add more details, or clarify the message."

I sometimes asked my parents to make a call for me. They did their best, but having one of them as the "middle man" was not ideal when things got too personal. Many friends liked my parents so much that they didn't mind talking to me through one of them. But I was as self-conscious as any teenager, so it bothered me. I tried to keep phone talk to a minimum, sticking to the particulars involved in making dates and plans.

Only a few friends, like Carlos, felt free to call my home and strike up a conversation with me through my parents. When friends didn't want to reveal something to my parents, they would call and make plans to meet shortly thereafter so we could discuss in private whatever we wanted to cover. All this required planning, and I was always grateful when a friend took the trouble to go this far in our friendship. Emails and texting have certainly simplified communication today!

Learning the art of complaining was another complicated process for me. In my junior and senior years, I worked on the yearbook staff as a coordinating copy editor with a girl named Eileen. Eileen and I got along well, but she loved to talk. Sometimes I grew impatient with her. One day she sat and talked with some of the other people on the staff while I wrote. It was distracting even though I couldn't hear her. Because of my curious nature, I didn't want to be left out of any conversation.

When I finished, I took everything I had written and everything everyone else had written to Mrs. Elliot for final editing. I complained to Mrs. Elliot that everyone else was too busy talking to come along. For some reason, she misunderstood me. She marched in to where Eileen and the others were and protested, "It's not fair for Paul to have to write everything. You should be ashamed of taking advantage of him like that!" She held up the papers I had turned in, and I realized that she thought I had written them all, which wasn't true.

Suddenly, I was on the spot. I tried to explain what I had meant by my simple complaint, but to no avail. Suddenly everyone was talking at once. The confusion took a long time to sort out. When I told my parents about the experience, my father said that it happened all the time. Breakdowns in communication were common even among hearing people and complaints were a frequent cause. My father warned me to tone down my complaints, to soften them before I expressed them, or they would be misunderstood in just this sort of way over and over again.

I was a bit envious about how freely some people complained. I wished that I could clean out all the garbage from my system as easily as some people did. But then I also learned that chronic complainers were unpleasant to be with and that you have to complain to the right people at the right times and in exactly the right tone, or it would create a conflict even bigger than what you were complaining about in the first place. This was a good example of having to learn through painful experience what hearing people pick up unconsciously.

The yearbook experience gave me a new appreciation of my close friends. What a relief to be able to say what I meant! I loved to complain to Carlos when no one else was around. He would react strongly and encourage me to be more dramatic. Soon I'd run out of things to complain about and feel healed and refreshed at having my say, always grateful for knowing that Carlos would not betray me.

5

ACCEPTING YOURSELF

Believing in our hearts that who we are is enough is the key to a more satisfying and balanced life.

Ellen Sue Stern

Both of my parents believed it was important for Jonathan and me to stay in touch with deaf friends across the country. Our door was always open to our friends and other deaf adults. One day when I was in high school, a couple that were friends of Jonathan's visited us—Alan and Vicki Hurwitz. Alan was an engineer at McDonnell Douglas, a major American aerospace manufacturing corporation and defense contractor formed by the merger of McDonnell Aircraft and the Douglas Aircraft Company in 1967. Both Alan and Vicki had gone to hearing high schools and colleges and were highly educated, which was unusual for deaf people at the time. Alan went on to earn an EdD, and in 2010, he was named president of Gallaudet University.

It was great for me to spend time with adult role models like Alan and Vicki. They were tangible examples of what was possible for an educated deaf person. These role models, combined with the support of my deaf friends and the amazing love and encouragement of my deaf brother, Jonathan, cemented my confidence in myself as a deaf person.

My parents also encouraged me to visit my deaf friends across the country. They knew how important these relationships would be for me throughout my life. In many ways, our families were trailblazers in establishing support systems for young deaf people that otherwise did not exist then.

During the summer before my senior year of high school, my old CID classmate Erik and I traveled together to visit other CID friends in Indiana and Kentucky. One night, we went out to dinner with Linda and Sheila, and while we were eating, they told us that Keith, the former CID bully, lived near the restaurant. We had our waitress call his mother, who in turn relayed our message to him. Erik and I had not seen him for five years.

When Keith came to the restaurant, we were surprised at how tall and handsome he had become. The real surprise was that he wasn't very friendly but only tried to impress us. Keith flirted with the girls in a chauvinistic way, which turned us off. But he did offer to take us out for ice cream.

We went in his car, which had been modified to look like a racing car. He drove it like a racer too, and we were relieved to survive the trip. When we got to the Dairy Queen, he parked his car in the back, away from public view. We didn't understand this at all. Keith asked each of us what we wanted and told us to stay in the car until he returned. When he came back with our cones, we asked him, "What are you doing—trying to keep us out of sight?"

"You talk funny," he said. "Your speech is not perfect. People look at you as if you're oddballs. I don't want my friends to know I have such strange-speaking friends."

We were shocked into silence. His little speech certainly ruined our appetites for the ice cream. "Just take us to our car," I said. He did and then terminated the visit immediately.

As he drove away, he looked relieved that we were leaving *his* town. We were more disappointed than embarrassed. We talked about how sad it was that Keith could not accept his own deafness. His speech was excellent, but Sheila's was better. He apparently tried to pass for a hearing person with people he met. But this was self-defeating, because it prevented him from asking for the help he needed to understand what was going on around him. Keith's life must have been full of deceit. We wondered how long he could live with the illusion that pretending to be hearing was better than admitting to being deaf.

I have met a number of deaf people who, like Keith, have tried everything to erase deafness from their lives. They do not acknowledge their hearing losses, their deaf school classmates, and many facts about themselves. They are obsessed with speech lessons and try everything to appear to be hearing people. They study the mannerisms of hearing people and try to imitate them. For example, they try not to use their eyes as much. They try to control their voices and laughter so they don't expose that they have issues with volume. They feign understanding no matter how much they miss. Many deaf people consider passing-for-hearing behavior to be a sickness. Still, it's not difficult to see why some deaf people give in to the temptation.

During our trip that summer, Erik and I ran into a couple of situations where some deaf people would have "passed" if they could. Once we stopped at a restaurant for lunch. After we were seated, a waitress walked over and then realized we were deaf. Instantly, her smile and friendly manner disappeared. She took our orders in a way that bothered us; it was not how we were accustomed to being treated. Erik noticed she was friendly with other people at other tables, but every time she came to our table, she turned cold. We were irritated, and Erik decided to tell her so.

When the waitress came to our table again, he said, "You're so friendly with everyone but us. We can't stand your sourpuss face and negative body language. You're discriminating against us just because we're deaf." The waitress looked at him in shock and took off for the kitchen.

"I'm not going to leave her a tip," Erik said. "Do you think we should walk out?" I wasn't bold enough for that. I persuaded Erik to stay and finish the food, but I agreed: no tip for the waitress.

In a few minutes our waitress came back with the warmest smile we had ever seen. "I'm *so* sorry. I didn't know I came off so prejudiced. Please accept my apology." For the rest of our time there, we enjoyed the company of our waitress. In the end, we left her a big tip, after which she came back to thank us and apologize again.

Being with Erik was a wonderful lesson in the power of honest expression. It was a lesson I would have to learn again and again: to express my feelings when I was wronged to help people think about what they had done and increase their awareness. Saying nothing resulted in nothing—everything stayed the same.

Later that summer, Erik wanted to show me the BMW model his father had recently bought, so we went to a dealership. A salesman approached us, but when he realized we were deaf, he walked away. Erik was insulted and became even more so when the salesman started courting other young people in the showroom. Everything Erik did had to be first class. He wouldn't submit to anything less than VIP treatment. He went back to the salesman and said he had a few questions, but the dealer waved his hands and said, "I have no time for you." He kept talking to the other young people, and we grew furious when he continued to ignore us and talk to more potential customers who came in later. We were no different—only our speech distinguished us from them.

What happened next was an incident that makes me both satisfied and sad whenever I think of it. Erik, seeing a sign welcoming us to try out one of the new cars, asked to do so. We were denied the courtesy. Then, after seeing the other young people given the keys to a demo, Erik complained to the manager, but the manager preferred to stay out of the conflict. The salesman then threatened us with a monkey wrench from the garage. It was beginning to feel like an episode from *Hawaii Five-O*.

At this point Erik turned to me and winked. He produced a business card from his wallet from another BMW dealership and explained that his father, a powerful businessman, was part owner of the other dealership. "My father will be in touch with you soon," he said. We then walked away, leaving the salesman and manager dumbfounded.

As we got into our car, the salesman ran up and begged us to return to the dealership. "I'm sorry, I'm sorry," he kept repeating. "I misunderstood your intentions." We said nothing and Erik started the car. I felt sick to my stomach at the man's helplessness. He was begging for our forgiveness, but Erik ignored him and we drove away.

Later, we wondered how many sleepless nights that salesman spent worrying about Erik's father and the prospect of losing his job. We had played a monumental trick on him by using that BMW business card from another dealership. We had won a victory, but I didn't feel good about it. Erik convinced me that we had tried everything and only resorted to deceit when all else failed. He said that the man needed a harsh lesson so that he would respect deaf car buyers in the future. When I thought of the parents who had kept me from driving their daughters on dates, I didn't feel quite as bad about what we'd done.

A MATTER OF PERSPECTIVE

People who look through keyholes are apt to get the idea that most things are keyhole shaped.

Author unknown

Starting when I was in ninth grade, my parents and I went often to the Cinema Arts Society at the University of Charleston to watch foreign films with English subtitles. It was my father's idea for all of us to go to these movies together. I loved the films because most were better and more realistic than their Hollywood counterparts. The English subtitles also made them more exciting for me since I didn't have to depend on my parents to interpret. I liked watching without interruption and catching the subtleties. Whenever a movie was interpreted, I felt that my opinions were colored by the interpreter. I never knew how much of the film I had missed. Here I could form my own judgments and discuss the themes of the films from firsthand opinion.

One Sunday during my senior year, Carlos and I decided to go by ourselves to see a film at the Cinema Arts Society. I drove to pick him up at his church. When I got there, he was with two girls. He asked if I minded if they joined us at the film. The girls went to Charleston High School, which was Stonewall's sports and academic archrival.

Carlos introduced us. Rachel sat in front with me while he and the other girl sat in the back. I was surprised at how well Rachel and I communicated. Rachel was friendly and I was strongly attracted to her. After the film, I asked her for a date and she accepted. We got along incredibly well. She seemed to be the ideal friend for me—just the person I had been looking for in all my restless searching. Besides being easy to talk with, Rachel was bright, ambitious, industrious, fun, and sophisticated. We talked about everything.

After a few dates, however, Rachel's father, a highly respected, college-educated professional, put his foot down. He said Rachel couldn't date the same boy more than once a month. He was old-fashioned and authoritarian. Rachel's mother, who was fond of me, tried to change the rule but got nowhere with her husband. I saw a lot of Rachel at her home when her father wasn't around, and we managed to sneak away on secret dates. I was attracted to Rachel's personality. She was idealistic, a dreamer like myself.

Some of my friends couldn't understand why I would go for Rachel. They considered Natalie more beautiful and charming. It was hard for me to explain that I felt like a protective big brother to Natalie. Our conversations were not as deep, intense, or electrifying as those I had with Rachel. I remained good friends with Natalie, who knew I was seeing Rachel and hoped it wouldn't last. At that time, I was not very communicative about my feelings and didn't know how to talk about the situation. When I look back at that time, I am appalled by my lack of communication and honesty.

I saw Rachel on dates, at the public library, and in other places so that her father wouldn't know we were seeing each other. Every time we went out on our special once-a-month date, we made the most of it, starting with an early dinner and ending late at night. We always had fun.

It felt wonderful to play a bit that senior year, after three hard years of studies. My parents were always telling me not to work so hard. In fact, starting in the tenth grade, my father began offering a monetary reward if I got a B rather than an A. I took my father's offers as jokes and never saw the reward, since I earned straight As for three years.

In the middle of the second semester of my senior year, when I was seeing a lot of Rachel, my English teacher warned me that my grade had slipped to a high B. I tried to look concerned but thought, *Wow, that's going to surprise my father, and maybe even please him!* Yet when I told him about the B in English, he was upset, which I couldn't understand. I thought he hadn't been honest with me about the reward for Bs.

After supper, he revealed why he was upset. "Since you've maintained a perfect record for so long," he said, "you might as well conclude your high school years with straight As. Why should you throw away such a brilliant accomplishment when you're almost finished?"

After a pause, he went on: "There is a chance, Paul, a very, very good chance, for you to be the valedictorian of Stonewall Jackson High School. What a wonderful thing!" He explained that he'd heard I was one of three students in the running for the honor.

I could see that my father was moved. He had been class valedictorian at Davidson College in North Carolina. For me to achieve a similar honor would make him burst with pride.

This was the kind of challenge I loved. I would find a way to continue seeing Rachel and still work hard enough to make all As in English. With a little more effort, the role of valedictorian would be mine. (And it was; the school eventually named me, Carlos, and Marilyn as co-valedictorians.)

I soon faced a different type of challenge. When the time came for the Stonewall Jackson prom, I asked Rachel. I wanted to show her off to my friends. I couldn't believe it when she said, "Paul, I can't. I'm so sorry. My father won't let me go to a prom outside of Charleston High." I was naive and accepted her explanation. Trying to find some way to be with Rachel, I asked if I could take her to her prom. That was nixed by her father as well. I should have guessed the truth at that point.

I ended up going to the prom with Natalie. Rachel, I thought, went with a friend to her prom. It wasn't until the next week that I found out from Angela, her close friend, that Rachel had refused to go to the prom as a silent protest to her father for not letting her go with me. Angela had been so upset about the situation that she'd nearly had Rachel ask me to take Angela instead.

Rachel and I managed to continue dating throughout our senior year, and we kept in touch through frequent letters when we went off to different colleges. As is often the case with long-distance relationships, ours evolved into a friendship. We stayed in contact but went our own ways. Fifteen years after our graduation, after she'd become a lawyer and I had been teaching for some time, we met again. It wasn't until then that the truth about her father came out.

"It wasn't just boys my father was worried about. It was deaf boys," she said to me at our reunion. "It was you. He didn't want me to go out with you because you were deaf." I was amazed at myself for not having known. Of course. He was prejudiced against me despite all the evidence that I was capable of living productively.

More recently, Rachel revealed even more about her father's feelings at the time, as well as her own. "Once I started spending time with you, he got alarmed," she told me. "He agreed that you were very intelligent and a person of fine character with many wonderful traits. But you were deaf. He forbade me from dating you. He was afraid that I would fall in love with you and he did not want that. He told me that it would be 'a hard life' and that I was too young to choose such a difficult path when I would undoubtedly meet many other nice young men. He was very fatherly and kind when he told me this, but he was firm. He said, 'We want one with all of his senses, honey.'

"I've never told you that last remark because it is so painful. I have only summoned the courage to tell you now because you are writing a book. I remember him saying that painful remark only once, but the underlying message seared itself into me as if Dad had used a branding iron: falling in love with you would be dishonoring my father. And it was unthinkable for me to ever do that."

I realize now that a big writeup in our local newspaper about my accomplishments at school wasn't enough to impress Rachel's father. Nor was my status as a high school valedictorian. I would have been unacceptable to Rachel's father no matter what great goals I achieved. His bias and desire to protect his daughter blinded him to the truth.

I'm glad to finally know the whole story. I have thought many times about what would have happened if Rachel had told me everything about her father's feelings when we were still in high school. Would I have been able to overcome his prejudice? What would I have done differently in my relationship with Rachel? What if I had taken Angela, who was African American, to the prom? The 1960s was another era, though. Society did not tolerate interracial marriages and looked down on disabled and deaf people. My growing-up experience would have been entirely different had everyone accepted people for who they were or recognized American Sign Language as a bona fide language. Perspectives have changed to the point that today I often see hearing young people becoming friends with or dating deaf and hard of hearing peers. We have come a long way.

The episode with Rachel and her father was another example of my trusting nature. It may have had a negative effect on my life, but in the end, would I want to change my nature? I was brought up to be unsuspecting and, all things considered, I think I would rather not live a suspicious existence. Even so, I hope this book will make a difference for some other unsuspecting deaf boy—or for the family of his girl-friend. Perhaps after all these years, we can begin to view deaf people with new eyes.

7

THE FUTURE BECKONS

Behind the curtain's mystic fold,

the glowing future lies unrolled.

Bret Harte

When I sat down to consider my future after high school, the obvious choice was college. By this time, I valued education as much as my family did. But where would I go to school?

I asked Dunbar which colleges he thought I should consider. He told me to take a close look at Antioch College in Yellow Springs, Ohio. That was all the advice I got from him. This was amazing! Antioch was the same college that Ellen, the student teacher at Central Institute for the Deaf, had recommended to me so long before. Dunbar was impressed with the Antioch graduates he'd met at the University of California, Berkeley. Among liberal arts colleges, Antioch ranked at the top for undergraduates who eventually completed their doctorates. A doctorate was not even on my mind at the time, but Dunbar was already thinking of the possibility. Antioch was also close to where my grandmother lived. Ellen, who had gone back to finish her degree, was there too.

I was impressed with the cooperative work and study plan at Antioch College. Antioch students alternated between study and temporary jobs for five years before they graduated. The work experiences would broaden my world and help me find out what kind of work I'd like to do after college.

Jonathan, on the other hand, encouraged me to go to Gallaudet, the only liberal arts college for deaf and hard of hearing students in the nation. I decided to visit a few friends there and see the Washington, DC, campus for myself. Everybody there signed. For me, it was like going to a deaf country where the native language was American Sign Language. All the classes were signed. I didn't know American Sign Language, but I managed to communicate with other deaf students and to have a blast with everyone at some of their parties.

I flew back home confident that I had arrived at the right decision—to look closely at both Earlham College, a Quaker school in Indiana, and Antioch. I had done volunteer work with the Quakers and enjoyed them very much. I visited both colleges and finally decided to go to Antioch, which seemed the most challenging. I enthusiastically embraced the idea of having work experience in the United States and possibly overseas through Antioch's work-study program. If it wasn't a good match, I could easily transfer to Earlham or Gallaudet. I sent in my application for early decision during the second semester of my junior year.

We were supposed to be notified of the college's decision within two weeks. When that period passed without a letter, my anxiety skyrocketed.

"The letter didn't come today?" I asked my mother. "It's supposed to be here. I can't wait. I have to know. I have to plan the rest of my life right now!"

My mother injected a dose of calm into my increasingly frazzled state. "Paul, it's all right," she said. "Just wait. The letter will come. God knows what to do."

A couple of days later, I arrived home from school and found in the hallway a folding chair with a card in it. The card had an arrow pointing to the left and the words, "Go this way." I obeyed the instructions and came to another chair with another arrow and the directions, "Now go this way."

Three more chairs followed. Finally, with my patience nearing its end, I walked into the family room and discovered yet another chair, only this one contained a letter. My mother was there too. Her face did not display a hint of anxiety. Rather, her expression seemed to say, "Okay, let's just see what it says."

Although my father had taught me to open envelopes carefully with a letter opener, this time I grabbed the letter and ripped it open with my fingers. It was from Antioch. I'd been accepted for enrollment after my high school graduation.

Now, at the end of my senior year, it was again time to look ahead. I had done it! I'd made it through the grueling four-year test and was ready for the next step. All that remained was the Stonewall Jackson graduation ceremony, in which I was to participate as valedictorian. I was proud of Carlos, who was my co-valedictorian and had been accepted to Harvard with a full-ride scholarship. I felt as though all of us had come to the end of a long chapter.

Just before graduation, the local newspaper had written a story about my achievements. I'd wanted to make a good impression on the reporter, so I emphasized the fact that a deaf person could mainstream at a public high school and succeed. During that interview, I felt a strong responsibility toward other deaf students with the opportunity still in front of them. I wanted my story to encourage deaf students who might want to go to a public high school somewhere. That article went straight to the hearts of many people in Charleston, though I didn't know it then.

A huge crowd turned out for the graduation ceremony. Five hundred students were graduating, and their families and friends were there to celebrate. The guest speaker was a congressman who gave a boring speech. Normally, the class valedictorian would make the speech, but I was graduating at the height of the Vietnam conflict. Student speeches had been forbidden, apparently to guard against the possibility that one of us would express antigovernment sentiments and incite a riot. We were sentenced to an uninspiring, seemingly endless monologue.

I couldn't wait to get the diploma and be with my family and friends at the graduation party planned for later at my house. I felt like a racehorse trapped at the starting gate. Finally, the time came for me to go up to the platform to receive my diploma. It was a long walk through the crowd, up the steps, and across the stage. There I shook hands with different school officials and the congressman, received my diploma, and finally returned to the steps and then my seat.

It wasn't until twelve years later that my mother finally told me about the standing ovation I received when I went up to the stage to get my diploma. I had been oblivious to the display of appreciation.

"Why, the whole crowd rose up," she said. "A lot of people were crying." I guess I was so busy concentrating on getting to the platform and receiving the diploma that I didn't know it was happening. I didn't feel it, I didn't see it, and of course I didn't hear it. When I got back to my seat, everyone was sitting quietly. What irony—while the crowd applauded me for succeeding despite the obstacles erected by my deafness, that very deafness kept me completely unaware of the applause.

Yet this image is a perfect symbol of all I had learned from my mainstream experience. I am deaf. I have always been deaf and will be my whole life. Deafness sets me apart in some ways and affects every area of my life, yet I can use my eyes, my brain, and the rest of my senses to take in all I need to know. It's true that I missed some of what was going on that long-ago graduation day. It's because I was looking ahead. I am looking forward still, using all that I am to take in this amazing adventure we call life.

PART SEVEN

ANTIOCH

HUMAN CONNECTION

Communication—the human connection—is the key to personal and career success.

Paul J. Meyer

The art of successful communication has everything to do with connection. Our ability to share and compare thoughts and ideas with others depends a great deal on the bond we forge with the people we seek to communicate with. The closer the bond, the easier it is for us to understand them and the more open they are to receiving what we have to say.

Unfortunately, the year I graduated from high school—1968—was one of the most divisive periods in America's history. Our nation lacked connection, which led to tragic results. I remember vividly a moment a couple of months before my high school graduation. It was April 5, a Friday morning. We'd watched the evening news the night before, but my parents hadn't listened to the radio or talked to anyone outside our home for the rest of the night. I had been up late and gotten up early in the morning to do homework in my bedroom. I walked downstairs and saw my father sitting at the dining room table in his pajamas and bathrobe. For the first time in years, I saw that he was crying. "What's wrong?" I asked.

"I am so upset," my father said. "Martin Luther King has been assassinated."

I knew this was an awful blow to my father because he admired Dr. King tremendously. In addition to hosting Dr. King in our home and escorting him to the graduation of the first black student from Little Rock's Central High School, my father had visited him in a New York hospital after a deranged woman had stabbed him.

I was simply shocked. I sat at the table with my dad, where we prayed and discussed what a terrible time it was for America.

Two months later, this scene played out a second time in an eerily similar fashion. On Wednesday morning, June 6, I again walked downstairs and found my father sitting at the dining room table, tears in his eyes. He told me that US presidential candidate Robert Kennedy had been shot early that morning after winning the California Democratic primary.

This time, my first response was anger. "That's crazy!" I said. "What is going on? What is wrong with America? America is going to hell." The next morning, Robert Kennedy died at Good Samaritan Hospital in Los Angeles.

These events coincided with the start of a trip I was to take to England for a summer work-study experience before starting classes at Antioch. I'd arranged to stay with a friend in New York City before flying on to England. I canceled my plans to spend time with my friends in New York and instead went to St. Patrick's Cathedral, where Kennedy's body lay in repose. I sat for hours near his closed casket in one of the front-row pews. For much of that time I was unaware of the people around me. I felt completely alone.

I was not only angry but also overwhelmingly sad. Just a few days earlier, I'd watched this energetic man on TV speaking about the importance of civil rights and the changes he hoped to make as president. My close high school friend Tom McQuain was a volunteer for Kennedy's campaign and had recruited me to help on occasion. I looked up to Kennedy and felt he was the best hope for our country's future. Now, suddenly, he was gone.

God seemed absent as well. For years my faith had wavered between belief and doubt, plagued by fears and questions and damaged by inconsistencies I saw in the attitudes and actions of members of my father's congregations. As I grew older, I drifted away from my faith. I met an atheist friend who influenced me. I did not rebel openly against religion or my parents' views about God—my father was a pastor, after all—but I quietly pushed Him out of my life. For a long time, I felt no link to the Lord, no sense of communication or presence.

As I sat in front of Robert Kennedy's lifeless body, the spiritual void in my own life had never felt more pronounced.

God, where are you? I prayed. *What's wrong with you? How could you allow this to happen?* I thought, *Maybe people are right. Maybe there is no God.* It was a bleak time for the nation and for me personally. I entered my college years excited about the opportunity to grow and learn, yet with many questions about my place in the world and what I believed.

I left New York for England, where I had been accepted, along with a host of other college students, to join the Winchester Excavation Committee directed by prominent archaeologist Martin Biddle. For the next twelve weeks, I would assist in one of the world's pioneering efforts in urban archaeology. I was of course the only deaf student at the site. When our training started, I had difficulty understanding what was being said. I was thrown immediately into survival mode—I had to act quickly or I would fall hopelessly behind. There was no time for worry or fear. I went from one student to the next, asking, "Hey, can you help me?" One after another was either reluctant to cooperate or hard to lipread, so I moved on.

Finally, after about two hours, I approached a huge, bearded student from Northeastern University named Randy. When I quickly explained my predicament and asked if he could help, he said, "Sure." He was a nice guy of Italian descent who gestured often as he talked. His movements always seemed to match his words, which made him easy to understand. Randy also listened well, watching my face and lips closely. He was a huge help to me.

My team leader, Carolyn Heighway, was about six years older than me. I walked up and introduced myself. I had *a little* trouble lipreading her despite her British accent. She was easier to understand than Martin Biddle, who smoked a pipe and often talked with a pipe in his mouth.

Carolyn and those of us on her team were responsible for the ruins of the bishop's palace behind Winchester Cathedral. Our job was to discover and identify what was below what had already been excavated. In addition to careful digging, we took photos and cataloged everything that was uncovered.

I liked the work, but after a few weeks I began to grow restless. I didn't want to spend the whole summer in one spot. I approached Carolyn and asked if I could take on other responsibilities as well. She was reluctant.

"Paul, when I explain something to you," she said, "I have to explain it in more detail, two or three times more than for other people."

"No," I said, shaking my head. "I don't agree. You tell me exactly the same thing that you say to the other students. It just takes a little bit longer because you're more conscious of talking precisely and of your facial expressions. The number of words is the same."

Carolyn's face registered surprise as she thought about it. "Yes, yes," she said. "You are right."

I was fortunate that Carolyn was open to having her opinion challenged by a member of her team. She put me in charge of the water pump, which meant that I arrived an hour and a half before the other students every morning to drain any water that had seeped into our dig sites overnight. I took satisfaction in the new responsibility, and Carolyn came to appreciate that she could depend on me. As the summer went on, she entrusted me with more duties. I found myself communicating more easily with Carolyn. We had formed a connection.

I also formed a connection with a student named Alicia Campi. Alicia was from Smith College and has since become an expert on Mongolia and served as a diplomat in Ulaanbaatar. She was easy to understand—when we talked, she looked me in the eye, enunciated clearly, and had an expressive face. If I didn't understand something she said, she rephrased her words instead of repeating the same thing. Alicia was my best friend that summer. If I missed anything, she let me know what was going on, including any gossip about the other students.

I wanted to see a London discotheque, so one Saturday I persuaded Alicia to join me on a visit. We missed the last train that could take us home and were stuck in London. We walked the streets all night and then attended a worship service at Westminster Abbey the next morning. Westminster has been the site of numerous coronations and royal weddings as well as the resting place for kings, queens, and other notable figures from England's history. While sitting inside, I sensed the powerful concentration of past, present, and future, all in one place. Although my faith was tenuous at the time, I also sensed the presence of God.

In just three months that summer, we excavated material from the 1800s all the way down to Roman ruins, a period of more than a thousand years. One day another team discovered a human skull in the kitchen of a bishop's palace. The skull was from the Anglo-Saxon period, sometime before 1066. Everyone was excited and speculated on what had happened. Did this poor man get into a fight with the cook? Or was he the cook himself, and the bishop didn't like his food? There was no way to know.

My time at Westminster was a fulfilling adventure. Whether our job was digger, note-taker, photographer, team leader, or any of a host of other assignments, everyone had a role. I felt I belonged, that I was part of the team and of the significant work going on. The Winchester excavations have been described as among the most important in the world during the twentieth century.

The summer was also fulfilling to me because of the bonds I forged with people like Alicia, Carolyn, and Randy. Although many students passed through, some staying only two weeks, others worked as I did for twelve weeks. Looking back, I believe that the communication between us all that summer was stronger and more satisfying because of that sense of belonging and connection.

I would soon be reminded of how rare that feeling can be.

2

LETTING GO

Letting go doesn't mean giving up, but rather accepting that there are things that cannot be.

Author unknown

It was September 1968. I was back in the States, in Yellow Springs, Ohio, ready to begin my freshman year at Antioch College. Antioch was in many ways emblematic of the tumultuous 1960s. With the help of a grant, the college increased its black student population that year from nearly zero to one-tenth of its two thousand students. Most were recruited from inner cities. At about the same time, Antioch established coeducational residence halls with no adult supervision, a radical change at the time. Authority figures were "square" and the hippie lifestyle was "in," including sex, drugs, and rock and roll.

Equally in was a zealous idealism. Many Antioch students believed they could and should change the world. They wanted to stop the killing and put an end to the Vietnam War. They desired to bring racial equality to the nation. They agitated for a dramatic shift in the political landscape. They wanted to wipe out poverty in America and around the world. They launched protests supporting women's rights, making Antioch one of the forerunners of the feminist movement. Many of these attitudes resonated with me. I had discovered a group of people who cared about making a difference. I embraced their philosophy wholeheartedly.

These lofty goals were hatched in a picturesque setting. Next to campus was a beautiful thousand-acre nature preserve, Glen Helen. My mother had camped there as a child with her parents, who lived only fifteen miles away. For all these reasons, Antioch seemed a magical place to me.

My parents helped me move into Birch Hall, my new home. My father waved at many of the other students and introduced himself, which naturally embarrassed me. But we eventually got everything transferred from the car to my room and my parents finally said their goodbyes. I was on my own, the first deaf student in Antioch College's history. I was nervous but also excited. Who knew what adventures were in store for me?

I met my new roommate, Jason, and was immediately concerned. He didn't move his mouth much and was difficult to understand. If everyone at Antioch was like this, I was in trouble.

Fortunately, that was not the case. Each of us was assigned to a fifteen-member "preceptorial" group that would meet regularly throughout our college experience. These other students welcomed me warmly. After a week, I could talk comfortably with and easily under-stand five or six of them, which was a great relief. Several of these students are still dear friends today. Our P-Group leader was a new math professor at Antioch. Howard Swann had been the first Peace Corps volunteer from Harvard and had just earned his doctorate from the University of California, Berkeley. He was a wonderful adviser and friend who lived in an apartment reserved for single faculty on the ground floor just below us. P-Group members were always welcome to drop in for dinner, to watch television, or to just talk—we had access

At Antioch.

to Howard twenty-four hours a day. I later learned it was rare for the faculty to live on campus, so we were fortunate. Howard was like a big brother to us.

One of the first things students did on campus was take a three-day placement exam. If we did well, we would be able to waive some of our classes. I was a little surprised to not have any of my math or history classes waived, since those were some of my strongest subjects. I was equally surprised that my test results allowed me to waive three English classes: two literature and one composition. All those in-depth discussions with my parents about my high school English courses had paid off.

I missed having my father join me to meet my professors as he had when I started high school. My support system was gone; I couldn't go home to my parents and talk over my problems. I had to handle everything myself. But this time I had more experience and more confidence. For the most part, the students and faculty were also more mature and open to making the effort to communicate with me.

I made it a point to meet all my professors before classes began to explain that I was deaf and to make sure that I could succeed in their courses. I'd learned from my experience in high school and from my parents that it did me no good to play the role of victim if there were communication problems. It was my responsibility to assess my circumstances and make adjustments if needed. If someone didn't understand me, I tried not to blame them or feel sorry for myself. I just had to fix the situation.

At Antioch, math was no problem because Howard was my professor. I introduced myself to the ceramics professor and found her cooperative, expressive, and easy to lipread. My psychology professor was a different story. He was a thin man with dark hair and a pale face. When we talked, he often turned away from me to look at his papers. He said he understood my speech, but I had my doubts. I decided to drop that class to try another psychology professor.

At our first meeting, it appeared I would have just as much trouble with my new psychology professor. He wore a beard that obscured his mouth, making him difficult to understand. He had a great attitude, however. "You can sit in the front row," he said. "I can smooth down my beard." I didn't think "smoothing" would help much, but I was sold. I remained in his class. On the first day of class, I saw another man at the front of the room who I thought must have been a teaching assistant. Then I looked closer. It was the same professor—he'd shaved off his beard!

I was stunned. "Yes," he said, noticing me looking at him. "It's for you." Then he announced to the class, "Paul is deaf. He can't hear me, so I shaved my beard so that he can read my lips."

His statement caught me off guard and I blushed furiously. But because of his announcement, a girl in the class offered to help and agreed to take notes for me. The college did not provide note-takers or interpreters for me; I was on my own to arrange for help. I ended up enjoying both that professor and the class immensely. He even tried to convince me to become a psychology major, but I had set my mind on mathematics.

Antioch had no fraternities or sororities and didn't field sports teams. The extracurricular activity was politics. A man who worked in California with labor leader and civil rights activist Cesar Chavez spoke on campus and inspired several Antioch students. When the manager of a local grocery store refused the students' request that he stop buying fruit from growers that hired nonunion field laborers, I joined them in picketing the store for three weeks. I valued the feeling of belonging and of doing something about an important cause. I doubt we had a major impact on the plight of migrant workers, but we did convince a few shoppers to change their buying habits.

Another unique offering at Antioch was its co-op program. While half of the sixteen hundred students took classes on campus, the other half served in temporary positions with businesses and other organizations across the country, gaining valuable experience related to their field of interest. At the end of the term, the students on campus left for co-op positions and vice versa. I was already a participant in the program. When the Winchester opportunity arose, I'd contacted Antioch and asked if they would give me course credit for it. They viewed it as a rare and exciting chance to learn about history, science, and cultures of the past and present. They granted my request.

My co-op adviser, a woman named Dorothy Scott, suggested that for winter quarter I accept an opening with the Martin E. Segal Company, an insurance firm in New York City. I agreed, as did another friend in my P-Group named Debbie. We found a small apartment in New York with a third Antioch student, Wendy. We were on the fourth floor. My room had no windows but did include a skylight.

As was usually the case, I was nervous but also excited about my new adventure. I arrived in New York soon enough to go to Times Square for New Year's Eve. There were so many people there that I was nearly crushed to death. I hoped it wasn't a sign of things to come.

My concern deepened on my first day of work when I couldn't understand my immediate boss, a highly stressed insurance executive. He was often impatient. I couldn't read his lips and he didn't understand me. Fortunately, Debbie helped translate his words. We eventually found that writing notes back and forth was effective, though when he was in a hurry, Debbie still served as interpreter. Our job was to enter data into a machine similar to a calculator that enabled the company to evaluate risk and establish actuarial tables. As I developed my skills at the company, I was given more responsibilities. I was pleased to receive a high evaluation at the end of the term.

Less satisfying was a pair of incidents during my time in New York. The first occurred after a high school friend invited me to a wedding, where I met a deaf girl named Brenda. Like me, Brenda did not sign and only lipread. We hit it off and decided to go on a date. A few days later, we were on our way to a restaurant, crossing the street arm in arm. When we reached the middle of the intersection, Brenda was just a few inches ahead of me. Suddenly I found myself spinning and running to keep my balance—a driver had ignored the red light, struck Brenda with his car, and sent me careening across the street. After I regained my balance, I saw Brenda lying in the street and ran back to her. She had a cracked pelvis.

I stayed with Brenda until paramedics took her to a hospital and then returned to my apartment and cried. I felt that what happened to Brenda was my responsibility. The whole thing was a nightmare. Later, we learned that the driver had a criminal record that included many traffic violations. Brenda's parents sued the driver and wanted me to testify, but my parents refused to give their permission (I was twenty and technically still a minor). They didn't believe in lawsuits and felt people should work things out without suing each other. I was relieved that I didn't have to testify. I also learned an important lesson about my parents' belief system.

The other difficult incident that winter occurred in February after a huge storm dumped twenty inches of snow on the city. I usually walked to work. Debbie sometimes walked with me, while other times she took the subway. One of my favorite routes was through Central Park. I loved the trees and watching the people. When I saw all the snow that first morning after the storm, I decided I would walk through Central Park. Wearing my hat, coat, and gloves, I trudged through the drifts. I was sweating hard by the time I reached our building. I took an elevator to our floor and opened the door. To my surprise, the office was nearly deserted.

"Paul, we're closed," a coworker said. It hadn't occurred to me that the office would be shut down.

"We tried to call you," my coworker continued. "We left a message with Debbie."

"She didn't tell me!" I said, feeling confused and a little hurt.

I was too exhausted to walk back home, so I took the subway. When I got there, I asked Debbie why she hadn't relayed the message. She said she knocked on my door but that I didn't answer. "You should have banged on the door," I said. "I would have felt the vibrations."

Debbie never apologized and never fully explained why she didn't try harder to let me know. I wanted to get everything out in the open and resolve the matter, but I sensed it would strain our relationship to keep pushing. It was the beginning of my awareness that even when two people are close, they may still suffer communication breakdowns. In hearing culture, people often let such matters go. It's a line that you can't cross. In this case, I had to accept that Debbie didn't want to discuss it further. She may have simply been embarrassed. As I've grown older, I've gotten better at recognizing when it's okay to press for resolution and when I need to back off and drop a subject. I'm thankful that Debbie is still a close friend today.

At the end of our term in New York, I returned to Antioch for spring quarter. One of my favorite teachers that term was Warren Watson, a math professor. He was a classic hippie who had an enormous collection of movies, all reel-to-reel. His course focused on theoretical ecology, an exciting new field. We tracked the behavior of coyotes and rabbits in a restricted area and used mathematical models to predict how their population and behavior would change over time. I found it fascinating and fun work.

The downside was that I found Warren difficult to understand. When he talked, he barely moved his lips. It was a serious problem. I sat down with Warren and asked if he would talk louder in class so I could understand him. He agreed. From that point on, he spoke louder, which forced him to enunciate more clearly and made him much easier to lipread. I thought my problem was solved.

Then one day a couple of weeks before the end of the term, Warren rushed up to me in the hallway, his face red. "Paul, you lied!" he nearly shouted. "You don't hear me! People are teasing me because I talk so loud to you. You're embarrassing me!"

We retreated to his office. "Warren," I said, "I do understand you when you talk louder. It's because the movement of your lips is clearer."

Warren was so upset that it was a long time before my words sank in. Someone had told him that I was completely deaf. He'd been sure that I had tricked and manipulated him. Although he did eventually understand my point, for the rest of the term he was less enthusiastic about talking loudly. It was another communication breakdown and another example of an instance where I had to just let it go.

I was far less inclined to let go of another incident a few months later. I stayed on campus and attended classes that summer at Antioch. Dorothy Scott, meanwhile, lined up a new job for my next co-op assignment. I would spend fall and winter quarters, six months, managing the mainframe computer at Wayne State University in Detroit (I'd gained some experience with mainframes in New York). It sounded like a great opportunity. I rented an apartment in Michigan, and at the end of the summer I packed my things and prepared to leave. My parents drove up to Antioch to help me make the transition.

Two days before I was to depart, however, Dorothy Scott called me into her office. We both sat down. "Paul, the placement at Wayne State didn't work out," she said.

"What?" I said.

"We'll have to find something else for you."

I was shocked. "Everyone is leaving," I said. "I have no job. What am I going to do?"

"We'll work something out," Dorothy said. "Just a moment. I'll be right back." She got up and left the room.

My eyes rapidly scanned the room as if searching for a way out of this sudden predicament. I spied a letter sticking out of a pile on Dorothy's desk and grabbed it. It was from Wayne State. The words seemed to jump off the page: "We've just discovered that Paul is deaf. We cannot accept him."

Now I was even more shocked. It was the first time I'd experienced blatant institutional discrimination. When Dorothy came back into the room, she knew from the look on my face that I'd read the letter. She tried to soothe me. "I'm confident we'll find something else," she said. "It will be even better."

After I left the office, my parents and Howard Swann also tried to calm me down. "God has a reason for this," my mother said.

Howard told me, "You're building big dreams on toothpicks. You take one toothpick out and everything falls down." He was telling me that I was placing too much importance on one job, but I was too upset to understand his message at the time.

Two days later, I received a note asking me to return to Dorothy Scott's office. A new opportunity had just come in. An Antioch alumnus, Leonard Swanson, was the director of the computer center at Beloit College in Wisconsin. He was looking for a qualified student to participate in an innovative computer initiative called the Social Sciences Instructional Project. He said that taking on a deaf student was no issue at all. Given my limited options, it didn't take me long to say I would do it.

The project director was Dr. Michael Hall, an economics professor. With his neat goatee and bald head, he looked every bit the brilliant scholar that he was. Dr. Hall was a little hard to understand but patient with his explanations, which I appreciated. It was wonderful when he introduced me to his team, which included a married couple, Betsy and Joe, and another student named Lynn. The students were friendly and welcomed me enthusiastically. Betsy and Joe even invited me to go out with them a number of times.

My initial task was to learn a computer language called FORTRAN. I worked long hours at it, and after a couple of weeks of trial and error, I felt ready for the next stage. I helped develop a package of statistical programs that enabled Dr. Hall's students to choose one and enter data from their classwork or research on a teletypewriter connected to the mainframe computer. Several teletypewriters were hooked to the mainframe. At the time, it was rare for people to be able to share the mainframe at the same time.

I relished the work, as well as celebrating each new advance with our team. Dr. Hall brought me a Snickers bar after each milestone because he knew it was my favorite. I felt I was making an important contribution. It was one of the best jobs I ever had. I found it so stimulating that I considered changing my major to statistics and computers.

The irony is that when I returned to Antioch and quizzed other students about their experience at Wayne State, they told me it was boring and didn't challenge them. Dorothy Scott, my mother, and Howard had all been right. It had all turned out for the best.

About twenty-five years after I graduated from Antioch, I got together with Dorothy and told her how much I appreciated her support while I was a student, particularly after the Wayne State incident. Her response surprised me. "That was one of the biggest regrets of my career," she said. "We should have sued Wayne State. The whole campus could have helped you. We could have had the Americans with Disabilities Act twenty years sooner."

I told her it was just as well. I didn't think I would've wanted to go through the time and stress of a lawsuit, not to mention be the face of a national court case. Although such a lawsuit would have been for a good cause, I had come to agree with my parents that suing people was not the best method of working out problems. It is one of the most important lessons I have learned over the years: as much as I believe in promoting communication and advancing awareness of the deaf community, I've also discovered that after a breakdown or conflict, sometimes the best thing to do is to simply let it go.

3

TAKING THE INITIATIVE

Even if you're on the right track, you'll get run over if you just sit there.

Will Rogers

The fall of 1970 marked a new adventure for me—I set out for more than a year of study at the University of Manchester in England. I had been accepted by several universities for a study abroad experience, but I chose Manchester since my adviser said it had the strongest math program.

I was initially excited to be there, but my enthusiasm quickly faded when I realized that the people in Manchester spoke with a different accent than those I'd become familiar with in Winchester and London. They were difficult to understand. Although the people were nice, they were also quite proper and formal, not warm or open. Within two weeks of my arrival, I was depressed.

In addition, I felt oppressed by my heavy mathematics course load. I was used to the variety of subjects offered at American colleges; the British system called for students to focus almost exclusively on their major. I was enrolled in Advanced Algebra, Math Logic, Numerical Analysis, Statistics, and Polygon Theory—five mathematics classes.

I soon asked my adviser for permission to drop one of the classes and take Classical Greek instead. After four years of Latin classes in high school, I thought I would enjoy adding Greek to my language base. My adviser somewhat reluctantly agreed to my proposal, and I became the only non-major in Greek I. A couple of days later, I decided that four math classes were still too many. I went back to my adviser. "Do you mind," I said, "if I drop another math class?"

He frowned. "Now what do you want to take?"

"Anthropology," I said.

"Okay," he said, waving his hand, "go."

There is a saying—"Variety is the spice of life"—that sums up my attitude at that time. Two weeks into the term, I decided that even *three* math classes were too many. I returned to my adviser's office. "What do you want to take this time?" he asked with a sigh.

"The History of Russia."

"Fine," he said. I think I'd worn him down with all my requests. It turned out that the Russia class was full, so I signed up for independent study, which included a key to a small room at the library. My adviser may not have been thrilled, but I finally had a schedule that felt balanced.

My social life remained, on the other hand, out of balance. I had trouble connecting with the proper British students. I met a handful of international students I could understand and some nice deaf people, but it was a frustrating time. My frustrations deepened during the Christmas holidays. My friends from Beloit, Betsy and Joe, were in Africa with the Peace Corps. They wrote me a letter inviting me to join them in Amsterdam for the Christmas holidays. When I arrived, though, Betsy told me that their marriage was on the rocks and that they needed some time to themselves.

Suddenly I was on my own. I felt abandoned and hurt. Betsy and Joe should have contacted me and told me not to come. I walked the cold streets by myself, observing homes with gaily decorated yuletide trees in their front windows and families that had gathered for the holiday. I spent Christmas morning alone. Later that day, I again ventured into the streets and struck up conversations with strangers who didn't look too busy. Fortunately, the people of Amsterdam were friendly. Thanks to their location in the middle of Europe, they were used to a variety of accents and languages. I found them easy to talk with and asked about the history and details of the buildings around us. Near a bridge over a canal, I spoke with one elderly woman who had survived the Nazi siege of Amsterdam during World War II. She described growing gardens and bartering with others to keep from starving. Our conversation somehow comforted me.

Those interactions got me through the Christmas Day holiday, but I yearned for deeper connections and familiar faces. I decided to travel to London and visit an Antioch acquaintance named Steve. I stayed with him for three or four days. We attended a church service and on New Year's Eve visited Trafalgar Square with a group of his friends, some of them from Australia. I was surrounded by people, but I didn't know any of them well and couldn't communicate with them. I didn't have the energy to teach them how to maintain eye contact with me and enunciate clearly. I felt terribly lonely.

My loneliness intensified after I returned to Manchester. In January, British postal service workers went on strike. Both the university and my "flat" offered no telephone options for a deaf person. In those days before the Internet and texting, letters were my only means of communication with my family and friends. I felt cut off from the world.

The strike extended through February and into March. I was so down and lonely that I decided to quit school. I wanted to go home. I learned that to leave, an "exiter" had to sign a form authorizing my withdrawal. I boarded a train and four hours later entered an overseas administrator's office at the University of Essex. The official was uncomfortable talking with a deaf person and enlisted another Antioch student who happened to be studying there to "interpret" for us, even though she had no experience communicating with a deaf person. When the man understood what I wanted, he called each of my professors and my adviser. They were all puzzled. They'd heard nothing about my unhappiness and said I was getting As in my classes.

"Your grades are good. You're doing so well," the official said to me. "Why do you want to leave?"

"I'm homesick," I said. "I want to go home."

"Everybody's homesick," he said, shaking his head. "Go back to school. I will not sign the form."

I had no choice—I went back to Manchester. When I saw my adviser, he said, "You should have told me. My job is to take care of you." My professors were equally sympathetic. They all suggested that we meet after class to see how they could help. One even offered to meet with me once or twice a week for tea and a tutorial—I no longer had to attend his class.

The personal attention made me feel better. I realized I had been a poor communicator. I'd decided to leave and disappeared without seeking help or explaining any of my struggles. I began to understand that if things were going badly, it was my responsibility to reach out and try to make the situation better.

The postal strike ended in March and that also lifted my spirits. At about the same time, I saw a poster at the student union advertising a spring break trip for students from London to an oasis in the Sahara desert. It sounded like a great opportunity for an adventure and a chance to get some sun. I wrote to Steve, my friend in London, who agreed to go with me. Ten of us hopped into a van in London. We traveled through France and Spain to the Strait of Gibraltar, where we took a ferry to Morocco and then drove into the desert. It was a different world and I had a wonderful time. At the oasis, we camped under the stars, swam in a natural spring, and even studied for upcoming exams. More importantly, I had the chance to talk with Steve and a handful of the other students that I connected with. The shared experience made it especially fun. When I returned to Manchester, I was in a far better state of mind and my remaining time there was much more positive.

I further satisfied my itch to travel when my friend Tom and I spent the summer of 1971 in Europe and Eastern Europe. One country I especially wanted to visit was Russia. I had taken a course on the Russian Revolution that focused on the Bolsheviks and Karl Marx. I was particularly concerned about the exploitation of underrepresented people and found the idea of equal treatment and fair distribution of wealth appealing.

Tom and I spent three weeks traveling through the home country of the Soviet Union. What I saw and heard there did not match up with my idealistic vision of communism, however. Our Russian tour guide, for instance, seemed brainwashed. She said that Russia's agricultural system was much stronger than America's and described a nonexistent crop failure and famine in the 1960s that supposedly caused thousands of Americans to starve to death. When we told her this had never happened, she thought we must have been too young to remember it. She refused to believe us.

I was taken aback by other experiences in Russia as well. I observed long lines of people waiting to buy limited and inferior food and supplies. I met people who wanted to buy our things so they could sell them on the black market. The people were not as open and friendly as in other nations; many drank heavily. Police were everywhere. The flourishing country I had expected to see did not exist. Instead, the atmosphere was oppressive.

Despite this disappointing discovery, the trip was a great success. It was fascinating to explore different cultures firsthand. Once again, having a friend that I could communicate with easily made all the difference.

We returned to Antioch for the fall of 1971. Tom left for a new co-op job and I was stuck with a new roommate who had a negative attitude toward me and was almost impossible to understand. Because of my year in Manchester, I was also on a different schedule than my old P-Group friends—they were all leaving for out-of-state co-op jobs. Once more, I felt alone. I was determined this time, however, to do something about it. Tom had earlier introduced me to his folk dancing group, which included students as well as people from the community. On my own, I rejoined this group. On Friday nights, we would eat a healthy meal, dance at the campus Red Square (all the bricks in that area were red), and then go downtown for fresh doughnuts. I made several new friends, which helped renew the feelings of belonging and connection that were so important to me. One of them was a registered nurse employed by the college, Barbara Hardman. Near the end of the academic year, she sent me a copy of the best-selling novella *Jonathan Livingston Seagull*, along with a note that included these words: "[This] is a beautiful story of a seagull who was willing to take many risks to realize his potential. He reminds me of you."

I was learning a great deal from my studies in mathematics and other disciplines, as well as about the larger world. Yet more important than all of that, perhaps, I was also learning how to take responsibility for my own happiness. I would continue to face situations that left me feeling cut off from others. To establish satisfying relationships and build meaningful experiences, I needed to take the initiative. As Barbara said, I had to continue take risks to realize my potential. It might not guarantee success, but it would make a positive outcome far more likely.

4

MOTIVATED TO SUCCEED

The basic building block of good communications is the feeling that every human being is unique and of value.

Author unknown

At the beginning of my junior year at Antioch, my friends Christine and Tom and I decided to get an apartment together. We thought it would be fun to have a garden and learn how to cook our own food. Christine was very enthusiastic about our plan. I don't know where she is today, but I'm sure she owns a farm and sells what she grows. Unfortunately, Tom and I weren't much help with the garden.

In my case, there was a good reason. I had a heart condition that prevented me from doing too much physical activity. I'd learned as a child that I had a heart murmur. Then, when I was thirteen, my father took me to our family doctor for my annual checkup. During the exam, the doctor placed a stethoscope on my chest. He frowned and listened for a very long time. I saw the growing concern in my father's eyes. Finally, I was told to put my clothes back on and sit in the waiting room.

Through an open door to the doctor's study near the examination room, I watched the doctor talk with my father. Both had serious expressions. Intermittently, my father clenched his fists. This went on for more than fifteen minutes. I was so nervous that my own hands shook. I said to my friend who'd come with us, "The doctor kept listening to my heart. I think I'm going to die."

Eventually my father came out and said, "There's nothing to worry about. Everything is fine."

I didn't believe him.

Later, I asked my mother about it. She said that it was just the heart murmur and that I would be fine. I didn't believe her either. My doubts intensified during the following months and years when my father sometimes pulled me aside to say, "Paul, please be careful. You don't want to overdo things. You need to have a long life."

Although my parents were wonderful communicators in so many ways, the information they withheld from me after my brother David's suicide, and now this, led me to mistrust them on certain issues. It wasn't until later that I discovered my parents and the doctors knew there was a problem with my heart but didn't understand what it was or what to do about it. The technology to explain it didn't exist. Today, I know that I have a bicuspid aortic valve—one of the three parts to one of my heart valves is missing. It's not as serious a condition as I had feared it was back then.

Although my parents and the doctors didn't understand my heart issue, I wish they'd been up front with me about it. Instead, I grew up suspicious of doctors, doubting what my parents were telling me about my health, and expecting to die at a young age.

These suspicions intensified during my year of study in Manchester. I wanted new glasses, so I went in for an eye exam. After a series of tests, the doctors handed me a piece of paper that said I had a rare condition called retinitis pigmentosa (RP). The doctors seemed in a hurry and told me nothing more. I thought I must have acquired RP during my spring break trip to Africa. Research at the Manchester library revealed, however, that the disease is genetic. That made sense, since I knew my brother Jonathan had it also.

The prognosis was troubling. For most people, the disorder gradually gets worse. Many people with RP go blind by the age of forty or even thirty. There is no cure. I was twenty-two at the time and terrified by the idea of losing my sight. I depended on it for everything.

I was also disturbed by the thought that my parents might already know. I'd had regular vision exams while growing up. A family member or someone who knew me well had always accompanied me. Had the doctors discovered my condition and informed my parents while keeping me in the dark?

When I returned home after my year of study in England, my parents were at the airport to pick me up. I walked down the ramp and saw them, but I didn't offer a cheery greeting or give them a hug. Instead, the first words out of my mouth were, "Did you know I have RP?"

My mother burst into tears. It was true. They'd known all along.

"Why didn't you tell me?" I said.

My parents explained that since I was deaf and had a heart issue, they felt I already had enough life challenges to worry about. They didn't want to burden me with another serious medical concern.

I was still upset, but at the same time, I understood. *My poor parents. They've gone through so much. I'm not going to blame them. I'll do them a favor and say nothing more about it.*

In the years since, my vision has deteriorated a little, but it has been stable for some time. I've learned that my strain of RP is an unusual one and less damaging than the more common version. Nevertheless, I would have much preferred learning about it from my parents and having the chance to investigate the issue at a younger age. Their decision to again keep the truth from me caused enormous stress and inserted another wedge of mistrust into our otherwise trusting relationship.

Mistrust wasn't an issue at the off-campus apartment I shared with Tom and Christine in 1972. It was simply that Christine was exasperated with us since she got stuck with most of the gardening. We were little help, since I had to monitor my exercise and Tom had almost no clue about what to do. At least I was a decent cook.

You could say that I got a chance to make it up to Christine. She was enrolled in calculus and struggled with the class. I offered to help. She resisted at first, but she eventually gave in and allowed me to give her some tips. My advice must have been helpful, because one day she said, "Paul, why don't you apply to be a math tutor at Antioch?"

Hmm, I thought. *Why not?*

I sent in an application. I feared that the department heads would tell me, "I'm sorry, but you're deaf. You won't be able to understand the students and give them the help they need." To my pleasant surprise, however, they accepted me without question. While a few other applicants were passed over, I was one of two tutors hired. Brian and I were each given an office with a blackboard and were expected to keep regular hours to meet with students.

During our first week on the job, I soon noticed that most of the students went to Brian for help. It was a blow to my ego. It may be that they didn't want to deal with what they perceived as the drawbacks of working with a deaf person. So many students wanted to get in to see Brian that they had to wait in line. A few grew tired of waiting and visited me instead. Gradually, my list of "clients" grew. After about three weeks, I realized that I was now the one with more students. Some of them told me that I was the better tutor. It took a little while for them to get used to my speech, but once they gave me a chance, I was able to prove what I could do.

A few weeks after that, I realized that Brian and I served different needs. The students who did well in the class and needed only a quick clarification on some problem or theory usually went to Brian. Those who had more trouble in the class and needed more in-depth explanations usually came to me. They felt I was more patient with my descriptions. It dawned on me that Brian and I were not in a competition for students. We each had a valuable role within the department.

I deeply enjoyed my time as a tutor and interacting with the other students. I felt we broke down the usual communication barriers. Math is a universal language. If a student didn't understand the concept I was explaining, I could write it on the board or give him or her steps to work through until it made sense. I found myself coming up with creative methods for getting the message across, which I also enjoyed. Little did I know how important my tutoring experience would be to my future.

Christine was instrumental in another of my activities during this time. She was involved in a Yellow Springs food co-op, where people pooled their funds, bought food in bulk, and sold it in a market. Thanks, I'm sure, to her influence, one of the members approached me and said they were looking for an accountant. It was a volunteer position. I would keep the financial books and an inventory of the co-op food. I didn't know any of the co-op members well, but they were persuasive and seemed to need my help, so I agreed to do it.

It wasn't long before representatives at the bank that worked with the co-op discovered a discrepancy in the co-op's accounts. Since I was now the accountant, they asked me to come in for a meeting. It wasn't an inquisition at all; on the contrary, they were extremely cordial. They simply wanted to resolve the problem. They asked a number of questions, listened carefully to my answers, and understood me. I had discovered an error that had occurred in the co-op account before

I started my position, and we cleared up the matter. Throughout the meeting, the bank officials treated me like a first-class citizen.

We so often encounter roadblocks to free-flowing communication. Sometimes it's because information is withheld, either out of ignorance or, in the case of my parents, out of a desire to protect someone. At other times, communication fails because of prejudice and false assumptions, as was likely the case with the Antioch math students who initially avoided me as a tutor. But when both sides truly want to exchange thoughts and ideas—when they want something and are motivated to make it happen—they will find a way to succeed. That's how I felt while talking to the bank representatives. They embraced the idea that I was the person who could help them solve a problem, and they treated me like a valuable partner. It was a positive experience and another opportunity for me to contribute in a small way to the world around me.

5

A NEW PATH

It is never too late to be what you might have been.

George Eliot

During my high school and college years, I kept in touch with many of my friends from Central Institute for the Deaf. I shared important bonds with several of them. We'd graduated from CID together and gone on to mainstream high schools. It was like being part of a cultural minority together. I valued their friendship and the support system we established.

A few of those friends mentioned that it would be fun to see older deaf role models at an upcoming event in Chicago: the Alexander Graham Bell Association for the Deaf and Hard of Hearing convention, scheduled for the summer of 1972. I decided they were right and hitch-hiked there from Yellow Springs (I hitchhiked often in those days).

When I arrived and walked into a meeting at the convention, I was thrilled to see so many deaf and hard of hearing people. Many of them were less thrilled with me, or at least with my appearance. With my long hair and backpack, I looked more like a hippie than a serious professional. I'll never forget the warm welcome I received from Joe Slotnick, a Harvard graduate who had been deaf since the age of three after contracting spinal meningitis. Joe was the secretary of Telecommunications for the Deaf and Hard of Hearing (TDI), a national organization advocating accessibility to the world of technology for all deaf and hard of hearing people. Thanks to Joe's influence, more and more of the attendees became friendly with me. I was eventually invited to "camp" with my sleeping bag in a hotel room shared by four well-known figures in the deaf community, including a physics professor, a publishing house editor, and Bob Nicol, an architect and graduate of the University of California, Berkeley.

I was also surprised and thrilled to run into two of my CID mentors, Paul and Sally Taylor. Paul was a chemical engineer at Monsanto in St. Louis. In the late 1960s, he had helped combine Western Union teletypewriters with modems to create telecommunications devices for deaf people, known as TTYs. Paul played a major role in developing the manuals that showed people how to connect teletypewriters and modems. He was also working to create the first telephone relay system that would allow deaf people to call anywhere in the country. Sally supported Paul and his efforts, worked part-time, and devoted her remaining hours to raising their three children.

Paul was very excited about the upcoming debate between Dr. Audrey Simmons-Martin and Dr. McCay Vernon, two prominent deaf educators. I had been unaware of the debate, but Paul kept saying it could be a turning point in the field. The speakers held widely different viewpoints on the communication controversy that had plagued deaf education almost since its inception. Before 1880, most deaf students in the United States and Europe had been taught through the manual method, or sign language. But after 1880, oralism gained dominance and most deaf children learned to speak and lipread to communicate with the hearing world. The rare exceptions were when school officials determined that students lacked the ability to speak or lipread. In that case, they were permitted to learn sign language. In the early 1970s, a growing number of deaf people, like my brother Jonathan, believed that deaf children should be taught sign language rather than the oral method of speaking and lipreading—or at least that they should be given the opportunity to choose.

Although I had never learned sign language, I considered it a beautiful method of communication. Over the years, I had become more aware of the movement toward choice and found myself agreeing with it. At the conference, Audrey Simmons-Martin promoted the oral philosophy while McCay Vernon favored signing. The debate and subsequent discussions left me even more convinced that people should be able to choose the method that worked best for them. Paul Taylor and I recalled a good number of CID students who struggled with speaking and lipreading yet were not allowed to sign. It had to have stunted their language development, emotional development, and social skills. We'd felt sorry for them at the time and now saw how it could have been different.

It was exciting to be in Chicago and sense the spirit of change in the air. That conference *was* a turning point, as the option of sign language gained increasing favor among educators of deaf and hard of hearing people. Although I agreed with the movement, I did not expect to be part of it. I was still focused on computers, mathematics, and technology.

My thinking was about to change, however.

Dorothy Scott had lined up my final college co-op position for the fall and winter quarters. She described it as "the best co-op job you could ever dream of, the perfect way to culminate your Antioch experience." And it was a wonderful opportunity—a position working at Stanford under Patrick Suppes, founder of the Institute for Mathematical Studies in the Social Sciences (IMSSS) and famous for his leading role as a proponent of computer-assisted instruction (CAI). The concept of gaining advanced education through computers was one of the hot topics at the time.

At Stanford, I helped develop programs that compared what kind of computer-assisted instruction was most effective for people in different areas, such as mathematics or counseling. The work was challenging and rewarding, and my fellow students and I didn't mind that we worked long hours. In fact, when we attended what turned out to be a dull New Year's Eve party, one of us said, "Let's go to the lab to work," and that's just what we did. About half past midnight, the door to the lab opened and Patrick walked in, still wearing his bowtie. He'd been at the same event. "That was the most boring party I've ever been to," he said. Soon we were all at work. We stayed until six or seven in the morning and had far more fun than we'd had at the party.

It was about this time that I began thinking seriously about my life beyond college. Overall, my time at Antioch had been an excellent experience, but it would soon end. Graduate school seemed the logical next step for someone interested in math and computers, and I began filling out applications. But I wasn't excited about any of the opportunities I was looking at. *What*, I thought, *am I going to do?*

I was in my office at Stanford when a young woman poked her head in the doorway. "Excuse me," she said. "My name is Pat Lashway. I just wanted to say hello."

Pat was a speech, language, and hearing sciences lecturer from Oregon State University who was visiting the IMSSS. She sat down and we ended up talking for the next two hours. She was easy to converse with and clearly had experience communicating with deaf and hard of hearing people.

One of the topics of discussion was my future. We talked about the debate at the Bell Association conference in Chicago, the growing recognition of the significance of sign language, and what an exciting time it was in the field of deaf education. Near the end of our meeting, Pat said, "Paul, I don't see you in the picture you've described. You don't belong in statistics and mathematics and technology. Something's wrong with that picture. We need more people like you involved in deaf education, people who can talk with parents and show them the options as well as teach."

I was immediately intrigued by the idea. My parents had done so much to advance my education. How nice it would be, I thought, to share from my experience, support other parents of deaf and hard of hearing students, and explain the options they had today.

"Where would I go?" I asked Pat.

"You could get a master's and PhD," she said. "You could still do statistics, research, teach, whatever you want."

After Pat left, I thought, *She's right. I like teaching. I like working with people.* I liked my work with statistics and computers but wasn't sure I wanted to do it for the rest of my life. I'd seen so many people burn out in those fields.

It was highly unusual for me to make snap decisions about major life choices, but this was one of those times. *She's right*, I thought again. *I'm game.*

A large pile of applications to various graduate schools sat on the corner of my desk. I took my hand and slowly slid the pile over the edge. I watched the papers tip and fall into the wastebasket below. The space on my desk where the applications sat was now empty. Just like that, I had cleared away all my old plans.

Now what?

Graduate school still made sense. I talked to my immediate boss at Stanford, Dexter Fletcher, and explained my change of heart. He recommended Stanford, the University of Illinois, and a handful of other colleges. Dexter was ahead of his time in that he strongly believed in the value of interdisciplinary programs. He advocated that all students broaden their scope of study so they would have more to offer society. In my case, Dexter encouraged me to pursue educational psychology and linguistics in addition to traditional deaf education programs.

My first choice was Stanford because I wanted to stay on the West Coast to be closer to my family. Dunbar was teaching in Berkeley, and my parents had been invited to move there to help a church start a program for senior citizens.

I launched into a new round of applications. I would have to wait and see.

In the meantime, I had to finish my final quarter at Antioch. I was thrilled to room in a house with Moss, a friend from my original P-Group, along with three or four others. Every Friday night, Moss invited friends over to the house to play poker. They indulged in beer, potato chips, and other unhealthy snacks. I occasionally joined them but more often went folk dancing with my friends at Red Square.

Much less enjoyable was the division that exploded into conflict between many students and faculty on the one side and the Antioch administration on the other. Many of my friends and fellow students were angry about the Vietnam War, about the prevailing political establishment, about authority in almost any form. At the same time, Antioch was experiencing financial difficulties, in part because of ambitious and expensive programs aimed at low-income black students and at establishing satellite campuses across the country. As a result, the administration began to cut back on promised scholarships. During that last quarter, students and faculty upset about these and other issues—my friends and I called them "the radicals"—launched a strike that effectively shut down the campus. Some confrontations turned violent. A professor who tried to get to his classroom was sprayed with mace. A dean was pelted with eggs. Police were called to campus to tear down a barricade. The administration responded by expelling twenty students and firing seven professors who had taken part in a demonstration.

Although some professors continued to hold classes in their homes, most normal college business was suspended. While we sympathized with some of the views of the radicals, probably two-thirds of the student body was against the strike. We felt it was the wrong way to handle the problems.

The strike destroyed the respectful, supportive spirit that had been so prevalent at Antioch. The bad publicity turned people away from the college and led to a decline in enrollment that lasted for years. For me, it was all depressing and demoralizing.

During a psychology class that last quarter, I met a girl two years younger than me who went by the name of Peaches. She had just returned from a co-op job at the Colorado School for the Deaf. She was expressive and patient, so I asked if she would mouth the professor's words so I would know what was going on. She agreed and did a wonderful job. At the end of the quarter, I complained to Moss about all the problems on campus and said I wished I was more tuned in to the issues. "I wish," I said, "that I'd had Peaches to interpret for me earlier."

"No, no," Moss said, shaking his head, "you didn't miss anything. You are one of the sanest people here because you don't hear the extra noise. Your deafness saved your life."

I didn't agree with Moss at the time. I always wanted to know exactly what was happening. But today I believe he may have been right. The constant drone of negative or irrelevant news would have wasted my time and sapped my energy. Sometimes it's better not to know all the details.

Because of the turmoil, the administration announced at the end of the academic year that all seniors would graduate. Plans for a ceremony were thrown together. I decided to add some levity to a difficult time.

My parents, other family, and friends planned to come to the graduation ceremony. During graduation week, I told them, "The president of the college wants to have a private graduation ceremony with just me and my family and friends early in the morning before the official ceremony." Everyone who was coming to help me celebrate was excited about this news.

On the morning of the ceremony, we all drove to the Glen Ellen nature preserve. I led the group to a life-size statue of Horace Mann, which towered several feet above us. Mann was an education reformer, the first president of Antioch, and among the first college presidents to hire female faculty paid on an equal basis with their male colleagues, as well as to admit black students. My family and friends were surprised to see that the statue clutched a real, paper diploma, complete with a ribbon, in his right hand.

"Oh, there's the president," I said. "And he has my diploma."

Everyone burst out laughing. Our family often played jokes on each other, and they realized I'd just played a big one. I climbed up to "accept" my diploma and announced, "Horace has just given me some valuable advice: Be ashamed to die until you have won some victory for humanity." This was the college motto.

I had my college degree, but I had no idea what victories awaited me. I was disappointed with the results of my graduate school applications. Stanford accepted me but did not offer a scholarship. In fact, the only institution that seemed excited about me, offering a graduate assistantship and a stipend, was the University of Illinois.

Since I didn't want to go east, I couldn't decide what to do. I thought I might find an appealing job instead. I traveled all summer and put off making a choice. I was at my parents' home a week before classes were scheduled to start at Illinois when my mother asked, "Paul, have you let them know at Illinois that you want to go there?"

"No," I admitted.

"When is the deadline?" she asked.

"Oh, last month."

"Last month! What are you going to do? We have no money for you."

It was time to make up my mind. I decided I would go to Illinois if they would still accept me. I sat nearby in my parents' kitchen as my mother phoned the University of Illinois and asked if their offer was still available. To her great relief—as well as mine, but mixed with a sense of apprehension—they said yes.

"Okay," I said. "I'll be there."

I was bound for the land of Lincoln.

PART EIGHT

LASTING IMPACT

I

JOINING THE RANKS

We must reinvent a future free of blinders so that we can choose from real options.

David Suzuki

My new "boss" and mentor at the University of Illinois was one of the leading researchers in the field of deaf education. Stephen P. Quigley was a professor of education, speech, and hearing from Belfast, Northern Ireland. He was in his mid-forties and had blue eyes, wavy hair, a strong upper body, and a fondness for alcohol. He also was hard of hearing. He wore a hearing aid with a long cord that stretched from his ear to his shirt pocket or behind his belt. Quigley was the first person to perform detailed and objective language testing of deaf children. I was part of the new team that would advance his research.

Although I missed California, I enjoyed getting to know my five boisterous comrades. Each of us had been selected for our expertise. Mickey was one of the nation's top authorities on interpreting and American Sign Language. Bob was a teacher with a background in child development and school administration. Gerald was a principal at the California School for the Deaf in Berkeley. Barry was an administrator from New York with experience writing grants. Because of my background in computers and statistics, my job was to ensure the reliability and validity of our tests and research. Although none were deaf, each of my team members knew sign language. I found them expressive and easy to understand. We bonded immediately.

Stephen Quigley worked us hard, but the research was exciting. Up to that time, 1973, most deaf education studies were poorly conducted or flawed in some other way. One study, for example, supposedly showed that deaf people were incapable of abstract thinking. Quigley saw the need for new, valid research that would replace the old. With the help of graduate students like us and others, he developed the Test of Syntactic Abilities (TSA), which became the standard for assessing language and syntactic abilities of deaf children and youth.

I met Quigley on a Monday in his office. He was also my academic adviser. "Paul," he said after we'd sat down, "you need to take a sign language class." He said that I should be familiar with the options for language training of young deaf students so that I could share my knowledge with families struggling to make decisions. His comments echoed Pat Lashway's advice to me at Stanford. The tide was already changing; some schools for the deaf and hard of hearing were beginning to accept sign language as an alternative to speaking and lipreading.

I was excited by the prospect of learning American Sign Language (ASL) at the university level. For years, I'd observed people teaching sign language in churches, clubs, and the like. Most of these people had little or no training. Now I had the chance to learn ASL from an expert. I agreed that the time had come for me to join the ranks.

Like Dexter Fletcher, Quigley believed in the value of interdisciplinary study. He nominated himself as my adviser, so that the two of us could design an interdisciplinary graduate program for me. He said that many deaf education classes were based on outdated theories and were a waste of time. Quigley believed I should take linguistics and educational psychology, which would better prepare me to conduct research in the future. I felt good about this plan as well.

I thought it would be nice to have an interpreter for my classes, someone like Peaches. I put an ad in a newspaper requesting a volunteer who could mouth words clearly. The day after the ad ran, two mothers responded. Each had a deaf eight-year-old child, one a boy and the other a girl. I liked both mothers immediately. They confessed that they wanted me to serve as a mentor and kind of "older brother" to their children, which I was happy to do.

Neither mom had any experience with interpreting and each had her own style. Joan helped me in my education class. She would listen to the instructor's words, think about the meaning, and then relay the information to me. She did a great job. "Joan," I said at the end of that first session, "I don't even have to talk to the teacher after class. I have everything I need to know." It was so different from my experience at Antioch, where I frequently had to follow up with professors to make sure I hadn't missed something.

The professor of that class, a nice, grandfatherly type, was also helpful. At my request, he asked for a volunteer note-taker for me. A student raised her hand and ended up taking notes for me in other classes as well.

During the second or third week of that class, we divided into groups of eight or nine students for a special project. So often in the past, I'd been completely lost in group discussions. With Joan's help, however, I was able to both follow along and give my input. When the time came to choose a group leader, four or five of the students suggested that I do it. That blew me away. I never would have imagined they would pick me, but Joan's efforts made it possible. It felt good to have their confidence. I served as group leader for the rest of the semester.

The other mom, Glenda, was my interpreter for my curriculum development course and also did a good job. We would discuss after each class to make sure I had not missed anything. What I especially remember about that class was how stressed and competitive the other students were about their grades. It was quite a contrast to the pass/fail system at Antioch. The pleasure of learning was out the window. Here I am, I thought, back in the race. It was a different philosophy.

Mickey's wife Jeannie was my ASL teacher. She was fantastic. I learned so much more than the signs for English words. ASL has a unique grammar, and facial expressions play an important role in conveying a message. Jeannie took me under her wing, often inviting me to join her and Mickey for dinner and to meet deaf leaders and other prominent figures in the deaf community. After a lifetime of speaking and lipreading, I was totally immersed in sign language.

I'd always been good with languages, and thanks to growing up with Jonathan, I was already somewhat familiar with ASL, so I picked it up quickly. It felt natural. I wrote Jonathan a letter to let him know about my new form of communicating. He teased me with his reply: "It's about time." In December, I visited him and his wife, Dorothy, and enjoyed signing and discussing the intricacies of ASL grammar with them. I had picked up a few signs over the years from Jonathan and other friends and used them in our conversations, but now we signed almost exclusively—except when, out of habit, we went back to silently mouthing words and lipreading.

I could tell Jonathan was pleased that I was now signing. He hoped that I would favor signing over speaking and lipreading, but I continued to use both methods. I believed then, and still do today, that one method may work best for one person and the other method for another and that it makes the most sense for each person to experiment and choose the option that seems most effective.

When my second semester at Illinois was about to start, Jeannie said, "Why don't you find someone to be a sign language interpreter for you? I think you're ready." I agreed and had to tell Joan and Glenda that I was making a switch. Both were disappointed, but they understood. For the next two or three summers, I continued to spend time with their children. I taught them English, writing, and math and also introduced them to deaf people who I thought were good role models. At their parents' request, we communicated by speaking and lipreading, though today both know and use sign language as well. I valued the experience and being able to contribute something to their lives. It was another foreshadowing of my future life's work.

While looking for a sign language interpreter, I met two undergraduate students at a party who seemed fun and were eager to give it a try. Suzi and Karen were both just beginning sign language, so neither had training. At times, Mickey advised them. One day when Suzi was interpreting for me, I dozed off in class. Suzi kicked me and woke me up. I was less than grateful. "I thought I had the right to sleep in class," I said.

"You are embarrassing me," Suzi replied. "What am I supposed to do? The whole class knows you're not paying attention."

We took our difference of opinion to Mickey, who sided with me. "Paul has the right to fall asleep," he told Suzi. "And you need to keep signing because if he wakes up, he can follow what's being said at the time. He has that right just like anybody else."

I worked through similar issues with Suzi and Karen and appreciated their help. They were volunteers at first, but eventually I was able to convince the university to give them a stipend, which they were thrilled about. Both worked with me for the rest of that academic year and through the next, until they graduated. Their help made my course load feel much lighter compared to my years at Antioch. I understood so much more during class and didn't have to study as hard.

That was important, since I spent so much time working with Stephen Quigley and his team. In addition to helping develop what became the TSA tests, the other graduate students and I performed research that Quigley was interested in. For instance, I was assigned to delve into current efforts to communicate with primates using sign language. I wrote a one-hundred-page paper on the subject, far more than necessary, and concluded that while primates really did learn sign language, their language development at best matched the equivalent of a three-year-old human. The result was that Quigley said the hype about primate language abilities was overblown.

In some cases, Quigley's expectations exceeded what was appropriate. He asked us to respond to correspondence for him and to help write news and research articles. Quigley would even call members of our team if he was out somewhere and couldn't find his car after too many drinks. I was the exception to those late-night calls since I didn't have a phone. One member of our team eventually quit in protest to these practices. I had mixed feelings about what was going on. Although Quigley took advantage of us in some ways, most of us felt protective toward him. He was a brilliant man who did so much to advance research in the field of deaf education. I count myself fortunate to have known him.

I was also blessed to work with the outstanding team he assembled. In fact, those students, along with others who worked with Quigley around that time, have been prolific in publishing important books and research papers in the years since. It was the beginning of an incredibly exciting period in deaf education and in the deaf community, and I was right in the middle of it.

Equally exciting to me then was the ease with which I communicated with the undergraduate students I met from the deaf education program. Even though they were hearing, their knowledge of sign language and communicating with deaf people removed the barriers. I didn't have to educate them at all about looking me in the face or enunciating clearly. It was like we already knew each other.

The same feeling prevailed among the Quigley research team members. I was not the first deaf student to enroll in the graduate program at Illinois, but I was the only one at the time. Yet it wasn't an obstacle. I felt accepted by my colleagues and found I could communicate easily with each of them. It was wonderful to make those immediate connections.

After two or three years at Illinois, however, I was struck by an interesting realization: My friendships at Illinois were not as deep as those I'd forged at Antioch. I'd had to work hard at Antioch to forge bonds with others. To connect, we often discussed and dissected the "big" issues: politics, social justice, race, class, faith. I might focus on one individual and really get to know that person. At Illinois, I talked so easily with many people that I didn't feel the same urgency to pursue relationships with such in-depth focus.

The irony was not lost on me. It appears that the more we invest in our efforts to communicate, the better we succeed, regardless of the obstacles.

2

ANSWERS

Life will reveal answers at the pace life wishes to do so.

Donald Miller

As was true for most people my age, my college years were a time of seeking and exploration. I sought responses to life's big questions: What did I believe about God and the universe? What was my purpose in life? Was there someone out there who would share the journey with me? Where would I put down roots and make my contribution to the world? I didn't know it at the time, but I was about to uncover many of the answers.

I earned my master's degree in educational psychology from the University of Illinois in 1975. I decided to stay on and get my doctorate. I approached Stephen Quigley with a proposal for my PhD dissertation, and he said he didn't think it would work, that I should think of something else. A month later, I presented a second proposal. That was rejected too. A few weeks later, I tried again. Once again, the answer was no—but this time, Quigley said he'd actually liked my original proposal. If I made a few changes to that one, he explained, he would approve it. I was relieved when he finally gave his official thumbs up.

In the mid-1970s, many deaf education experts believed that private deaf education schools attracted students from a broad spectrum of socioeconomic backgrounds—that the mix of high, medium, and low ranges averaged out. Quigley believed, however, that private schools served a much narrower group—families from high socioeconomic backgrounds. Since no one had researched the issue before, my dissertation would show who was right. I was able to obtain alumni addresses from three of the top private deaf education schools in the nation. It took two years to gather the data on parents' incomes, education levels, and jobs, but I did it. The results showed that Quigley was correct. He was, of course, elated.

It was the kind of project I enjoyed and was good at, working with and analyzing statistics. Quigley saw a bright future for me in the field of research and statistical analysis. But in the fall of 1976, my fourth year at Illinois, he made a "mistake" that changed my life. He asked me to teach a class for him.

Total Communication Principles was an undergraduate course. I was only a part-time lecturer, but it was a major step beyond tutoring calculus students. I had my own class to instruct in whatever manner seemed best to me. I found myself adopting the Howard Swann approach that I'd so appreciated at Antioch. Instead of adhering to a formal professor-student relationship with strict office hours, I encouraged students to get together with me after class and at other sites on and off campus. Our meetings were casual. When we met, I had the students practice signing to further develop their skills. I relished the entire process of teaching a class—planning lectures, handing out tests, grading, and connecting with and helping students. In fact, I loved it. I woke up each morning looking forward to seeing the eager faces of my students. Although I didn't tell Quigley, I realized that I'd found my calling. I wanted to teach at a university.

I was connecting with undergraduate students, and I was making other exciting connections as well. Since it was so rare to see a deaf student in a PhD program, I was treated as a minor celebrity by some members of the deaf community. Some people even said to me, "You couldn't have been born deaf. You must have been born hearing and become deaf later in life." My "status" gave me greater opportunities to meet deaf leaders and role models from across the country, sometimes when I traveled and sometimes when they visited Illinois. The relationships I developed this way led to a lifelong support system that has blessed me many times over.

Graduate school was also the time when I experienced an upswing in my social life. I began dating more. One of those dates was with Kelly, who was pursuing a master's degree in recreation. She was a national archery champion. She was also paraplegic and used a wheelchair. We shared a class, and Kelly brought up the idea of having dinner together. I agreed and said I would pick her up. After class, however, I began to stress about our date. "How will she get into my car?" I said to my friend Shelley. "Do I pick her up? What do I do with the wheelchair?"

"Oh, Paul," Shelley said. "Just ask her and learn."

Which is exactly what I did, and our date went fine. Kelly was able to lift herself into my car on her own and I was able to collapse the wheelchair and put it in the trunk. The restaurant didn't have a ramp, but I was happy to simply carry Kelly up the stairs and then bring up the wheelchair. It helped that Kelly was outgoing and personable, which made both of us comfortable. Going out with her was no big deal. I later realized, however, that my anxiety over what to do was likely similar to what many people experience when dealing with a deaf person for the first time. It gave me a new perspective on the challenges we all confront when facing unfamiliar circumstances.

That date didn't lead to a long-term relationship, but another one did. In 1973, I met Naomi, a beautiful girl with long black hair, from Morton Grove, Illinois, who was studying deaf education. We seemed to be a perfect match. We talked about and agreed on everything, and we always had a good time together. I found her one of the easiest people to communicate with I'd ever met. I was smitten.

The fact that Naomi was hearing and I was deaf didn't bother either of us. Nor did the fact that she was Jewish and I was still seeking to define my beliefs. We both said that if we got married and had children, it didn't matter what religion we'd choose to raise them by.

I discovered, however, that religion mattered very much to Naomi's family. They were completely against our relationship because I was not Jewish, and deaf besides. Once, when we were at Naomi's parents' house and she was calling for me to reserve a rental car, her parents began saying things to Naomi, literally behind my back. "You see, the boy can't even make phone calls for himself," her father said. "You'd have to be his interpreter for life!" Although I didn't understand why at the time, Naomi burst into tears. Naomi's grandparents, meanwhile, threatened to disown her if she married me.

After we had dated for more than a year, the pressure from Naomi's family became too much. She broke up with me. I was devastated. I had a hard time accepting that a relationship that seemed so perfect could collapse just because of family disapproval. Because of her family, Naomi could no longer picture herself being happy with me. She lost faith in the idea that we could have a future together.

Soon after the break-up, my friend Shelley and I visited her family, and I complained about Naomi's family to Shelley's mother. Shelley also was Jewish, and her mother was blunt with me. "Paul, I don't think

I would want Shelley to date someone who wasn't Jewish," she told me. "Our religion and culture are so important to us. We wouldn't be able to handle that." I was still heartbroken, but those comments did make me a little more understanding.

It took me a while, but I eventually realized that Naomi wasn't the right girl for me. Little did I know that the solution to my search for a soul mate was just around the corner.

At Christmastime 1976, I was back in California, where I attended a party in an upscale, art deco home high in the hills of Pasadena. The host was Dr. James Marsters, a successful deaf orthodontist who was famous in the deaf community. He had worked with inventor Robert Weitbrecht, providing financial, legal, and emotional support, to create the teletypewriter and modem that combined in 1964 to make the TTY. I'd recently started using a TTY myself in Illinois and had obtained them for my parents and Jonathan. My mother was especially thrilled to be able to call and communicate with Jonathan.

Dr. Marsters wasn't the only distinguished party reveler that night. There were deaf pilots, an accountant, a social worker, and an occupational therapist. I recognized a few of the guests from the Alexander Graham Bell convention in Chicago, including Joe Slotnick, the man who had been so friendly to me. I also was singled out for pursuing my doctorate from the University of Illinois.

And then there was a young woman named Anne Keenan, among the first hard of hearing registered nurses in the country. While Anne was out of the room, Dr. Marsters passed around an article featuring her that had appeared in a hospital trade magazine. She had applied to twenty colleges. All of them had turned her down because of her hearing loss save one, the Saint Anthony School of Nursing in Rockford, Illinois. "She's tough," our host said, obviously admiring her persistence.

I, however, was more impressed by the picture of Anne that accompanied the article. She was dressed in her nurse's uniform and had an inviting smile on her face. Even in black and white on a flat magazine page, something about her expression conveyed both softness and unusual depth. I felt I could see into her soul.

I had good reason for my interest in Anne that evening: we were on our first date together. We'd met two years before at a youth leadership conference in Atlanta. She lived in Long Beach, California, but we were both elected to two-year terms as officers with the organization that

Anne's graduation photo at St. Anthony
School of Nursing, Rockford, Illinois.

sponsored the conference, so we stayed in touch. I found myself occasionally sending Anne short notes that had little to do with our duties as leadership officers. I was delighted when she responded. There was a familiarity in the way we talked and wrote to each other that made it seem as if we'd known each other for years. When I let her know about my trip to California, we decided to get together.

We hadn't seen each other in two years, but when Anne and I drove up to the party from Long Beach, it was as if we were continuing where we had left off in Atlanta. The conversation flowed easily. That comfortable communication continued at the party, both between Anne and me and with the other guests. Dr. Marsters and his wife, Alice, went out of their way to make sure everyone was having a good time.

There was just one problem with the evening: Anne seemed to be avoiding me. Anne and I would chat and laugh together for a few minutes, and all seemed to be well, but then she'd find something to eat or someone to talk to and drift away from me. The first couple of times it happened, I tracked her down and tried to resume our conversation. But after she disappeared for the third time, I changed my strategy.

I'm not sure what's going on here, but I'm not going to follow her anymore, I thought. *I don't want to scare her away.*

For someone who prided himself on communication and thought he'd found a kindred spirit, it was a puzzling situation. Only later did I learn the explanation for Anne's behavior: nerves. She'd decided she liked me and thought I might even be someone she could fall in love with, but she'd promised herself she would never fall for a deaf person.

After the party, at Anne's apartment, the two of us sat at her kitchen table drinking coffee. I was about to learn that when Anne has something on her mind, it doesn't take her long to express it. She wrapped her hands around her mug and locked her blue eyes on mine. "So, Paul," she said, "what do you want out of this relationship?"

I leaned back a few inches. *Wow, I can't believe she just asked me that*, I thought. *She's very straightforward.*

"Well," I said, "I think if we're going to date again, we should get to know each other better to see if we might be right for each other. I believe if you want to have a good relationship with someone of the opposite sex, you have to learn to communicate well with that person over a long period of time. That way you become bonded.

"Unfortunately," I continued, "people start too fast. They don't communicate for very long, the companionship isn't there yet, and then they have sex. That complicates everything. They miss the opportunity to get to know the other person well and enjoy them for who they are. Too many people jump into sex. It messes things up and leaves them with hurt feelings."

Anne just looked at me, absorbing my words. "That's true," she said. "I'm not interested in games. I agree with you."

There was something else I needed to discuss with Anne. Recent personal research and reflection had led me back to my parents' beliefs and faith. I explained this to Anne and discovered that she'd recently made a similar spiritual journey.

It seemed that we did have much in common. We were talking openly and easily. My interest in this young woman was soaring higher than the hills above Pasadena.

So much in my life was changing. Just before that date with Anne, I'd sat down with Stephen Quigley in his office. He knew how long it was taking me to gather the data for my dissertation. I wasn't going to finish analyzing and writing it up before my doctoral program funding ended the following June. Quigley had recently granted funding and

Honeymoon in Vancouver.

a one-year extension to another doctoral student in a similar predicament. I was sure he'd do the same for me. But I was about to find out there was a problem with my plan.

"Paul," he said, "I'm sorry to have to tell you that federal funding is being cut off everywhere. No one in federally supported doctoral programs is being allowed to continue past their current funding."

What? I thought. *I need one more year! Now I have to leave and support myself? What am I going to do?*

When I overcame my shock, I realized I had no choice but to find a job. I decided to pursue a community college position somewhere on the West Coast so I could be closer to Anne and my family while I finished my dissertation. I sent resumes to several colleges. In April 1977, I also attended a conference in Sacramento for California community college administrators who worked with disabled students. Gary Johnson, the administrator of the disabled student services program at College of the Sequoias, in Visalia, California, approached me and said, "You are the person here I want to talk to." I liked him immediately, and soon afterward, I interviewed for and was offered a job to start a deaf and hard of hearing program at the college in the fall. I would also teach a class. I happily accepted. After four years in Illinois, I was a Californian.

The highlight of those first months in California was not, however, my new assignment at College of the Sequoias. Anne and I continued dating and quickly fell in love. We were married in January 1978 in a ceremony on the beach, with my father officiating. Anne wore a beautiful dress in the style of *A Midsummer Night's Dream*. She also went barefoot—it was the 1970s, after all.

I was confident that Anne and I would have a strong marriage. It was as if we'd been on parallel paths. Like me, she had gone to mainstream schools and become a professional. We both understood the unique challenges that arose while making our way in the hearing world. In addition, we both approached discrimination by the hearing in a similar way. If a restaurant waiter ignored us, our response was not to confront and scold but to educate—we assumed he was simply ignorant and needed to learn how to deal with people who were deaf or hard of hearing. Anne and I even had a similar sense of humor.

Perhaps most important, though, was that we communicated easily and with the same approach. Anne enunciated clearly and naturally, so we mostly talked and lipread, with signing reserved for more difficult subjects or when we were physically farther apart. In addition, we had a similar attitude toward communicating with others. Rather than quickly judge people we met, we both preferred to listen and look for clues on whether they were comfortable with us and whether they understood our message. It was as if we had developed an extra sensitivity that made communication much easier, both with others and between ourselves. It helped that we got off to a good start in our relationship. The "ground rules" that we established during that conversation in Anne's kitchen on our first date—avoiding games and simply being frank and truthful with each other—would be among the foundations of our marriage.

Although I had been building toward finding the answers to many of my most important questions for a long time, I found them in a surprisingly short period. I now understood what I was passionate about doing as a career. I had resolved my doubts and beliefs about faith and God. And I had found and married the person I wanted to share my life with.

The answer to one of the last of my big questions—where I would put down roots—was soon to come.

3

PUSHING THROUGH

Nature makes trees put down deep roots before having them bear fruit.

Vincent de Paul

Part of my new job at College of the Sequoias (COS) was to help the faculty accept the presence of interpreters for the deaf students in their classrooms. Most faculty were receptive, but a few resisted. They thought the interpreters would be a distraction, even though the hearing students quickly tired of watching the interpreters. Part of the issue, I suspect, was that some professors just didn't want to share their stage.

My biggest ally and model for the other faculty in this effort was a popular physical education professor and swim coach. Daniel Anderson was enthusiastic about the idea of having deaf students on campus, so I asked him to share his enthusiasm with other faculty, which he was happy to do. Although Daniel was a great role model for the faculty, I still had to educate them at times. I once visited a vocational class and noticed a poster on the wall that portrayed a deaf, blonde girl in a scene similar to the style of a Playboy pinup. It said she would not hear what her husband said or tell what he did—she was the "perfect wife." It was an insulting, sexist message. Without making it into a confrontation, I brought the poster to the instructor's attention. He apologized and agreed to take it down. Although I suggested we keep the matter between us, I found out the next day that the instructor was apologizing about the poster to everyone on campus. As I'd seen often in my life, a few quiet words presented in a friendly manner had again had a big impact.

One winter day after I'd been on the job a few months, Daniel came into the disabilities office with tears streaming down his face. He'd just come from the hospital. His two-year-old son, Gary, had spinal meningitis and had permanently lost his hearing. Daniel was devastated.

I mostly listened to Daniel that day, though I did tell him that his son could still have a good life. In the ensuing weeks, I tried to help and encourage Daniel and his family. I was surprised when he told me that they had enrolled Dale in my old school, Central Institute for the Deaf, in St. Louis. I wished they had talked with me about it first. Daniel was confident that his son would receive a fine education based on the fact that I'd attended CID, but he would be a long way from home. Daniel's wife moved to St. Louis and lived with Dale until he was old enough to stay in the dorms, which undoubtedly eased his transition. I've stayed in touch with Dale and am happy to report that he has indeed had a good life, which includes a wife and family of his own.

It wasn't long after Daniel's family crisis that Anne and I faced a different kind of crisis. We were in Fresno running some errands in our two-door, yellow Capri. I was driving on Blackstone Avenue, a busy street in a business area, when I saw a flashing light from what I thought must have been a police car. I stopped the car and got out. I was used to standing up and talking with police officers since Anne had accumulated several speeding tickets in the short time we'd been together. To my surprise, however, I didn't see a uniformed police officer behind me. Instead, I saw two sedans with four men in business attire jumping out of them. They each had guns drawn—pointed at me!

We must be in the middle of a shootout! Where are the cops? I thought I was about to die.

I put my hands up. The men were yelling something. Anne got out of the car. She was yelling back at the men. While my heart beat double time, one of the men finally pulled out a police badge and showed it to me. Now I understood—they were plainclothes policemen.

"I'm not moving!" I said. "I don't want to make a mistake. Come to me." I was afraid that they would tell me to move or sit, I wouldn't see the message, and they would think I was resisting.

The police officers made both Anne and me place our hands on top of the car. I was a nervous wreck, but Anne was in control. "Paul is deaf," she told the policemen. "I am hard of hearing. Look me in the face when you talk to me." After a minute, one of the officers said, "Everything is fine." Apparently, a yellow Capri like ours had just been involved in a robbery and the officers thought we were the robbers.

"You can't point guns at me like that," I said. "My life flashed before my eyes."

"We're sorry," the officer said. "We can't take a chance."

A minute later, the policemen left. Anne had been firm and confident throughout the incident, but now that the officers were gone, she began shaking and crying. "Paul, they could have shot you!" she said. Anne didn't sleep well that night because she kept thinking about what could have happened. It was a frightening experience.

Fortunately, my job at COS was not too stressful. I liked the work but found it left little time for working on my dissertation. One year stretched into another. I eventually finished a first draft—more than three hundred pages of text, tables, and research data—and sent it to Stephen Quigley. Not surprisingly, he recommended changes. We dialoged by letter until he was satisfied. Finally, in March 1979, I was ready to fly to Illinois to defend my dissertation before a five-member committee. I thought I'd already taken care of the hard part—I'd analyzed the data and written my conclusions. I was wrong.

The first problem occurred when employees at United Airlines went on strike, grounding my flight. After several phone calls, Anne and I found we could arrive in Illinois in time for my Monday meeting with the committee by taking six flights, but the timing was so tight that I felt we were sure to miss a connection. Instead, I asked Quigley to delay the meeting until Tuesday and took a flight that would put Anne and me in Chicago on Sunday night.

We arrived at midnight, nearly five hours late because of a flight delay. The temperature was zero degrees. We planned to stay with Anne's brother in Chicago, but our rental car broke down a half mile from the airport. It began to snow. I said to Anne, "I guess I'm not going to get my PhD."

"No, no," she said. "We're going to keep pushing through."

We waved down a driver who took us back to the airport. In our second rental car, we attempted to locate Anne's brother's place, but in the snow and darkness, we couldn't find it. Finally, at 1:30 in the morning, we came across a man shoveling snow who knew where the housing development was. After a short night's sleep there, we left for Urbana, arriving on the Illinois campus in the afternoon. I immediately tracked down Stephen Quigley.

"I'm here!" I said. "The meeting is tomorrow, right?"

"Paul," he said, "I have bad news for you. I couldn't get the committee to agree to tomorrow. They can meet in two weeks."

Two weeks! At that point, I was ready to give up. Yet I needed the committee's approval and I needed that PhD—not just for my personal satisfaction or to enhance my resume but also because my next job depended on it.

I hadn't been looking for another position; it had found me. Several months earlier, I'd run into an actor who performed with the California Shakespeare Festival, which was based in Visalia and performed at our campus theater. During our conversation, I suggested that the festival invite the acclaimed National Theatre of the Deaf (NTD) to perform on campus. My new friend thought it was a great idea. Both the festival members and college staff also embraced the notion. We were all thrilled when NTD accepted the invitation. I was soon involved in promoting the event, which included conducting interviews for television and newspapers. NTD's performance at COS in October 1978 was sold out and attracted people from throughout the region. It was a sensation among both the deaf and the hearing attendees.

One of the people who saw my promotional media appearances was Karen Jensen, a professor of deaf education at Fresno State University who was trying to raise the profile of her program. She came to some of my lectures on campus and talked to me about the idea of joining the faculty at Fresno. I enjoyed my duties at COS, but I missed working at the university level. I was also excited about the idea of becoming a full-time teacher. I eventually interviewed at Fresno State and was offered a position—contingent on completing my PhD.

I feared my plans were falling apart. I didn't have the money to fly to California and come back again in two weeks. Anne and I decided I had no choice but to stay in Illinois. I spent the time sightseeing and visiting with friends while I waited for the next meeting. I also had to make the difficult phone call to my boss to explain that not only was I not coming back for two weeks, but I also was leaving the college for another position.

By the time the two weeks had passed and I finally appeared before the dissertation committee, my anxiety level was through the roof and I was exhausted from lack of sleep. After two hours of presentation and discussion, however, they all agreed to pass me once one question about my data was resolved—one of the committee members wanted to see the source analysis.

I mailed that source material to the professor right away. I should have realized by that point that getting final approval would not be a simple matter. I waited four weeks without hearing anything and then called the professor's office. His secretary said, "Oh, actually, he's out of town. His mother is sick. He won't be back for another one or two months."

I wanted to tear my hair out, but Anne remained patient and optimistic. "Just wait it out," she said. Sure enough, two months later I did hear from the professor and was told everything was fine. I was given permission to publish my dissertation. It was a big relief. The whole experience had been an ordeal, but at last I had my PhD in educational psychology. A dream had been fulfilled.

I felt a different kind of fulfillment in June at the COS graduation ceremony. Our first deaf student walked onto the stage and received his diploma. He was a role model. He showed that anyone who was persistent, motivated, and had the right support could earn a community college degree. I was proud of him.

My work at COS was done. Starting in the fall of 1979, I would be a professor in the deaf education program at Fresno State University. I didn't know it then, but I had found the answer to the last of my big questions. I was about to put down some very deep roots.

4

THE NAIVE PROFESSOR

We must accept finite disappointment, but we must never lose infinite hope.

Dr. Martin Luther King, Jr.

I was naturally excited about my new position at Fresno State and pleased to have staunch support from the other two faculty members in the deaf education program. I discovered, however, that their opinion was not universal. I soon found myself in conflict with a few of the other faculty in my department. My first year as a university teacher turned out to be a rocky one.

The problem had little to do with me personally and everything to do with differing philosophies toward deaf education. Although American Sign Language was gradually gaining acceptance as an alternative or even preferred method of communication in deaf education programs at colleges across the country, the rate of progress was slow. For many educators who had favored and taught the oral method for years or even decades, change was difficult. That was certainly true at Fresno State. Even the title of our department—made up of the deaf education, speech language pathology, and audiology programs—reflected old-school terminology: the Department of Communicative Disorders.

I openly shared with my students that the deaf community has a distinct culture and language and that ASL had been shown to be a language by William C. Stokoe in 1960. I realized from my experience at Illinois that ASL was slowly on its way to widespread approval. Not everyone agreed with me, however. One department faculty member often complained about what I said or did. Another, in discussions with students, told them that I was wrong, that "ASL is not a language at all. It's just a gesture system." He was outspoken in his opposition to

240

my views. It was confusing for the students; they weren't sure who to believe. It also was difficult for me. I felt ineffective as a teacher. My supporters among the faculty told me to ignore the naysayers, but I didn't find that so easy.

I was a bit naive in my attempts at resolving the problem. I sent my outspoken colleague books, papers, and other publications that made a convincing case for ASL as a language. I believed that he would sit down with an open mind, read the materials, and realize the error of his philosophy. But he never responded, and I doubt that he read any of the publications.

In my second year at the university, I faced another trying experience. I represented the communicative disorders department on a college committee that approved or rejected funding requests and made recommendations for changes to faculty proposals for research projects. I got along well with most of the members of the committee. They seemed to appreciate my feedback and efforts, for example, to encourage the library to stock more books in our respective fields. There was an exception, however. One committee member from the Department of Social Work Education never spoke to me and seemed irritated every time I said anything. I did not understand his attitude, but I didn't react to his negativity.

At least that situation had a happy ending. Near the close of the academic year, this committee member began showing me more respect. He even started talking with me during coffee breaks. Finally, at one of our final meetings that year, he approached me and said, "I want to apologize." He explained that he'd had a bad experience with a student who was deaf and was sorry he'd taken it out on me. I was surprised but pleased to accept his apology.

In those first years at Fresno State, the majority of faculty and staff were nice to me, and several were extremely supportive. Only a few showed their ignorance and rejected me, but dealing with those few left me feeling deeply frustrated. What kept me going were the students. The classroom was my place to escape, and when I walked in the door, the stress melted away. I loved teaching, and I developed a strong rapport with my students. They appreciated having a deaf professor who taught classes other than sign language, which was rare. When I began my career at Fresno State, I was the only deaf faculty member, although we did have a part-time lecturer who was deaf and taught sign language. Except for the faculty at Gallaudet College, I was one of perhaps only ten deaf people in the country who was a full-time faculty member at an accredited university.

As I had at College of the Sequoias, I tried to be as available as possible to my students, which allowed me to develop relationships with them and help them. I explained my willingness to see benefits in multiple education methods. A few urged me to publish a book to increase exposure of my views. They weren't alone. Since I had participated in a number of newspaper and television interviews as part of a deaf awareness campaign, many parents of deaf children also came to me, asking for more information and wanting to know the best education approach for their kids. I'd already had the idea of writing a book that would be a guide for parents of deaf children and would cover the benefits and drawbacks of both the oral and manual methods of communication and education. No one had yet published a book that was comprehensive and evenhanded. The demand for useful information from parents and students, along with the resistance and ignorance I detected among some of the faculty, pushed the idea from the back of my mind to the forefront. Following the end of my first year at Fresno State, in the summer of 1980, I began researching and writing.

The project took many months and carried into my second year at the university, but I finally finished a draft. I called it *The Silent Garden: Raising Your Deaf Child*. I wanted the best possible product, so I mailed copies of the manuscript to a handful of well-known educators of deaf people and leaders in the deaf community. I'd met each of these people, and I asked them for honest feedback.

One of the first responses I received was from a hearing educator and high-ranking administrator at a college program for deaf students. I eagerly began turning pages. I saw that he had used a red pen to make comments. To my dismay, he'd crossed out entire sections of the manuscript and written long notes expressing his disapproval, using phrases such as "No such thing as deaf culture" and "ASL not a language." The pages virtually dripped with red ink until they suddenly stopped—he didn't even finish reading the manuscript. I was devastated. I hadn't expected this response at all. I felt as if someone had stabbed me in the back.

Feedback from other reviewers began coming in. The members of the deaf community didn't like it either. One wrote, "We are not vegetables—why use 'garden'?" But most of the comments centered on my inclusive philosophy. Unlike the hearing educator, they didn't like my favorable comments about the oral method. They wanted me to support sign language only. In fact, none of my reviewers said I had produced a good book.

I was discouraged and explained the situation to Karen Jensen, the head of Fresno State's deaf education program. "Obviously, Paul," she said, "you've written the perfect book."

"Huh?" I said. "What do you mean?"

"Those people will never agree with each other, but you can educate everyone about the benefits of other approaches." Other friends and colleagues gave me similar encouragement, saying that I couldn't please everyone. I decided to push on. Despite the criticism from the "experts," St. Martin's Press published *The Silent Garden* in 1982.

To promote the book, I handed out copies at a conference that year. At one point during the gathering, I saw the "red pen" reviewer coming my way, clutching a copy of the book. "Paul, I loved your book," the man said. "I want to help promote this wonderful volume." I was surprised, but then I realized his apparent change of heart was really about politics. My former critic must have believed he would look bad if he denigrated my work. He had decided to get on the bandwagon. I politely accepted his praise.

More gratifying to me was the response from parents. Many moms and dads told me then and over the years that I had given them an invaluable resource, providing them with detailed information, different perspectives, encouragement, and viable options to consider for raising and educating their deaf children. This was exactly what I had hoped to accomplish. I am grateful that today *The Silent Garden* (the 2016 third edition is available from Gallaudet University Press) is considered a classic in the field of deaf education.

When the book was published, though, I did not know it would be so well received. I was troubled by the resistance I continued to encounter from a handful of faculty members. I also had begun thinking about how nice it might be to join my brother Dunbar on the faculty at the University of California, Berkeley, where he was a professor of dramatic art. I was seriously considering leaving Fresno when I had an unexpected and life-altering conversation.

It was graduation day in 1982, always a joyous time of celebrating an important milestone with students and their parents, other family, and friends. It was also an opportunity to visit with Fresno faculty members I rarely saw. On this day, I sat under a bright sun with the rest of the faculty on folding chairs arranged on Jim Sweeney Field, inside the football stadium. Next to me was a woman named Glen Doyle, a member of the university's nursing department. As we talked, I told her about my dream to move to the San Francisco Bay area and join my brother Dunbar at Berkeley. She responded by arching her eyebrows and asking, "Do you really want to lock yourself in the ivory tower? It's true, you could do all the writing and publishing you want. But you'd have limited contact with students. You'd be focusing on yourself—that doesn't seem like you.

"I've known you just a short period of time," she continued, "but you seem to belong in this area. You can share so much more of yourself here. People love you. People need more role models like yourself. You seem to be the kind of person who thrives on being with people. Why would you want to take yourself away from here?"

I sat back, stunned. I sensed that God was talking to me. I knew that my life had again taken a dramatic and permanent turn. Later, when I explained Glen's comments to Anne, she was quick to embrace the idea as well. It confirmed what my heart had already told me. Everything Glen said made sense.

I decided I would stay on at Fresno State and devote myself to teaching and to my students. This was where I could have the greatest impact. I have never regretted that decision. I was also about to discover that a shift in my communication strategy would smooth the road in other relationships as well.

5

BECOMING SAVVY

Strategy is about making choices, trade-offs; it's about deliberately choosing to be different.

Michael Porter

I had an active professional life in my early years at Fresno State. In addition to publishing *The Silent Garden*, I wrote a play that won a Ford Foundation playwright award and was performed at College of the Sequoias. During my second year at the university, I also decided to use an interpreter in the classroom and in some meetings. Some of the faculty had seemed against the idea my first year, believing I should use my own voice. But I found that I sometimes missed things in meetings and group discussions. Karen Jensen and Bette J. Baldis, the other Deaf Education faculty, occasionally interpreted for me, but I felt that was a duty that distracted them from concentrating on their own work. As a result of having my own interpreter, I was better able to contribute in discussions and on committees.

In 1985, I applied for academic tenure, which would provide me with a permanent position on the faculty. My friends on the staff said that with my book and other accomplishments, I was a shoo-in to be approved. I too was confident about my application.

The first hurdle in the process was the department committee. Unfortunately, two of my advocates on the committee missed the meeting when my request was addressed. Even more unfortunate was the fact that the chair of the committee was the same professor who opposed my views on sign language. Soon after they met, I received a letter with shocking news—my request for tenure had been denied.

To have my own department reject my application was quite a blow. I was extremely upset. That night I called Dunbar and told him what had happened. As a twenty-year veteran of life among the faculty at a

245

major university, he sympathized with me. The next day, he wrote a fifteen-page letter—single-spaced—filled with insights and wisdom on how to deal with university politics. It included advice on how to work better with people, network, prepare better proposals, and not grow complacent about my progress.

Anne had similar thoughts. As one of the first hard of hearing people to complete a nursing degree, she had plenty of experience with politics herself. Some of Anne's professors and the medical professionals at her school were skeptical of a hard of hearing person's ability to succeed as a nurse. They attempted to fail Anne but could not because she passed all her coursework. She told me, "You can learn from this."

I realized that I had to become more politically savvy. It wasn't that I had to change my views, but I needed to become more aware of how people responded to me as a deaf person and of how I could most effectively educate and communicate with them. My approach had to be strategic. I also had to learn to not take things personally, which was hard for me. I needed to give others the chance to change their attitude toward me and other deaf people.

I was soon encouraged by a surprising development with my tenure request. The denial letter was passed on to the College of Health and Human Services tenure committee, the next step in the process. This committee had the option of accepting or rejecting the department's recommendation. Normally, a rejection by the department meant a rejection by the tenure committee, which would officially put an end to my application. But the dean of the college, Richard Ford, happened to see the letter sent to the committee. We had served on committees together and he knew me well. He was surprised by the conclusion of the department committee and called the chair of the committee—I'll call him Dr. Doane—into his office.

"Can you explain this?" the dean said, pointing to the rejection letter. "I've been looking through the paperwork and can't quite pinpoint what Paul's weakness is."

"Well," Dr. Doane said, "he can't teach these classes." He mentioned several courses that were outside of the deaf education course list.

"Yes, that's true," the dean said. "But you can't teach sign language. You can't teach deaf education. You can't teach deaf history. Those are all in Paul's area of expertise. These other classes are not."

Dr. Doane did not have an explanation. When Dean Ford said that the committee's finding appeared to be blatant discrimination, Dr. Doane was silent.

The dean overruled the department committee's rejection. My application was then approved by the college tenure committee, a university committee, the university vice president, and the university president. I'd been granted tenure after all. Like the process of earning my PhD and like so many other challenges in my life, it had not been easy. Yet my efforts had been rewarded. I was at Fresno State to stay.

Two years later, Anne and I grew tired of our long work commutes from our home in the country and decided to move closer to campus. We bought a home with a swimming pool in a residential neighborhood. When a neighbor came over to welcome us and I told her that I worked at Fresno State, she said, "Oh, someone else who works at Fresno State lives next door to you."

I hoped it wasn't someone in my department. Our mystery neighbor soon stopped by and revealed his identity. It turned out to be both better and worse than I'd hoped—it was Dean Ford! I had a great relationship with him, but I wasn't sure that I wanted to live next door to my boss.

A few weeks later, Anne and I hosted my sign language class for the weekend. Every year, I invited the class to come over for food, fellowship, games, and now, thanks to our new pool, swimming. It was a "silent retreat"—everyone had to use sign language rather than their voices. It was a great way for them to have fun and bond as a group while also practicing their signing skills.

A couple of days after the retreat, Richard Ford and his wife stopped by with a strawberry pie. The four of us sat down to chat. At one point, Ford said, "I understand you had some people over last weekend. We could hear them laughing, but we couldn't hear any talking." The expression on his face was one of concern. I wondered what he thought we'd been doing.

"We weren't stoned," I said, which drew a hearty laugh from the Fords. "It was a group of my students. We were practicing sign language."

The Fords looked relieved. I suspect the dean wondered whether his decision to support my tenure application had been a terrible mistake.

I was happy to put his mind at ease. The Fords turned out to be great neighbors, and the four of us got together on many occasions.

Soon after my application for tenure was approved, I began to implement my new, strategic approach to life at Fresno State. Dunbar had advised me to work on faculty committees to bring about change. With that counsel in mind, I volunteered and was appointed to chair the department curriculum committee. It was in many ways a thankless job comprising much reading and filling out of paperwork. No one else wanted the awful task. But the added responsibility put me in a position to better support the deaf education program, including some of my new ideas. I learned, for example, how to navigate the complicated process of changing course names and class sizes. As a result, in 1988 the title of our sign language course changed from Manual Communication to American Sign Language. It also became a required course in our department.

That same year, I encountered another opportunity to establish myself in the department. Without realizing what the other was doing, my two colleagues in the deaf education program had submitted requests to take a yearlong sabbatical to do research. When they found out that they had both made the same plans, neither was willing to withdraw her application. The chair of the personnel committee didn't want to make a decision that would alienate one or the other. He asked who I would choose. I said I needed time to think about it. I realized this was a chance to prove myself. I wanted to show what I was capable of.

After discussing it with Anne, I gave the personnel committee my recommendation: Let them both take the sabbatical. Hire a full-time person for one year and let me run both the undergraduate and graduate programs. The committee members were taken aback, but they approved my proposal. It meant that I would be mostly unavailable to help Anne at home, even though she was also working full-time. It was going to be a busy year.

Our year became even busier when I received a phone call from Anne's hospital at the end of September. Anne had injured her knee at work and needed immediate surgery. I had to call her mother and insist that she fly out to help. Anne's recovery took eight weeks, making for a difficult period in our lives. But at the end of the academic year, as well as after my colleagues had returned from their sabbaticals, more than one faculty member told me that I'd demonstrated my talent as a leader. I had gained more stature and respect in their eyes.

In 1990, I joined the College of Health and Human Services curriculum committee, which had jurisdiction over not just our department but also seven others. I had fixed my sights on a bold goal—to make American Sign Language a General Education course that could fulfill the core language requirement for all university students. No other college in California—and perhaps even the nation—had made ASL part of its General Education curriculum. If my proposal was approved, it would effectively declare ASL a legitimate language.

I first took my idea to our department curriculum committee. I made the point that ASL had already been recognized as an official language by many linguists and educators across the country. But in keeping with my new, strategic approach, I also described a financial benefit. If more students signed up for ASL to fulfill their language requirement, it would mean more funds for our department. Not surprisingly, the committee liked the sound of that. They approved the proposal.

The next step was the General Education curriculum committee. Before the meeting, I sat down with the chair of the committee. Because his father was a pastor who ministered to deaf people, I was sure the chair understood the significance of ASL. He said he would support my proposal, which had me feeling confident going into the meeting. The session did not go as I'd hoped, however. The representative for the linguistics and foreign languages departments felt threatened by my idea. He said that fewer students would take traditional language courses such as Spanish and French. Even worse, the committee chair went back on his word. He said that his father believed ASL was only a refined system of signing, not a true language, and that he wouldn't support my proposal.

I had been shot down. But I wasn't giving up. If I had learned anything from my experience with my PhD dissertation, it was that persistence can win the day.

In 1991, I again filled out all the paperwork to make ASL a General Education course and again found myself before the GenEd curriculum committee. This time I brought in books, articles, and other materials that demonstrated ASL's standing as a language. I showed them to the committee members. The committee had a new chair, but it was made up of a number of older faculty who were resistant to change.

One of them stood, pulled down a world map that hung from the ceiling, and said, "Where is ASL spoken on this map? There is no country that speaks ASL. It is not a language."

My proposal was rejected a second time.

In 1992, I made my third attempt and third appearance before the GenEd committee. By this time most of the old guard faculty had been replaced by new, younger members. I passed out research articles from a linguistics journal that established ASL as a language and made my presentation. "Oh, yes," one of the committee members said. "I have a deaf student in my class right now. It's fascinating to see the interpreter interpret into American Sign Language."

Another committee member spoke up: "I know someone who knows sign language." Suddenly the atmosphere in the room was friendly. These people were open to hearing what I had to say. When it came time for a vote, the proposal was approved. Now that it had the blessing of the GenEd committee, it passed through the remaining steps without trouble. ASL officially became a core language at Fresno State. It was an exciting achievement and one of my proudest moments.

I was able to help instill other advances in the deaf education program as well. I occasionally had to make compromises to win approval of the new proposals, but our progress was remarkable. In 1998, I became chair of the college curriculum committee. That same year, the university approved our Deaf Culture class as an upper-division course in the General Education curriculum. In 2000, we added a sign language program option—later the interpreting program—for students who wanted to study sign language but weren't interested in deaf education. In 2003, we added another course to the General Education curriculum: Intro to Hard of Hearing and Deaf People. For me, the course was symbolic and representative of my philosophy. It showed that we welcomed anyone who was deaf or hard of hearing, including people who did not sign, who had varying degrees of hearing loss, and who were from all age groups. It demonstrated the diversity of the deaf community.

During those years, I had a few more successes as well. One of those was the publication in 1992 by Little, Brown and Company of my book *Chelsea: The Story of a Signal Dog*. It described the experiences Anne and I had with our beloved Belgian sheepdog, a professionally trained canine who served for years as our ears and as our companion.

Paul and Anne with their first professionally
trained, fully certified hearing dog, Chelsea.

In 1995, sixteen years after I joined the faculty at Fresno State, I was
named "Outstanding Professor of the Year" by the university's faculty,
staff, and students. It was a great honor, and it meant I was nominated
for the same award for the entire California State University system.
At a banquet, I learned that I was second choice for the state award. I
was in many ways relieved that I didn't win. Although it would have
been a tremendous honor, it also would have required me to do a great
deal of traveling and speaking, adding stress to my life and distracting
me from my family, friends, and students. I also feared being chosen
because I was deaf. I wanted to be known as a strong teacher and communications professor, not as the "deaf professor." Finally, when I saw
the accomplishments of the winner, I felt that he was the right choice. I
did not want to win ahead of someone more deserving.

I had come a long way in my time at Fresno State, both personally
and professionally. Thanks in part to my brother Dunbar's sage advice,
I had become more savvy and effective in my communication with the
university's faculty and staff, enabling me to help enact significant and
lasting changes. My greatest satisfaction remained working with my
students in the deaf education program, who now had more opportunities to pursue careers in the field than ever before.

As I looked ahead to the remaining years of my teaching career, I wondered what challenges awaited. I would soon find out.

HOME

Home is not where you live but where they understand you.

Christian Morgenstern

In November 2007, I attended a conference in San Francisco and stayed overnight with a family friend. At breakfast that morning, I noticed I wasn't feeling well. By the time I reached the airport for my flight home, I was a little concerned. My backpack felt heavier than usual. More worrisome was that my heart seemed to beat erratically, occasionally adding an extra beat. I hadn't experienced anything like it before, which made me think it wasn't related to the heart valve issue I'd been aware of for years. I got on the plane hoping the problem would go away.

Instead, it got worse. When the plane landed in Phoenix, where I was supposed to connect to another flight, I texted Anne to explain what was happening and then took a taxi to an emergency room. The ER staff admitted me right away and also provided a professional interpreter, at my request. I answered a barrage of questions and was submitted to a host of tests.

Several hours later, with me hooked to a heart monitor and IV machine and oxygen tubes plugged into my nose, a doctor entered my room. He explained that I had an ascending aortic aneurysm—a balloon-like bulge in my aorta, near my heart. It was a dangerous condition. If the bulge was another half centimeter larger, it would warrant immediate surgery. If the aneurysm ruptured, it could easily prove fatal.

I'd dealt with a variety of health issues throughout my life, but this was a huge blow. I was lying in a hospital bed, alone in a strange town, facing my mortality like never before.

Through my interpreter, I called Anne and told her what the doctor had said. It was an emotional conversation. We both realized that my heart was degrading. I had mentally prepared my whole life for the idea that I would eventually need to slow down and be less independent. Now, at age fifty-eight, it appeared that moment had arrived.

Back at home, my doctors and I agreed to postpone surgery for the time being. I was put on medication that reduced the risk of rupture. It also left me with less energy than before. I reluctantly concluded that I had to retire from full-time work.

Richard Ford had retired years before and now Benjamin Cuellar was the dean of the College of Health and Human Services. I met with Dean Cuellar to briefly describe my heart condition and ask if I could take a half-time position. He was less than eager to grant my request. "Paul, I want to retire first," he said. "Then you can retire. You can't leave before I do."

I met with the dean three more times with the same request and received the same result. Finally, in our fifth meeting, I had my interpreter make my request in Spanish to honor the dean's Mexican heritage. This time he granted it. With more than a little sadness, I ended my full-time teaching career in June 2008.

I was fortunate to have such a good relationship with the dean. I was indebted to him in more ways than one. Three years earlier, he had called me into his office and asked an unexpected question. "Paul, tell me your dream," he said. "What would you like to do in the remaining years of your career? Something special."

I replied that I had a few books in mind.

"No, that doesn't count," Dean Cuellar said. "What if funds were not a problem, time was not a problem, and you could do anything? Think about it."

I went home and talked to Anne about it. I had some ideas, but nothing felt quite on the mark. Then one morning about two weeks after my meeting with the dean, I woke up with a new vision in my head. During my years at Fresno State, I had been able to support teachers, parents, interpreters, and other professionals with my knowledge about the latest research and findings in deaf education. But I would not always be there. In addition, the field was changing so fast. It was a great challenge for any one person to keep up with the explosion of information. What was needed, I decided, was an endowment that would fund a permanent, revolving position at the university. It would attract experts on various topics related to deaf and hard of hearing people. The plan called for a different expert to come each year. It would be a way to extend our support on a permanent basis to everyone who needed it.

I would call it the Silent Garden endowment.

When I explained my idea to Dean Cuellar, he was enthusiastic. "That's great," he said. "I'll have you work with a university development officer to start figuring out an endowment. We will raise the money."

I was excited too, though the feeling was mixed with a sense of trepidation. I had just given myself a new challenge that I knew little about: fund-raising. My initial thoughts on the process were a bit naive. I figured I would invite a few wealthy people to dinner, ask them to make a large gift to the program, and I would be done. In fact, that's exactly what I tried to do. But when I sent out invitations, everyone turned me down. I realized that my task was going to be a little more involved than I'd originally thought.

Over the new few years, I worked with the Fresno State development office. When I went to a part-time schedule, I continued to teach one class. I missed the opportunity to teach more frequently, but I was also excited about my new challenge. I had much to learn, so I took classes on fund-raising. They were like an advanced course on communication. I should not have been surprised to discover that for successful fund-raising, just as for successful communication, developing strong relationships is vital. That fit perfectly with my philosophy. As I told one university official, "I want our donors to be my friends. I want them to be involved for the duration of the program. I can't just say, 'Thank you for the check,' wave, and leave. That's not me. I want to keep in touch with our donors, have a relationship and a rapport with them. To me, that's how development should work."

I already knew how important relationships were when a sensitive subject needed to be discussed. Several years earlier, for example, the university had hired a new chair for our department. He was a man we all liked. After two years in the position, however, our new chair seemed to be struggling. A few faculty members weren't pleased with the quality of his work but didn't know what to do about it. Since I had a good relationship with him, I decided to take a bold step. I invited the chair to coffee on a Saturday morning. With the help of a professional interpreter, we discussed a number of things. Then I asked him, "How do you feel about being chair?"

"I don't enjoy it at all," he admitted. "But I feel stuck. The reason I moved out here was to be chair of the department."

"Would you rather be just a member of the faculty?" I asked.

"Yes, very much so."

I encouraged him to share his feelings with the faculty. I knew that they respected him and was sure they would welcome him as another member of the team. I told him he didn't need to feel obligated to continue as chair and that the rest of the faculty would understand. Eventually, that's just what he did. The situation was resolved without conflict in a way that made everyone happy. But I would not have risked talking with the chair, and he would not have risked sharing his true feelings, if we had not already had a good rapport.

The more I learned about fund-raising, the more I believed in a relationship-first philosophy. Even so, I was sometimes impatient. At one point I shared my frustration with Peter Smits, the university's vice president for advancement. I told him that I felt I was making little progress. No one had yet made a million-dollar gift to the endowment. Peter said that on average, it took six years to develop a relationship that could lead to a million-dollar gift. That made me feel better. I asked if I should change my approach at all.

"No," he said, "don't change a thing. Stay persistent and you'll be fine. Just keep going and be yourself."

That was the advice I needed. Thanks to a little persistence and the help, support, and generosity of a wide array of friends, the Silent Garden program now includes the Robert Duncan Nicol Silent Garden Endowed Chair, the Joseph S. Slotnick Distinguished Professorship, the Silent Garden Educational Fund, the Silent Garden Scholars, and Scarlett's Park, which serves deaf and hard of hearing children and youth with special needs. The Silent Garden has grown into a rich and bountiful educational program touching the lives of countless deaf and hard of hearing children, youth, and adults in the region and throughout the state. The varied branches of the program offer unique resources and training opportunities for families, students, and professionals in deaf education and sign language interpreting with the common goal of allowing everyone, regardless of needs or abilities, to grow and thrive. I was thrilled when my old friend, Dr. Alan Hurwitz, delivered the first Silent Garden Lecture on campus in 2012.

One of Paul's classes with the Deaf Education faculty and students.

Many professionals in the field of deaf education now consider the Silent Garden a model for the rest of the nation. Today, I continue my work to support and raise funds for the program. It is tremendously rewarding.

As I look back on my career, I'm gratified to see how much the deaf education program has grown at Fresno State. By 2008, when I retired from full-time teaching, we had nearly twice as many faculty and four times the number of part-time lecturers. In addition, the number of undergraduate students had grown significantly, and hundreds more took American Sign Language and other classes to fulfill their General Education requirements. We had made so much progress.

In addition to my strategic approach to communication, I realized I was different from some of my colleagues in another way. Many of my fellow faculty members moved from college to college. They advanced their careers by taking more prestigious teaching, research, and/or administrative positions every few years at another institution. There is nothing wrong with this approach, but it wasn't me. Over the years, I had gotten to know so many of my colleagues in other departments across the university. Sometimes that was through my work on committees, sometimes through connections with students who took our deaf studies classes, and sometimes through simply getting out of my office and exploring what was happening on campus. I realized that developing those deep relationships was very important to me. What began as a survival skill had turned into something more, something I'd been doing and relishing all my life.

I couldn't imagine leaving the university after working so hard to build up our program and those friendships. As a younger person, I had appreciated the chance to travel often and have experiences with other people, countries, and cultures. Despite my early struggles at the university, Fresno State had become my home. I had helped create an environment where I felt connected and where I had a meaningful, lasting impact on the lives of students and families with deaf and hard of hearing children.

The university had become more than my workplace. It was the place that I belonged.

I was truly blessed.

EPILOGUE

In 2012, I received a Lifetime Achievement Award at the annual conference of the California Educators of the Deaf. Awards and honors are always nice, but far more rewarding for me has been the opportunity to interact with and advise hundreds of deaf and hard of hearing students over the years. Watching these talented and dedicated young men and women grow into the people they were meant to be and seeing how much they have to contribute to our world has been one of the great joys of my life. My desire to guide and teach was born in the classrooms and dormitories at CID, thanks to the example and encouragement of several wonderful teachers, housemothers, and others. I hope I have continued this fine tradition in the years since.

The smartest decision I ever made had little to do with my choice of profession, however. It was asking Anne Keenan Ogden to be my wife. She is a wonderful, open, and honest communicator—and my best friend. I have been married to the love of my life for nearly forty years.

I cherish many other relationships as well. Although my parents, David, and Jonathan are gone, I keep in close touch with Dunbar and Annegret, and their growing, extended families. I also stay in contact with many of my friends from my years at CID, Lincoln, Stonewall, Antioch, Illinois, and of course, Fresno State. Their encouragement and support have blessed me over a lifetime. I am also grateful for many other friends across the country who are valued members of my social circle.

All these relationships have been built on communication. I have enthusiastically studied and practiced the art of communication my entire life. Being deaf has perhaps given me a unique perspective, but successful communication is crucial for everyone: hearing, hard of hearing, and deaf. We cannot thrive without it.

One of the questions people ask me most is, "If someone offered you a pill that allowed you to hear, would you take it?" I have three answers to this question. If you had asked me when I was sixteen, I would have said, "Sure." At that age, I was searching for new and better ways to grow, to advance, to gain advantages for my life, relationships, and career. I would have grabbed the opportunity to join the hearing population.

Today, if you offered me a pill that gave me the ability to hear for twenty-four hours, I would again happily take it. What fun it would be to hear the lilt of Anne's voice, to experience a classical symphony, to go to the beach and discover the sound of wind, waves, and birds, to go to Berkeley and hear my brother Dunbar give a lecture to his students at UC Berkeley! After all these years, I think I would be happy to satisfy my curiosity and understand what so many others experience.

If the pill you offered would grant me a lifelong, irreversible change to be hearing, however, my answer would be "No, thank you." I've lived a long time and worked hard to get where I am. If I could hear, I would have to start over, learning to recognize unfamiliar noises and sounds. I'm comfortable with who I am and with my personal challenges and issues. I'd rather not trade them in for a new set of issues.

The truth is that I'm grateful for my deafness. I think it strengthened my faith by keeping me humble. I might have otherwise grown arrogant and unwilling to depend on anyone else. It also has given me greater empathy for those who struggle with their own unique challenge in communication. It is a foundational part of who I am. I find it difficult to imagine who I would be or what my life would be like if I were not deaf.

When I look back over the years, I feel the satisfaction of knowing that my deafness is an important part of who I am but certainly not all that I am, and not something that has prevented me from living out my goals and dreams. I hope the words in this book have in some way inspired you to reach for your own goals and dreams and given you new strategies for helping the young deaf people in your life to do the same.